Backstage Stories

edited by Barbara Baker

continuum

Continuum
The Tower Building
11 York Road
London SE1 7NX

80 Maiden Lane, Suite 704
New York
NY 10038

www.continuumbooks.com

British Library Cataloguing-in-Publication Data
A catalogue record for this book is available from the British Library.

ISBN: 978-08264-9247-0

Library of Congress Cataloging-in-Publication Data
A Catalog record for this book is available from the Library of Congress.

Typeset by Servis Filmsetting Ltd, Manchester
Printed and bound in Great Britain by
Cromwell Press Ltd, Trowbridge, Wiltshire

For Robin

Contents

Acknowledgements

As always, I am indebted to the encouragement and advice given by my husband, Robin. I would like to thank all the people who helped to arrange interviews: Neil Black, Susie Cordon, Juliet Manners, Mary Parker, Ewan Thomson, William Nedved, David Watson and Nada Zakula. And I am very grateful to Anna Sandeman and Continuum for commissioning this book.

Introduction

There is a Chinese proverb that says, 'Tell me and I'll forget, show me and I may remember, involve me and I'll understand.' To a great extent the ultimate experience of people who work in the theatre, as well as those who watch the performance and, I hope, the readers of this book, is one of involvement.

This book offers a rare insight into the jobs and characters of the large number of people involved backstage in the theatre. It reveals who they are, what they do and why they do it. It is about the people who often take the stick rather than the laurels in their profession.

Most audiences do not realize that a medium-sized theatre may employ about 50 people who work behind the scenes. Large companies employ many more, and small ones manage (often brilliantly) with very few – each doubling up, and some being brought in on a freelance basis. But however many people there are working backstage, each one requires a special commitment and vision. Oscar Wilde said, 'The stage is not merely the meeting place of all the arts, but is also the return of art to life.' This book includes interviews with people from artistic director to wig-maker – someone from almost every department involved in the art of theatre, other than the actors. Each has a creative part to play in what eventually happens on stage during a performance.

Another apposite (though extremely self-deprecating) quotation comes from the Afterword of *Camino Real* by Tennessee Williams:

> The color, the grace and levitation, the structural pattern in motion, the quick interplay of live beings, suspended like fitful lightning in a cloud, these things are the play, not words on

paper, nor thoughts and ideas of an author, those shabby things snatched off basement counters at Gimbel's.

So how does this wonderment come about? The answer is usually months of preparation. The first people to become involved with putting on a performance are the artistic director (in subsidized or not-for-profit theatre) or a producer (in commercial theatre). It is their job to choose the play (perhaps with the help of a dramaturg or literary manager) and the director. The director will then help choose the cast (often with the aid of a casting director) and the designers. The set designer will then make a model box of the set, and consult the costume and lighting designers. The sound designer will get involved too, as will a choreographer if needed.

The scale model is presented to the production manager, who will start costing everything and relaying information to a construction manager or set builder, and other departments, such as scenic artists and wardrobe. Next the set will be built and painted; props made or sourced; costumes, shoes, jewellery, hats, armour and wigs made or bought. The stage manager will schedule rehearsals as well as costume fittings; the deputy stage manager will facilitate the rehearsal process, and relay more information to other departments. During rehearsals a voice or dialect coach may be required, as well as others with specialist skills, such as musical directors, fight arrangers and flying directors.

Often just a few days before previewing, the set will be ready on stage, lamps will be rigged and the actors will move out of the rehearsal room. In the technical period that follows, electricians focus lamps, and sound levels are set. At the dress rehearsal designers, costume supervisors, wig, make-up and wardrobe departments will check their work. Finally, everything from all the teams comes together.

During the performance the deputy stage manager runs the show, and the lighting and sound operators create the effects designed for that production. The wardrobe department will see that costumes are clean, wig and make-up artists and dressers may help the actors get ready, and be available for quick changes. A stage crew will get scenery in and out, might move furniture around and may be responsible for flying sets as well as people. After the final performance the crew take the whole thing down. As Martha Graham (American dancer and choreographer, 1894–1991) said, 'Theater is a verb before it is a noun, an act before it is a place.' Theatre is the result of many people working together to achieve a common end: it is live, active and full of possibility.

In *Notes and Counter Notes* Eugene Ionesco (French-Romanian playwright, 1909–1994) wrote:

> I personally would like to bring a tortoise onto the stage, turn it into a racehorse, then into a hat, a song, a dragon and a fountain of water. One can dare anything in the theatre and it is the place where one dares the least.

I love this flight of fancy, and agree that a tremendous amount is now expected of good theatre, but I would contest Ionesco's last comment, and say that frequently, it is also achieved. To do this requires creativity, craft, organization, hard work, patience and perhaps above all, good communication. Almost all the people I interviewed stressed the importance of this. For anyone working backstage, knowing precisely what is required is half the battle, and unless each department and individual communicates, the whole enterprise breaks down.

Linked with communication is collaboration, and a desire to share in a common purpose. Choreographer Susan Stroman says, 'Everyone is in the same swimming pool together: you all drown together, or get an Olympic medal together.' Producer David Ian says, 'It is really always about teamwork.' Virtually everyone interviewed mentioned what Andy Keogh, production manager, put into words, when he emphasized the importance of creating an atmosphere 'where people feel that they are listened to and are contributing, and where they all have a value'.

Another vital thing that backstage workers share is passion. As designer Bob Crowley explains, 'It is hard work and it is a religion: it becomes your life, for good or for ill.' Everyone involved in the theatre works unsocial hours, and generally gets paid badly. One thing they are not in it for is the money. So what keeps them going? Each person gets something slightly different out of it. Some enjoy the buzz of a new play, some savour the gratification of getting something just right, or interpreting another's vision, some thrill when they hear applause and an appreciative audience. Voice coach Deborah Hecht gets most satisfaction when she works on 'a play which really has something potent to say [and] you feel that your work is more than just entertainment: you realize the importance of the theater'.

But people who work backstage are also rewarded with a ravishing experience. Stage manager Trish Montemuro expresses this particularly clearly:

> You are backstage, and not in the limelight, like other people in the theatre, but I wouldn't want to be. I love the fact that there is so much to see from the vantage point of backstage.... An audience that sees a limited run of a great play with a wonderful cast is very lucky. But the joy of working in a theatre is being in that special place at a specific time and being able to see something unique.

American Actress Tallulah Bankhead (1902–1960) famously said, 'It's one of the tragic ironies of the theatre that only one man in it can count on steady work – the night watchman.' There are two main groups of people who work backstage in the theatre, those who are employed by a company full-time, and those who work freelance. This brings out certain differences in character. The first enjoy the family atmosphere that work in theatre often generates. The second, however prominent in their work (like Bob Crowley), suffer from a certain amount of job insecurity, but (especially in the case of fight arranger Terry King) delight in the fact that no job is ever the same.

Finally in this brief summary of the characteristics of the people I interviewed, a few started as actors; a good many got in by chance, or through knowing someone; but the majority had formal training of some kind. With more relaxed trade union rules in Britain, it is not as hard to get into the theatre as it used to be. Nevertheless, sadly, there is still racism and sexism in this business (as attested particularly by Paul Tazewell and Paule Constable).

Theatre, as Richard Eyre says in his interview, 'in some ways . . . replicates society, and is theoretically a utopian microcosm of society'. What is also evident is that theatre is a small world, and the names of people with specialist skills recur, so their stories link together. Irish freelance designer Bob Crowley praises Canadian-born stage manager at the National Theatre, Trish Montemuro. In New York, dramaturg Anne Cattaneo reminisces about the pleasures of discussing a Tom Stoppard play with Bob Crowley. As prop-maker and welder Ewan Hunter puts it: 'Over time you carve your life and environment out of people you like to work with.' Or to quote George Devine, founder of the English Stage Company at the Royal Court in the 1950s, 'policy is the people you work with'.

Choosing the people to interview for this book was naturally subjective. I omitted administrative staff and those who work in marketing and education; they all support the production process and the work that takes place on stage, but are less directly involved with it. I included people with as many different jobs as I could, performed in a great variety of venues. I interviewed people who work in the West End, at the Royal Opera House, in national, regional and fringe theatres in England, Ireland and Scotland. I also interviewed people who work in Chicago, and at the Lincoln Center, on Broadway and off Broadway, in America. And I interviewed freelancers who work in many, if not all, of these places. All the interviewees are highly regarded experts in their chosen field, who additionally possess the eloquence and humour to impart fascinating information and amazing anecdotes. I am extremely grateful to each of them for being so generous with their time, and for honestly sharing their stories. I also apologize to those who, for reasons of space, were not included.

The 'Selected Production Credits' section gives a brief overview of each interviewee's work, often chosen by them. These credits are arranged chronologically, ending with the most recent. Where a play, opera, ballet or musical is performed frequently (for example Shakespeare's plays) the date has been added so the particular production can be identified.

Theatre and live music are the only art forms that are transient and are never the same twice. Andy Keogh says:

> I love the fact that it doesn't last. I think change is a good thing. The work that goes on before, and after a production to get rid of it, is never really seen by most people. But when you are there from the first day till the end, you see the entire process happening, like an arc, and then it is gone.

This aspect of the theatre is also expressed by Richard Eyre in his book *Utopia and Other Places*:

> I like the fact that it happens in the present tense, that it's vulnerable and it's changeable. I like its sense of occasion, the communal event: going in as an individual and emerging as part of a group. . . . And I like the singular combination of magic and moral debate.

Elsewhere in his book Eyre states:

> Each art form has its unique properties. There is no art that uses time, space, gesture, movement, speech, colour, costume, light and music in the way that the theatre does. It thrives on

metaphor: things stand *for* things rather than being the thing itself, a room becomes a world, a group of characters becomes a whole society.

Watching a play the audience experiences the real and the unreal simultaneously. Being allowed a glimpse into how that world is created, as I was, cannot fail to fascinate. The stories of those who work beyond the stage door intrigue and inspire. But the real magic happens when all the elements involved come alive, as the houselights go out.

Artistic Director and Actress

Martha Lavey

Martha Lavey is an exceptional woman. First seen nude on the stage at Steppenwolf Theatre, Chicago, in a play directed by John Malkovich in 1981, she is now an ensemble member and artistic director of the theatre. A more usual career path for an artistic director is via directing plays, not acting in them, and the customary gender for that job title is male. Yet Lavey is responsible for scheduling all the plays at Steppenwolf, and is also highly regarded as an actress: Richard Christiansen wrote in the Chicago Tribune *of the 'mesmerizing magnetism she brings to the stage'. With quiet intelligence off stage, she brings commitment and energy to all she does. Her interview with me was grabbed between appointments, whilst she ate a salad, yet it is full of intriguing insights.*

Steppenwolf is no ordinary theatre either. It started in a church basement in Chicago with 88 seats and a donation box, and now has 24,500 subscribers, a large budget, an expensive building with two stages and a third (the Garage) down the street. As well as administrative and technical staff, the company consists of 35 ensemble members who are actors, directors and writers. According to their official literature:

> *Steppenwolf Theatre Company advances the vitality and diversity of American theater by nurturing artists, encouraging repeatable creative relationships and contributing new works to the national canon. The company, formed in 1976 by a collective of actors, is dedicated to perpetuating an ethic of mutual respect and the development of artists through ongoing group work.*

Selected Production Credits

Buried Child (Broadway), *One Flew Over the Cuckoo's Nest* (Broadway, and the Barbican, London), *Lost Land, Glen Garry*

Glen Ross (Theatre Festival, Dublin), *I Never Sang For My Father*, *The Pillowman* (all Steppenwolf productions, some transferred as indicated).

*   *   *

My first encounter with Steppenwolf Theatre was as an actor in 1981, when I was in a play called *Savages*, which John Malkovich directed. I became an ensemble member in 1993, and have been the artistic director since 1996. My job as artistic director is to develop programming at Steppenwolf for what goes on our stages, and maintain the ongoing programs, like our work in arts education. I also interact with our 35–member ensemble, our board of 60 trustees and our staff. So there is the generation of internal artistic life, and being the face of the theater with our trustees, staff and audiences.

It is unusual to be an artistic director and an actor, and it speaks to what is unusual about Steppenwolf Theatre, in that it was begun by a group of actors, and has maintained leadership by an actor for its 30–year history. But ensemble members are actors, directors, writers and adaptors of plays. There is nothing formulaic about becoming an ensemble member. What we value is repeated creative relationships with artists. It might be that we feel that an actor in one of our plays, or a director with whom we work, makes a special contribution to our existing pallet of abilities that live within the extant ensemble. And if there is a cultural fit in the way this person works too, then they will be asked to join. The ensemble has grown incrementally, without exact design, over time. It is very infrequent that an ensemble member leaves. Early on there were a couple of people who elected to leave, and more recently an actress, Glenne Headly, had no interest in working on stage anymore, and felt it was misrepresenting herself to stay since she now works in film and television. Other than that, it is a membership for life.

An important part of Steppenwolf is encouraging new talent, including less experienced actors, which again, is unusual. We are in a position here to mentor or give opportunities to younger people, either working with them, or inviting them as guest companies. We also have a very active commissioning program for new plays at all levels: emerging playwrights, mid-career playwrights, and we commission for our program called 'Steppenwolf for Young Adults', which is for student and family audiences. So there is a lot of commissioning and workshopping. We are marking this, our thirtieth anniversary season, by doing five new plays in our subscription series. But in general the mix of our programming includes new work, projects from the American canon, and some English language work generated in Ireland or England, for example, we are doing *The Pillowman* [by Martin McDoagh] at the start of the next season.

We are always attentive to new work. I say 'we' because there is myself, the director of new play development, Ed Sobel, an associate artistic director, David New, a casting director, Erica Daniels, and Hallie Gordon, who is in charge of the Steppenwolf for Young Adults program. This group of people are the artistic office, and the 35 ensemble members suggest plays as well. We have a geographical dispersion, with ensemble members located in New York, Los Angeles and Chicago, but the members resident here in Chicago are designated associated artists. They attend our artistic office meetings and have a more intimate life in the institution of the theater, coming to development events and things like that. We are all always circulating plays among ourselves, cultivating the work of new writers, and introducing emerging work and new artists. We might think, 'This would be a great project for person X!' So we give it to them, and another time director X might come to me and say, 'Gee, Martha, I really want to direct this!' So it is a two-way conversation.

We are also committed to the development of new plays by writers of international prominence. At the moment we are working with Cormac MacCarthy, trading drafts back and forth, and we have worked with people like Sam Shepard and Tony Kushner. The giftedness of those writers is patent, and they are wonderful people: very dialogical and permitting of engagement back and forth – it is a privilege. There is also a consciousness here to encourage women as writers and directors. If you look at the early history of Steppenwolf, one of the things said about it was that it was a bit like a boy's club, and was a very male-dominated company. A lot of the profile of the theater that was crafted early on was masculine, and somewhat adolescent. But now a lot of the foot-forward artists in the company are women.

My own career path was haphazard. I was interested in theater from when I was a child, and then I studied theater at Northwestern University. After graduation, in 1979, I signed up for an acting class taught by John Malkovich. That was a fun experience. Over the years John has become a good friend of mine, and in fact last spring we were in a play here together, called *Lost Land*, by an English playwright, Stephen Jeffreys. John is a wonderful actor and his coaching of acting has the same kind of unique perspective and point of view that he brings to his own work as an actor. He is very intelligent and sensitive.

After the course with him I went away, and worked in various performance ensembles, not necessarily in dramatic performance, but rather in performance art. I worked with composers and musicians, and was also in some plays. Then I decided, in 1985, to return to Northwestern to get my degree in performance studies, which is a sister program to the theater program at Northwestern, surveying a larger arena of literature for consideration for the stage: prose fiction, non fiction, poetry, and looks at things like ritual and performance in everyday life. I got my PhD, wrote my dissertation, and was looking in two directions – at an academic life, and life in the theater.

I was made an ensemble member here just after I got my degree, and was asked to be artistic director a number of years later, through good fortune. My predecessor, Randall Arney, was ready to move on, and the founders of the theater, Terry Kinney,

Jeff Perry and Gary Sinise, were looking to build a larger artistic office infrastructure, and have a new leader, and to my surprise, they asked me to do it. I still act as well, usually in one play per season. I start rehearsals in about a month for a new Don Delillo play called *Love-Lies-Bleeding*. I acted in another of his plays, *Valparaiso*, a couple of years ago, and previously John Malkovich adapted Delillo's novel *Libra* for the stage, and Mr Delillo came at that time.

So I work with some marvelous writers, and also actors, for instance some of the actors who were in *Lost Land* with me, like Yasen Peyankov and Amy Morton: any actor from the ensemble is just a thrill to work with. Certain plays that for me, as an actor, were particularly gratifying include Wallace Shawn's *Aunt Dan and Lemon* [a black comedy showing how educated, refined groups of people can display horrific behaviour. The character Lavey played, Lemon, defends Nazism]. That play was so provocative to the audience, I think in a very valuable way, generating conversation. There have been any number of plays which we have done that are remarkable in various ways. Frank Galati has adapted Haruki Murakami's short story *After the Quake*, which is currently in our Upstairs Theatre, and is a beautiful piece of work. Tina Landau took William Saroyan's classic *The Time Of Your Life*, which is a piece known never to work, and breathed new life into it and animated it with music; that was a gorgeous experience – there are millions of them!

I am one of the really fortunate people on earth in that my work is totally integrated with my life. These are the ideas and activities that excite me, and these are the people that I most want to be around. There is a complete fluidity between what moves me as a person on all levels, and what I am able to do to make a living. It is a kind of impossibly fortunate circumstance, and I am very, very grateful to it.

There have also been challenges, like the economics of making theater, particularly when you are pressurized to negotiate a balance between innovative ideas, and those that can more easily gain support. There is always that leading, following question about theater as an art form. All that is challenging. And it is also a very people-intensive job. So the very thing that makes it so beautiful, and such a gift, is also, of course, the thing which makes it most rigorous. I think the question of what constitutes right livelihood is always an active one for me. I feel that I am able to make a contribution that I respect in this job, and there is a kind of wish that it will always be true, but I have to keep that under examination.

Body Control Instructor

Jane Paris

I would like to say that waiting inside the stage door of the Royal Ballet at the Opera House in Covent Garden, there were no beautiful people calling each other darling and kissing, regardless of sex – but that would not be true. From this stereotyped picture of theatrical glamour, I wound my way along corridors and into a lift, guided by Jane Paris: 'I worked here for weeks before I found the canteen', to her studio. It was large, empty of people and a little clinical, with charts on the wall of 'The Human Spine – Disorders', 'The Muscular System' and 'The Skeletal System'. There were also various machines that you might expect to find in a gym, except that they seemed to have more coils, springs and hooks above flat beds, and to a sedentary writer, looked a little like instruments of torture. Jane Paris, however, is small-framed, attractive and calming: clearly no torturer. She is one of the only people employed by a theatre to teach Pilates full-time.

Both the National Theatre and the Royal Shakespeare Company advocate the benefits of Pilates, and Sir Ian McKellen has said in an interview: 'The only times I have taken exercise seriously have been in training for specific jobs e.g. three months of Pilates preparing to play the super-athletic Coriolanus [National, 1984] on stage.' But Pilates is particularly appropriate for dancers – both for strengthening and toning their muscles, and in helping to recover from inevitable injuries. Pilates was developed by Joseph Pilates in the 1920s and involves exercises designed to strengthen muscles, improve posture, provide flexibility and balance, create a streamlined shape, unite body and mind, and improve endurance and stamina.

Selected Production Credits

Anastasia (1996), The Nutcracker (1999), Marguerite and Armand (2000), Tryst (2002), Cinderella (2003), A Wedding Bouquet (2004),

The Sleeping Beauty (2006) (all at the Royal Opera House, Covent Garden: dates refer not to first performances but to new productions or revivals of repetoire of particular interest to Paris).

*   *   *

I work here as part of the medical team. We have two full-time physiotherapists and a full-time and part-time masseur. We have quite a few people who come in from outside when needed, like a podiatrist, orthopaedic surgeons, a doctor and a nutritionist. We have our own occupational psychologist, who is a regular member of the team and comes in about two days a week. And there is me, and I have been here for about 12 years.

My job title is Body Control Instructor because about eight to ten years ago there was a therapist in New York who took out a law suit against anybody using the word Pilates. He said he owned the name and trademarked it in America. So for a long time nobody in the UK would use the word Pilates because we were absolutely terrified that he was going to turn up and sue the pants off us. He tried very hard in America and won the first case, and then he lost on appeal. Now Pilates is considered a generic term and more or less anyone can say they teach it. But at the time I didn't want to put Pilates Instructor or Pilates Coach in the programme in case it caused the company any problems, and I just never got around to changing it.

Pilates is particularly good for ballet because it doesn't go against the aesthetic in any way, or the rules of classical ballet technique. So it is not like going to a gym and suddenly sprouting muscles. It tends to give an elongated physique: strong muscles but quite sleek, rather than bulky. Pilates also has a lot of emphasis on flexibility, which other exercises, apart from yoga, don't have. You can also work in isolation, controlling particular muscles and muscle groups. I think Pilates first became popular with classical dancers because of rehab in injury. It meant you could safely work your whole body, and keep yourself completely in shape, while you were rehabilitating your injury.

I can't think of any principal dancers who haven't been injured at some point in their career. Some I have worked with for years and years, like Darcey Bussell, who has now written her own book on Pilates, and Miyako Yoshida. Miyako has been with me twice a week now since she joined the company from Birmingham Royal Ballet. She likes Pilates, but also she did have a back injury many years ago, which still comes back to haunt her occasionally if she doesn't keep very strong. So she does it more as a preventative measure as well as thoroughly enjoying it, to the extent that she has now been partly responsible for opening studios in Japan, so it is now growing in Japan in popularity. Hopefully I have partly contributed to her, and Darcey's, love of Pilates.

Most of Pilates is done against the resistance of springs and pulleys, so you have springs of different lengths and strengths to guide your body through different movements. You are still in control of the equipment, which either, for example, helps to pull you into a stretch, or you work against it to build strength. Balanchine originally sent his dancers in New York to Joseph Pilates, because he saw patterns of repetitive injury happening. So even before the recent explosion of interest in Pilates by the general public, it has been popular with dancers.

I went to ballet school and started as a dancer, but quit dancing professionally when I was about 28. I don't dance at all any more, except occasionally, when the door is locked at night, I might do a skip round the room, or do a ballet bar, just to keep myself ticking over. So I only danced for about ten years, mainly in France and Portugal. Then I did some commercial theatre work in London and some television. Next I decided to go into acting and did a little bit of that, and at the same time was getting involved with Pilates, and really enjoying it, and wondering if I could have a career in that. So I trained to teach the Pilates method, and quite coincidentally, my husband was offered a job in Scotland, so we went to live in Edinburgh, and I opened my own studio there, and ran that for a few years.

Meanwhile there was a Pilates instructor for the Royal Ballet who had trained at the same ballet school that I trained at, and we had met a few times at health conferences and that sort of thing. I wrote to her when we were moving back to London, just to say I was coming back and it would be nice to meet up again, and I got a phone call back from her saying, 'Could you come in for a job interview tomorrow?' They had been looking for someone to take over from her for about a year, and hadn't found anyone suitable. So I went off for an interview, and had another one the following week, and I have been here ever since. Originally I wasn't based in the theatre; I was based in our rehearsal rooms in Barons Court, where the Royal Ballet School was. Before the Opera House was refurbished there wasn't enough space for the opera and ballet to be here at the same time.

The Pilates we do at the Royal Ballet follows all the same rules and principles as anywhere else, and you would do the same exercises at your local Pilates class. You can do Pilates mat work, just on the floor, which is quite widespread because it is cheaper. But there are also many Pilates studios with similar equipment to here, where the investment is quite high. The difference is that here what I teach is more specialized in that it is more functional towards classical dance. The aesthetic has to rule everything here, and so you have to be very careful how you change a person's body, because it must be pleasing to someone with an eye for classical ballet.

Even though most people might think a particular dancer is fit, slim, healthy, strong – that dancer may feel that there is a body area that they really need to change, and if that is possible, we might work on that. For example, someone may feel they need more calf muscle, or a higher calf muscle, and they want to sculpt that area; or they may feel their thighs are too large and maybe there is something we can do to make it a better line aesthetically.

So whereas in a normal Pilates class you might aim for a flatter tummy, here we really try to engineer the body. And of course all the people I am working with are supremely talented, with fantastic physiques, so it is the top end of the work, and the more refined, advanced exercises. I don't usually have to go right back to basics with most of the dancers. For example, we can work with strengthening muscle and control, but flexibility is not generally an issue.

I would love to work one-on-one with the dancers, but usually I work with about three or four people at a time. The dancers make appointments to see me. Generally I get here at about 8.30 in the morning to get ready, and the first dancers come in at about 9.00, because their daily ballet class is at 10.30. One, to one-and-a-half hours is about right for a Pilates session, and many of them like to do it before their ballet class; they feel it sets them up for the day. I get just as many men as women; in fact recently, it has been solid men all day long, but it goes in cycles depending on injury, and the repertoire and so forth. It is entirely voluntary, although a few might be steered in my direction if the ballet staff felt they were having problems with something, or needed some extra strength somewhere.

I work full-time for the Ballet. Very occasionally I will see outside people – a few Olympic athletes and Premiership footballers have been here, but that tends to be a one-off special sort of thing. It is still quite rare for a ballet company to employ someone like me on site. Most dancers have to pay, and go outside to see somebody. I am quite friendly with my opposite number at Boston Ballet, and they do have their own studio, not in the theatre, but at their rehearsal rooms. Otherwise, even members of major companies, like New York City Ballet, have to pay and go outside to do Pilates. A few musicals in America use Pilates – I know Celine Dion, who is in a big show in Las Vegas, has her own private Pilates studio backstage, as do Cirque du Soleil, who have a special wagon to tour it around with them.

In commercial theatre there may be a little more money for that kind of thing, but at the moment, as far as I know, I am the only one working in a theatre in London, if not the world. I think for anyone interested in Pilates it is important to have a good teacher. It is much more rewarding to work with someone than to just read a book, or watch a DVD. The very basic exercises you find in books are a bit like watching paint dry. If you really want to work with the method, go and find a good teacher. And if you want a job like mine, push for it. I think more theatres should have facilities like this to help people. It would be fabulous at somewhere like Sadlers Wells, where they have so many visiting dance companies. It would be nice if there were a few more of me in other theatres! In older buildings you would never have the room, but with modern ballet, and with musicals, it would be fantastic for the dancers involved to have something like this on site. Commercial theatres might even save themselves money in the long run, rather than having to pay for injuries to be investigated, and have artists off sick.

It would be nice if all dancers were well looked after in the future. They work incredibly hard, and musicals have matinees twice a week with the same cast for months on end: at least here it is repertory. I do not go on tour with the company because it is difficult to find somewhere with the same facilities. And of course there are also always people left behind, because they are injured, or coming back after a baby, or something like that. So there are always people to work with.

Having been a dancer, it is lovely for me to still be involved in that world. If I was outside, I could be working with people who are office-bound or work in a bank all day, and I wouldn't be able to push them in the same way that you can really work an elite classical dancer. They work to the limits, and you can really see fantastic results from what you are doing. It is rewarding working with the general public, when you see people's posture change, or they say, 'Oh! It is so much easier for me walking up stairs now.' That is nice, but to actually see an elite classical dancer improve something is even more amazing. They are trying to achieve perfection, and so you have to work really hard to make tiny changes.

I enjoyed working with Sylvie Guillem very much because she is so quick to take new ideas on board and to change things. It is something I see across the board with really elite performers and athletes. But Sylvie always pushes herself anyway. You give her something to do and she will slightly change it, and possibly make it better or more interesting. So I actually learn from working with people like that. I feel I get as much back as I give. I have also worked with Mark Morris, the American choreographer. I have worked with him for many years when he is in London, and he has actually been doing Pilates longer than I have been teaching it. And I find I learn from him every time. They are very open to trying new things, and are so experienced in movement that they say something like, 'If I just did that . . .' and it opens up a whole new possibility of how you might take that exercise further.

One of the things I really enjoy about working here, and which wouldn't happen anywhere else, is that I invent or adapt exercises around our repertoire. Consequently we have these weird exercises named things like 'Godmother 1' and 'Godmother 2' and 'Bronze Idol Turn Exercise' and 'Arabian Exercise'. 'Godmother 1 and 2' are for a particular movement within a solo that the fairy godmother has to do in *Cinderella*, and one dancer was having issues with that step and needed some help. She said, 'When I do this, the line isn't correct and I don't feel stable enough; have you any ideas?' So I adapted two existing exercises, one of which involved a lot of extreme side bending, where you have to be very stable on your other leg. That is something I would never be able to do somewhere else.

I get lots of special challenges, like someone saying, 'I have to be lifted in this particular way, and I can't quite get that position. I need to be able to practise that position, without my poor partner having to lift me all the time.' Then I might find a way of putting that dancer into the same position, which is actually quite fun. One of the male dancers who was going to be dancing the bluebird in our recent new production of *Sleeping Beauty* was having trouble getting his back in a certain position on a jump. So we had to find a way for him to practise it without him having to jump all the time, because jumping is really exhausting, and it is over so quickly that you don't really have time to adjust your back position. So we developed an exercise on a piece of equipment that would enable him to practise it slowly, and see in the mirror how he would look in the air. That is a fascinating side to my job that is only possible because I am working with dancers at this level.

Another dancer I have very much enjoyed working with is Lauren Cuthbertson, one of our English dancers who has recently had quite a lot of prominent roles – she is very good fun. She has even been known to rush in here, in costume, just before a performance, to do a favourite exercise. It gives her confidence so she can think, 'I've done that. That's good. I know it's not going to let me down now.' It is quite a strange sight to see someone in full stage make-up and costume in here. Health and safety would probably have a fit at the thought of the costume getting caught in the equipment.

It is almost unfair to name people because on the whole they are such a fantastic group. They are so talented and so motivated that pretty much all of them are a joy to work with. Not 100 per cent, and not all of the time – everyone has their up days and their down days. It is nice when you work with people over a number of years, because that is when you see real changes. It is great when a dancer comes to me as soon as they join the company, because then you can see them on the way up. I suppose one that springs to mind, who I have worked with a lot, is Brian Maloney, who is one of our American dancers.

Brian came to me straight away. He had already done a little bit of Pilates in America, but felt he needed quite a lot of help technically still, and so we started from day one and I have seen him every week since. He has also been through some quite serious injury since he has been here, and when a dancer is off injured I see them every day, and then you work really closely with that person. You really see things change and see them alter. And I have seen him get promoted, which is lovely. You can't take any credit for that, but it is nice to be on that journey with them, and feel that you have contributed something towards it.

I used to work with the Royal Ballet School and more members of the company when I was in the old rehearsal rooms, but now I pretty much only work with the top dancers. Quite often my job is to get someone back after surgery, with a particular timeframe in mind. For instance, when a principal dancer is off, it is much more challenging than when one of the Corps de Ballet is off. The first person I did a serious rehab on was Stuart Cassidy, who has since left the company and is dancing in Japan. He was my first big test. He had had foot surgery, which initially hadn't gone terribly well, and he had to have a second operation. So he was off for nine or ten months, and I worked with him almost every day. As a principal dancer you can't come back on in the back row of something; you are on in a leading role or you are not there at all. He came back in *Swan Lake*, as Prince Siegfried, and I remember sitting out front with my heart in my mouth watching that first show. It is incredibly exciting doing that whole journey with a dancer from almost day one after surgery to seeing their first performance. It is fantastically rewarding, and has happened many times now over the years.

Feet and ankles are the most common injuries. We get quite a few ankle sprains, which can be quite serious. We have fractures, usually a stress fracture from overwork, although we occasionally get trauma fractures from bashing into scenery. We don't get many problems with knees, which is unusual, although I am in the middle of a fairly serious knee rehab at the moment. We also get some back and shoulder problems. We get lots of statistics from around the world about classical dancers and injuries and we come out pretty well.

People are often at a very low ebb when I start working with them after an injury, so I am very grateful for the rest of our support team, like our psychologist. I like people to feel very secure in this room and safe and valued. It is very difficult for a dancer who is off for any length of time to see their work going to other dancers, and if they are not careful the whole structure of their day falls apart – usually they are so busy going straight from one rehearsal to another and then a show at night. They don't have a minute to themselves, and suddenly if they are injured, the whole day is their own. And although they want to get back as quickly as possible, you have to consider what is safe. If you push back too quickly, are they going to re-injure? So it is quite a responsible position. We do try to educate all the dancers on how to look after themselves, so ultimately the decision is theirs as to whether they feel ready to do something, although we always give advice.

When I am watching a performance here I can never really relax. I can enjoy watching other companies a lot more, but when I am out front here, I am watching individual dancers to see if something we have been working on is getting corrected, or if it is still a problem. It might be something about the way they hold their neck, or something about their elbows that I will be looking at, and of course you miss half of the performance. Alternatively, I suddenly see something like a wobbly ankle on someone, and think, 'Oh, no!' And I am worried that they will go over on it. So I am always a bit on the edge of my seat.

I try to watch some rehearsals and sometimes we can pre-empt problems. I remember some years ago Darcey [Bussell] came to me when something was being choreographed and said, 'I am having real problems with my right thigh.' And I said, 'It must be something you are rehearsing.' And it was a particular move-ment in a Pas de Deux that she was trying over and over again to get correct. It was something quite unusual that the choreog-rapher wanted, and consequently the repetition, rather than the movement itself, was a problem. So we had to try to add in little stretches and things that would help to alleviate that situation. Usually it is the dancer who will highlight a problem, and they might say, 'Could you just pop along to the rehearsal and stick your head in the door and watch me do that, and see if you can come up with some ideas to help.' That is quite a nice relationship to build up.

We do not have time to work directly with choreographers early on, so they take responsibility and know the risks they are taking. Most of them are alert to the possibility of injury when you repeat something awkward, or something that is very unfamiliar to the dancer if it is very modern choreography. Pilates is actually just as important with modern ballet as with classical – and in modern ballet the body needs to be especially flexible, and also one is often more aware of the appearance of the dancer. For example, if you see Sylvie Guillem in a new ballet, here or elsewhere, the way she is dressed now on stage shows a lot. She is very thin, so you tend to notice the musculature more, but she often now has bare legs, and quite often a bare midriff and arms. The use of very specific lighting, with strong shadows, also highlights the musculature.

I don't think her body has actually changed much over the last few years while she has been doing more of that type of work, I just think it is more visible than when she wore pink ballet tights and point shoes. She has always had a very toned, sinewy body: a racehorse kind of physique with the wonderful definition that you get with very low body fat. Obviously, some of the look of dancers is genetic, and down to body type, and the fact that the selection processes at this level are quite severe. So we are working with fabulous physiques in the first place, but then those physiques always need to be pushed more. It is interesting to think how far one can push technique. Where does it go from here?

At present I am supposedly doing a PhD, but I am terrible for putting things off. It is about ballet rather than Pilates: it is great to have something a little bit outside what you do. A few years ago I did a Master's Degree in ballet, and that really helped to broaden my view of the context in which I work. I'm not quite sure what I shall be doing in the future. I am happy doing what I do, and it is very hard to leave a job like this – it would have to be something really special to move from here. There *are* downsides to working here; I am not going to pretend it is perfect. It is tough to keep going all year, because we work from the end of August right through till the end of the next July, and you can't really take any time off during that time. So mentally and physically it is quite a draining job, and you need quite a strong constitution to keep going. But I think it would be hard to find another environment where I felt I was working at such a high level within a profession. I don't think I could go back to working with the general public any more. So I don't know where I might go from here, unless the PhD eventually takes me off into other areas, like writing about ballet – on technique maybe.

Some of the dancers I have worked with say they should have a T-shirt saying 'Body by Paris' but I think most of the general public would not know that a job like this exists. I don't think they bother to read through all the credits in the programme. And when I tell people what I do, although they are fascinated, I think they wonder if a job like mine is necessary. They come to a performance, and see how fabulous all the dancers are: they are thinner and more toned than anybody they know, strong and yet flexible, and they think, 'What could there possibly be to work on?' But then I think, 'Maybe I have done my job quite well!' People are not thinking, 'Oh dear! The dancers all look a bit out of shape: they look like they are struggling to get through this.' But maybe more people will understand about it now, if it is in your book! Perhaps I'll have queues of people applying for my job. I would like to think I would have to retire before anyone else gets my job, but I could do with an assistant!

Casting Director

Joyce Nettles

The job of casting director involves several contradictions. It might be some people's dream: going to the theatre virtually every night, talent spotting. In reality the job is extremely hard work, and after a full day in an office or rehearsal room, you are expected to attend performances in which you might have very little interest. Moreover, the decisions of a casting director can determine the success of a play, and yet it is always the director who has the final say.

Joyce Nettles is an intriguing mix of contradictions too. With such an illustrious career, I expected her to be relatively old. Working it out, she must only be in her fifties, and she looks younger. One might imagine someone who has worked in theatre, television and film to be quite affluent, but she lives in a modest house in north London. Unlike many people who work in film, who have signed photos of stars on the walls, the only evidence I could see of her profession were a lot of video tapes on the shelves (of, for example, Foyle's War, which she casts), and a poster with Roger Rees and the cast of Nicholas Nickleby from the production at the RSC, where Joyce Nettles worked for ten years. And finally, although she does not shy away from stating that she has good taste, it was only when I asked her specifically whether she had discovered any actors (and thereby influenced the face of British theatre and film in a significant way) that she very casually listed some names. The list was awesome.

Selected Production Credits

Macbeth (1976), *Nicholas Nickleby* (both RSC), *Hamlet* (for the Almeida at the Hackney Empire, 1994), *Richard II*, *Corialanus* (both for the Almeida at the Gainsborough, 2000), *The Seagull* (Edinburgh International Festival, 2003), *Julius Caesar* (Barbican Theatre and world tour, 2005), *Blackbird* (Edinburgh International Festival and West End), *Death of a Salesman* (West End, 2005).

*   *   *

I got into my job by chance. I was always interested in acting, but I just wanted to be Julie Christie. I didn't want to go round the reps understudying and playing maids. That is why I am quite tough when I meet young actors and talk about what they want to do and how dedicated they are. I clearly wasn't dedicated enough: I gave up at the drop of a hat. While I was still at university I met a casting director, Miriam Brickman, through my husband, who was an actor [John Nettles, star of *Bergerac* and *Midsomer Murders*]. She asked me if I wanted a temporary job answering her phones, and because I was just about to graduate, and was broke and needed something to do, I took it.

Miriam was a fantastic casting director: one of two great casting directors of her time. She did films directed by people like Karel Reisz, while Maude Spector did the Hollywood blockbusters. Miriam is sadly dead now, but she kind of invented casting in the theatre in this country, starting off as George Devine's assistant at the Royal Court. She had such a good eye for actors that he made her his casting director. She was brilliant, and I stayed there 12 years. I stayed so long that when I was invited to go to the Royal Shakespeare Company, I didn't really want to, because I liked working with Miriam so much. She became a really close friend, and I loved her. It was the best kind of experience, and everything I know, and everything I have passed on to assistants since, I got from her. I went straight from working as Miriam's assistant to working as casting director at the RSC. It didn't seem a big leap to me then: I certainly was unaware at the time how important a job it was. It is only with hindsight that I think, 'Bloody hell, no wonder everyone wanted to know me!' I thought it would be just doing what I did at Miriam's only somewhere else, but it didn't quite turn out like that.

Casting for a company, rather than for a specific play, is different. It is enormously hard to do, and one of the reasons that I left the RSC after ten years was that enough time wasn't given to the casting department to organize that company. A company of 90 actors, going across three theatres, is like Hannibal going across the Alps. You need to plan it very, very, carefully, and you can't just do it in a couple of weeks. And it gets harder as less people want to be committed to being in Stratford for a year or two, as more openings come up for actors in the industry, like television and film. The world of acting has changed, and casting a company is very difficult.

Even the National Theatre rarely cast a company now. Most of the actors go there to do one play. Getting a body of actors together involves pleasing all the directors, and trying to get a company that will happily gel for a two-year period and not all kill each other in the first six months. The first year that I worked at Stratford I cast every part in every play before the first day of rehearsal, because that is what I thought I had to do, and then I imagined I could have 11 months' holiday. It was partly because I was new, eager, committed and passionate. And it was partly because it was a very well-organized season, planned well in advance. It never happened again. Not because I lost the commitment, but because we never knew what all the plays would be in time.

When I left the RSC, in 1985, I went freelance. I did a season at the National, when Gillian Diamond took a sabbatical, and I worked a lot at the Almeida, doing almost everything that Jonathan Kent directed there and subsequently. He is a director who I admire hugely, and also he has become a very good friend. I also worked for Peter Stein, one of the greatest living directors. I have done two things with him now, and I did lots of one-offs at different theatres, and worked for film and television. Theatre doesn't pay very well, so television is the bread and butter, but theatre feeds your soul. Last year I did a year at the Old Vic for Kevin Spacey's first year as artistic director. I left there for complex and personal reasons, and it is still a little bit too close for me to properly analyse.

I don't think I could ever go back to doing theatre full-time again; I just wouldn't want to, but I would miss it dreadfully if I didn't do any. In the last 18 months I have done an awful lot of theatre: four plays at the Old Vic, and also *Death of a Salesman, As You Desire Me, And Then There Were None,* the Agatha Christie directed by Steven Pimlott, and I have just done a play with Michael Blakemore, and I have three more plays I might be doing in the next six months. One is *Troilus and Cressida* directed by Peter Stein. There has been arguably too much theatre, but that is just the way it has turned out. Usually it is the director who will ask me to work on a production, although sometimes it is the producer. There are a few directors with whom I have hopefully got a long-term relationship into the future as well as from the past. I would, I hope not arrogantly, assume that if they were directing something, they would ask me to work with them, although that might not always prove to be the case.

Directors are not all easy to work with; we often have a healthy, rigorous and volatile debate about things, but the ones I have enjoyed working with most, in no particular order, are Trevor Nunn, Jonathan Kent, Peter Stein – always a difficult casting process, but worth it with him. I have also worked with Peter Brook, which I feel is an honour, and I learnt a lot. I worked on *The Mahabharata* and *The Cherry Orchard* with him. I like people I can *learn* from. I like people who are cleverer than me; who know more than me. I genuinely mean that. I don't want to work with people who I've got to teach.

In casting, the first thing I do, obviously, is read the play. The second thing I do, is talk to the director, and get a feel for the period that the play will be set, and the age of the people, and then I will do a list for each part. I would type out anything between one and 30 names for each role. It is sometimes only one, because someone comes at you so strongly that you can say to the director, 'I *know* who should play this part.' Now the director might say, 'No, you are completely wrong,' in which case you probably offer up some other names. It is usual that somebody is already attached: the producer or director has already lined them up. For instance, when I did *As You Desire Me*, [Playhouse Theatre, Jonathan Kent] Kristin Scott Thomas and Bob Hoskins were already attached – they were part and parcel of the play being done.

When I did *Embers* [Duke of York, Michael Blakemore] Jeremy Irons was attached. When I did *Death of a Salesman* [Lyric Theatre, Robert Falls] Brian Dennehy was attached, as were a couple of other actors, because it was transferring from New York. That is usual, because the West End is like any other business, and we are in show *business*, and much as I don't like the star system, I have to acknowledge that you can't just put on a play in the West End without something that will draw an audience to it. When I did *And Then There Were None* [Gielgud Theatre] with Steven Pimlott, there was nobody attached, so we started with a completely blank sheet. And we knew, because we discussed it, that we wanted a *company* – an ensemble of ten actors – and we succeeded in getting that. We didn't want someone looking at the poster saying, 'Oh, he must be in it because he's famous.'

For the Peter Stein *Troilus*, which I am about to embark on, Peter has said to me that he wants a very young Troilus and a very young Cressida. Now even if I disagree with him, as I *do*, that they should be as young as he wants, I know that I can't suggest someone of 35, even if they look 25. So even though I might not be going to 16 or 17, I know that I have to think of people who are either just about to come out of drama school, or who have come out last year. I am definitely thinking drama school, because they are very difficult parts, and the actors need training and the ability to do Shakespeare.

The process here is a bit of an exception. Peter is German and he doesn't know British actors, so for me to do lists is a complete waste of time. And also because of the nature of the job, which is rather bizarre, what I will probably do, is make a list of actors who I think would respond to this kind of work: maybe 200 or 300 actors. Then I will go through that list and think, 'Is there anything in this play that they could do?' So I will think of an actor who would enjoy the working process with Peter Stein, which is eclectic and not to everybody's taste: a brilliant experience for some actors, and absolute misery for others. Peter Stein rehearses at home, in his twelfth-century castle in Tuscany, which is great, but you are stuck there for two months, just with a bunch of actors. You can't get anywhere; there is not another town for miles, and not every actor would respond well to that experience of being enclosed. So on something like that, you need to know the actor's personality as well.

When I did *The Seagull* with Peter Stein two years ago, I think I knew everybody we cast pretty well. I don't mean that I go out clubbing or partying with them, but I had known them all over a period of time. So casting *Troilus* will be interesting for me. Who are the actors who would enjoy, and/or benefit from this kind of process? Simon Russell Beal would. And he is brilliant, but first, he is not available, and also he has played Thersites. So it is a brilliant idea that can't work. But that is how I shall approach it.

Sometimes, when a director has gone through my list, there will be straight offers made to an actor, through his or her agent, if they have one. I *like* directors who know actors, which is why I like working with Jonathan Kent so much. He knows actors really well, so we can talk about the actor without having to meet them. Working with directors who don't know actors well happens less in the theatre than it does in film and television, where the degree of knowledge of actors on the part of the director is *staggeringly* depressing.

The next round after the straight offers is the meetings and auditions, and how those are conducted depends entirely on the project. Some directors just like to meet and talk, some actors like to meet and read from the play. Some actors might, rightly, be too grand to come in and read, and yet the director feels that he has got to meet them, because it is a very intimate process. It can be quite delicate, getting a senior, leading actor in to meet a director. You have to handle it with sensitivity. I am constantly aware of how heartbreaking it is that even actors in their 80s still have to go and parade their talents, and face the possibility of being told they haven't got the job. But I do think I have got great taste in actors. If I lost faith in that, I wouldn't be able to work. Having worked for a very, very long time, I have something practical in my life, like a CV, and something resembling a bank balance, that can support my instinct.

I either want to remember an actor, or I don't. I can't remember them all. I remember going to RADA and seeing Anton Lesser walk across the stage, and I wrote his name down and thought, 'Who is that?' Actors don't like stories like this, because they would say, 'That's not fair! How can you judge an actor, literally, by the way he walks across the stage?' How can I justify saying, after seeing an actor once, 'I want to remember and pursue that actor, rather than another one.' What right do I have to make that judgement after only a meeting or seeing them in a very small part? The answer is I have the right because I have the job to cast this play, and presumably people wouldn't come back and ask me to work for them again if I had got it all wrong. So *I* think I have got very good taste, and I usually make very quick judgements as to whether someone is worth remembering.

The longest period there was between me seeing, and casting, an actor, was something like 28 years! I meet actors, and they say, 'You won't forget me, will you?' and I say, 'No, but it might be that I remember you again in five years' time.' Obviously, I have a very good memory, as well as files. But I saw a Polish actor, Wojciech Pszoniak, in Peter Daubeny's World Theatre Season, who was brilliant: 28 years later Karol Reisz asked me if I knew a middle-eastern European actor who could play the doctor in *The Deep Blue Sea* and I said, 'Well, I do, actually.' And this actor, who I had very loosely kept in touch with over the years with the odd Christmas card, had gone to Paris from Poland as a political refugee, and Karol flew to Paris and met him, and cast him, and he came over to London to play at the Almeida. Subsequently I cast him in an episode of *Kavanagh QC*.

I find it very frustrating if I have a strong view about someone and the director disagrees, because he has the final say. But I suspect that the director finds it as frustrating as me, if not more so, because I tend to be quite outspoken. I might say something like, 'Well you are making a terrible mistake!' Or, 'Of course I can do a longer list, but I can't do a better one.' But because most of the theatre directors I work with now, I have worked with before, we do have a kind of shorthand, and they trust me enough that if I say, 'You've got to meet this person: *please* meet this person', they will generally do it. And then, of course, if it works out well, it is great to be proved right. Casting is a very ephemeral job. Casting directors, in an ideal world, should not exist. They do, because there are too many actors, and so getting it right is being vindicated.

For instance, *The Seagull* was a great thing to do. [The first time Peter Stein worked with an English-speaking cast, opening at the Edinburgh Festival in 2003.] We got a fantastic cast [including Fiona Shaw and Iain Glen]. One of the people who has done well since is Cillian Murphy, who played Konstantin, and was absolutely wonderful. He was about to take off in movies, and it was touch and go whether we would get him, because there were movies around for him at the time, but I am thrilled that we did, and so was Peter. Other young actors in it were Charlotte Emmerson, Eliott Cowan and Jodhi May, who played Nina, and then went on to do *Blackbird* with Peter, which is a production about to come into the West End.

I have discovered a lot of young actors and actresses. A lot of people came into the RSC while I was there: many of them in their first jobs. People who all came early in their careers were Mark Rylance, Anton Lesser, Juliet Stevenson, Fiona Shaw, Ken Branagh, Ruby Wax, Jane Horrocks, Alan Rickman – he didn't come straight from RADA, but was certainly an unknown quantity to the world in general when he came to the RSC – there were loads of them, who came straight out of drama school. I went to see drama school productions and suggested that the RSC employ them. But I doubt if I'll be there when these actors appear on that television programme *This is Your Life*. Actors, whom I very frequently adore, tend always to think that they got the job themselves. I don't think that is 'malice aforethought'; maybe it is partly because they *have* to, to keep having the necessary confidence to carry on. But I don't think many of them say, 'Good old Joyce. I'm really grateful to Joyce, because if it hadn't been for her, I wouldn't have got that kick start to my career!' I don't think they think like that.

I discover actors in everything I do: I watched some television last night, and saw an actor I didn't know, and wrote his name down, and looked him up in *Spotlight* [a UK directory of actors with names and photos] this morning. I never switch off. I enjoy going to the theatre for pleasure, but only if it is in a foreign language do I think, 'Thank God, nobody is going to write to me tomorrow, or send me their *Spotlight* pin number, or a video or DVD (which now tend to pile up till I have to watch 20 or 30), and I haven't got to remember who they are.'

My favourite thing in the world is seeing Shakespeare in a foreign language. I know the play, so I don't have to worry about understanding it, and there is some kind of release about seeing it in a foreign language. I haven't worked out the logic of this, because Shakespeare is the greatest dramatist who ever lived, and it is all in the words, so how can I like it, if it is in Japanese? They could be saying, 'Can I have a packet of frozen peas please?' And yet, for me, it is intensely satisfying. I hope not, but do not know, whether it is a really bad translation. But ironically, some of the best Shakespeare I have seen has been in foreign languages, which does disturb me. There is, for instance, something about Eastern European productions of *Richard III*, where they understand in a way that we don't, suffering under political dictatorships.

I saw a Romanian *Richard III* which was just breathtaking, and a Japanese *Macbeth* directed by Yukio Ninagawa – that and Trevor Nunn's, with Judi Dench and Ian McKellen – are my two favourite *Macbeth*s. I was very lucky because I was at the RSC in a golden age. That is nothing to do with rose-tinted glasses, or getting older or sentimental. There has been a recent RSC period that has been far from golden: it's *tarnished*. But I was there when Trevor did *Macbeth* [1976] and *Nicholas Nickleby* [1981, with a cast of 40]. I consider myself fortunate, because he is a brilliant director, and was going through one of his many golden periods. It was thrilling to work with him.

But one of the reasons I don't feel I could do full-time theatre again is not only does it not pay very well, but it is very demanding. I am starting work on *Troilus and Cressida* now, in January, and rehearsals only start in June. At the RSC in particular, the process was *endless*. First there is the pre-production process of all the casting, and then I would go to some of the rehearsals, then a preview, and press night, and understudy run, and the last night in Stratford. Then the play would go to Newcastle, and I would see it there, and then again in London. It is a full-time job keeping up with the show you have cast, let alone going to the theatre to see other things, after an eight-hour day. Last week I went to the theatre five times. I am not a workaholic, and I didn't plan it like that, and it was a real killer. It is really hard, but it is my job. I'd much rather be a novelist!

There used to be more women casting directors than men, but it is changing a little now: there is a man at the head of the National Theatre's casting department. But it can be quite a subservient job. My job is to serve the director, and to some extent, the producer, but I like to see it as serving the director. So I am not the boss, the director is, and I think women are better at serving. I am not suggesting I am not a feminist, or that I am docile. Yet looking back at my time at the RSC, I don't know how I got through it, having a small child, too.

For people coming into casting now, it is rather different. Now television companies don't have in-house casting directors, they bring people in from job to job, and there are hundreds and hundreds of casting directors. The BBC has almost no one in house in any department, because so much is made for them by independent companies. The BBC is crumbling before our eyes. Also, there are promotions, and adverts and videos that all use casting directors now, and a whole world that I don't know about, or want to.

The natural path into becoming a casting director is to work with one. I have had four assistants in a long life of casting. My first and second assistants are now casting directors, my third is PA to Victoria Wood and my fourth, Louise, is with me now. They have all, hopefully, got the kind of training I got with Miriam Brickman. You just pick things up when you are working with someone who does good work, as I hope that I do.

I shall carry on for as long as I can, and then I'll write my novel! I like doing it when the conditions are favourable; not in a howling storm. I like working with talented people. I am a snob, but I am quite proud of that, because in this world of *Celebrity Big Brother* somebody has to wave the flag of good taste. I *love* working with Jonathan Kent, and I am very excited about working with Peter Stein. I know it will be very difficult, and that there will be tears at bedtime, possibly blood on the carpet.

I watch an episode of *EastEnders* from time to time, but I don't get Soaps. I think it would be much more interesting for the people who watch them to go out and have a bit of a life. I get a great buzz out of working on wonderful texts, and that always brings you back to Shakespeare, who is the best without a doubt. It is thrilling and challenging. But I enjoy the freedom I have now. I am about to do two episodes of *Foyle's War* on TV, and I love that too, because it is classy telly, with very good scripts, and we get very good actors, and it pays me well enough to allow me to do the theatre.

Theatre is more personal than film: there is more of a journey. You bring in the actor, have an audition, see them grow during rehearsals, watch them during the run, see their ability, and stamina, and a relationship is built up. When I cast a movie, I probably never see any of them again, until in two years' time, I catch it on the telly. Something like *Nicholas Nickleby* is still unbelievably special to me. When I last went to Stratford, I bought myself the DVD of it. It remains brilliant. There was a fantastic company of actors, and Trevor Nunn directing, who has the ability to bring out the best in everybody. You come away from seeing it and think, even though you may be wrong, that you have seen the best 30 actors in the country, nay in the world! You probably haven't, but Trevor has this inspirational gift. It was a wonderful version by David Edgar, fantastic music by Stephen Oliver – it was inspiring. I would like that on my tombstone: 'She cast *Nicholas Nickleby*.' It was fab.

Choreographer and Director

Susan Stroman

Among Susan Stroman's awards are five Tonys, two Oliviers, eight Outer Critics Circle Awards, five Drama Desk Awards, four Astaire Awards and the Drama League's Distinguished Achievement in Musical Theatre Award. She has choreographed and directed for stage and screen. Born in 1954 in Wilmington, Delaware, Stroman majored in theatre at university, before moving to New York to pursue what she already knew she wanted to do: choreography. She worked with touring companies and then received her first break as a choreographer in the revival of John Kander and Fred Ebb's Flora, the Red Menace. *Soon after she was discovered by Broadway producer Harold Prince, who asked her to choreograph his 1989 New York City Opera production of* Don Giovanni.

Stroman went on to choreograph many Broadway and off-Broadway shows, later directing as well, and recently choreographing and directing the film of her stage success, The Producers. *Mel Brooks, the show's writer, said of her, 'She'll look at something, look so intensely that it's scary. I mean, she is something. If she were a laser beam, she would destroy whatever she was looking at. It's such energy and focus when she's studying it.' Stroman is known for her vision. In her interview, what came out most forcefully is her ability to visualize music and her love of collaborative work.*

Selected Production Credits

Don Giovanni (New York City Opera), *Crazy for You, Show Boat, Big, Contact, The Music Man, The Producers, The Frogs* (all Broadway), *Oklahoma!* (West End).

*   *   *

When I was five years old I went to dance school. Also, my father was a wonderful piano player, so the house was always filled with music. That passion for music, given to me by my father, was what propelled me into the theater. He would play the piano, and I would dance around the house and choreograph! Even at a very early age, more than performing, I loved creating. As I got a little older, I started to choreograph in community theaters, and in the high-school band. I would perform in the different shows, and loved to sing and dance, but it was really creating choreography that gave me the most joy. To sit at the back of a theater, and hear an audience laugh, or cry or see them put their arms around each other – to see how choreography affects an audience is very fulfilling.

I am a choreographer of the theater, which is different from being a choreographer for a dance company. In the theater one has to know about dance through the different decades, in different class systems and societies, in order to service the plot and the story. To be a choreographer in the theater is to be a storyteller. You create a dance for a *specific* man, whereas in abstract dance companies you are creating the role of *everyman*. And if I am just choreographing, it is very collaborative with the director and composer. We must all see eye to eye.

I immerse myself very much in the decade and the geographical situation. For example, when I did *Crazy for You*, I immersed myself in the 1930s and that style, and how people danced in the east and the west. In *Show Boat*, it was dancing at the turn of the century in America, and the north and the south. But for *The Producers*, it was more a matter of immersing myself into the world of Mel Brooks. I had to try to make the comedy carry all the way through. So, for example, Mel would say, 'I am writing a song called, "I want to be a producer" and I want Leo Bloom to be surrounded by beautiful girls.' Then it is my job to figure out how to get those girls on stage. So I would say to Mel:

Why don't I hide some girls in the file cabinets? Then Leo Bloom can turn around, and all of a sudden, girls pop out of the file cabinets, and the set can blow away, and we can do a big production number where Leo Bloom is surrounded by beautiful girls.

That comes out of a strong collaboration, where the writer or composer (Mel was both in this case) writes the number, and then I visualize it. An important thing from an early age, for me, was visualizing music. When I hear music I have always imagined all sorts of pictures, and that is still true today. If I hear music I see a whole scenario, with costumes, and fights and story.

Another thing you have to do as a choreographer is to take on the role of a character while you create it. So while I am creating 'I want to be a producer' I am imagining myself as Leo Bloom, as I am making up the routine. I am also imagining myself as the actor, Matthew Broderick, knowing what his strengths and limitations are. So you have to take the actor's talent into consideration when you are choreographing. It is different with a show like *Contact*, which is a show about dancers, and took place in a dance club. There I was able to have great freedom, knowing that these dancers were true athletes.

But when something seems difficult, I see it more as an opportunity than a challenge. When I create a show, I love the collaboration between the composer and lyricist, and the whole creative and design team. I also think that with every show I do I become stronger, because I learn more about everybody else's department. For example, even if I create the greatest dance step of all, if it is not lit right, or if it doesn't have the right costumes, it won't work.

I loved working with Mel Brooks: he is a great collaborator, and he loves music, so opening up the music he wrote for *The Producers* was wonderful, because he is so receptive to ideas. For example, he wrote a wonderful song called 'That Face', and there is a line in the play when Leo Bloom says, 'I want everything I have ever seen in the movies.' So being inspired by that line that Mel wrote, I created a dance that paid homage to Fred and Ginger. However, we never leave the comedy, because Leo Bloom is never going to be a strong dancer: it has the partnering of Fred and Ginger, but it remains comic, because that is the nature of the play.

I also adored working with Harry Connick [composer and lyricist] on *Thou Shalt Not* because he is a wonderful writer, and I was inspired by the music of New Orleans. Another show I loved doing was *Crazy for You*. For that, the Gershwin Estate allowed me to open up the music for dance, because what I also sometimes do as a choreographer is alter the music to create the dance arrangement. For instance, in *Crazy for You*, the song 'Shall We Dance?' comes to me as a simple melody, but I manipulated the time signature to help the emotion of the story. So if Bobby and Polly are coy and shy with each other, I play it in a soft shoe rhythm; if they want to chase each other, I play it faster; and if they fall in love, I play it as a grand waltz. So changing the time and rhythm of the music helps express the emotion through dance.

I think the show that is most dear to my heart is *Contact* [where Stroman was writer of the book, director and choreographer]. It was really based on something I saw. I was in a club in downtown New York, and into a sea of New Yorkers who only wear black, stepped a girl in a yellow dress. She would step forward when she wanted to dance with someone, and retreat back when she was done with them. And I thought to myself, 'This girl is going to change someone's life tonight!' And it was only a couple of weeks later that I got a call from André Bishop at the Lincoln Center, saying, 'If you have an idea, I will help you develop it.' So I replied, 'Well actually, I do have an idea!'

I went down into the basement of Lincoln Center, and had 18 dancers, and created a short story based on that visual that I saw. Rather than being based on an existing book, or a movie, that show was based on my gut emotion of seeing this girl. Having that opportunity to create something is rare, especially in American theater. Here the theater is less supported than it is in London, so it is very commercial, and it is very unusual for someone to say that they will help you develop an idea. Usually someone is handing you a script for an old revival, to play it safe. Sadly, we don't take as many chances as in London. So I had this opportunity to do something with no expectations: no one was saying, 'You need to create a hit,' or even whether it had to be a musical, a dance piece or a play. So when it did become a hit, and ran for three years at Lincoln Center, it went beyond any dream.

Winning awards has given me some of the chances to work on projects that I might not have had before. So for me, it is the opportunities that have been the most important thing. I have been lucky to work so much on Broadway. There is so much talent out there from people who can really act, dance and sing. There is nothing like live theater; and when you see some of these performers, who can belt it out, and do it all, it is quite moving. If you walk through Schubert Alley, you can feel the electricity: it is like all the talent that has come before is zipping down the alleyway. The lights of Broadway, the concentrated area, the history of all the musicals, make it special.

In film it is very different. It is very technical, and doesn't have the same kind of heart. In the theater, everyone drives towards an opening night, and everyone is in the same swimming pool together: you all drown together, or get an Olympic medal together. When you direct a film, there are very many technical categories. You start with the shooting crew, and when you have finished shooting, you never see them again. Then you get passed to the editing team, then the sound mix team, the Foley team [who add sound effects such as doors shutting, or shattering glass] and then the colorization team. It is like you have this film under your arm, and knock on the door, and meet a new group of people who add something to the image that you caught. It is not as live, as alive as the theater. Although I admired and *adored* the technical team that I worked with on the movie of *The Producers*, it still did not have that feeling of a team finishing together, which one has in the theater. The director is the only constant in film, and carries it through for a year and a half.

I have just finished the film and the DVD, so I am just taking a little time off to decide what to do next. I have been offered more films, and some theater, but I have also been creating some new things myself, and I think I am probably going to go back to the theater and work on an idea I had before I started the movie. It is not that I wouldn't do a movie again, I would, and in fact I have been asked to make *Contact* into a movie, so that is a big possibility. But I think I am going to go back to theater first, and do a show, and then do a film. I feel I am a writer of dance in a sense, and a dramaturg [works as advisor to the director on the background and historical relevance of a play, edits and revises scripts and advises on the suitability of scripts for a company], as I work on these different pieces, so some day it might be nice to write, as well as choreograph and direct!

I have a great passion for the theater, and I love working with the actors, but I really adore the collaboration with the design team, the composer and the lyricist. There is something so wonderful about a team of people giving birth to a show: there is nothing like it really. I enjoy doing different themes, different time periods, and I feel very fortunate that something I had a passion for when I was very young has actually followed through. Because I visualize music, I think if I hadn't become a choreographer, I probably would have gone crazy! Even to this day, when I hear music, I see hoards of people dancing through my head.

Costume Designer

Paul Tazewell

Paul Tazewell is a tall, slim, elegant 42–year-old African American. When I met him he was wearing blue jeans, brown leather shoes and a soft grey suede jacket. Under the jacket was a tight-fitting beige jumper with co-ordinating sleeveless jumper on top. The latter was by Save the Queen and sported a subtle-shaded, stitched appliqué abstract design suggestive of skyscrapers. In conversation Tazewell comes across as a passionate realist: an unusual combination which has served him well in his chosen career.

Tazewell has over 18 years' experience in costume design. He has received a Princess Grace Theater Fellowship, three Helen Hayes Awards, the Lucille Lortel Award and several others. He has designed costumes for many critically acclaimed Broadway and off-Broadway productions. He has also designed extensively for regional theatres across America as well as internationally. Paul is at present taking a leave of absence from an associate professorship at Carnegie Mellon University in order to work full-time on costume design for plays, musicals, opera and ballet.

Selected Production Credits

One Flea Spare (Public Theatre), *Bring in 'Da Noise, Bring in 'Da Funk, On the Town, Elaine Stritch At Liberty, The Color Purple* (all Broadway), *Harlem Song, Flesh and Blood* (Lincoln Center), *Margaret Garner* (Michigan Opera), *Caroline or Change* (Broadway and National Theatre).

*   *   *

Originally I wanted to be a dancer or singer, but I thought I would not be typecast in the same way if I were a costume designer. If I had joined a company it would have been different, but my focus was the Broadway stage, and there were roles that being African American, I felt I would never be up for: it just wouldn't happen. So I thought I would have a fuller, more creative career as a designer. And when I look back on it, if I had chosen to be a dancer, my career would have been very short. I can design as long as I care to, although I have found I still get typecast in the work that I am asked to do. There have been disadvantages and advantages. Being African American has created a career for me because there are very few African American designers working in theater, or in film. When I was coming up there were maybe three or four other African American designers who were working, and we all got to it in a different way.

I grew up in Akron, Ohio, where my father was a research chemist for Firestone, the tire and rubber company. I went to a high school that had a performing arts program, because at that point I still hoped to be a dancer and singer, but I also designed the costumes for the high-school productions. Then I did one years' undergraduate at Pratt Institute in Brooklyn, doing fashion design, because I felt being in New York I could start taking dance classes and do auditions, but also I would at least get a degree that I could fall back on.

But soon I really gave up the idea of dancing and started focusing on costume design. I went to North Carolina School of the Arts, in Winston, Salem, and then did my graduate work at NYU in costume and scenic design. A year after I graduated I got a job designing a production for the Arena Stage, a regional theater in the States. I was working with the associate artistic director, a man named Tazewell Thompson – we share a name but it is his first name and we are not related. He liked my work and we worked a lot all around the country in different regional theaters. That gave me more exposure, and I started to get noticed by George C. Wolfe, who later became the artistic director of the Public Theater. He asked me to do a production of *Blade to the*

Heat [by Oliver Mayer] in his first year there, and that started a relationship working with George. I did a couple of shows there with other directors, and then George asked me to design the costumes for *Bring in 'Da Noise, Bring in 'Da Funk* [by George C. Wolfe] and several other productions.

At that time there was a grant that went to regional theaters for cultural diversity. There was also a thing called 'Blind Casting' aimed at diversifying theater companies, so there was a lot of casting done according to talent rather than, for example, trying to create a family that looked like each other. Some of that was good, and produced some wonderful work, and some of it was abysmal, where decisions were made according to filling the quota rather than to make an excellent production. But with that, I was invited in.

Of course, I think costume design is much more important than many people feel that it is. It is my task to make a visual image of who a character is. Through research, and given the physicality of the actor, my job is to give clues to the audience in support of who the character is, or will become, or how the costumes will play poetically within the piece itself. The decisions made are multi-layered, and of course they incorporate the director's point of view. Some directors are more comfortable than others talking about clothing. I was going to say that as a generalization, if you are dealing with a male director, their connection with clothing tends to be fairly minimal, but that is not necessarily true. I suppose that directors have more of a sense of space and how they want the actors to move around the space, and what that environment needs to be, than they do of the nitty-gritty and the detail of creating a costume. But directors, actors and costume designers, all have to do some of the same work in making a character live.

As a designer, you have to love people in order to do the work well. You are always collaborating with an actor, or another designer, or the people who are building your clothing, or the director. I enjoy working with all directors so long as they communicate, and there is a trust that is built. All of them work in different ways, and therefore I work differently with them. I think certain parts of my personality come out more with certain directors. For example, because I started working with George when I was so young, certain buttons are pushed – sometimes that is good, sometimes not so good, but in general it is much more casual. With other directors it might be like walking on eggshells while they are trying to figure out my personality and style, and I am trying to figure out theirs. You always have to communicate where you are coming from, what your idea is, what the style is. So you need people skills to make others feel comfortable around you and to pull the best out of them.

Oftentimes, the set designer and director have already been collaborating, and I get brought in at a slightly later stage. For example, I have just done a production called *The Wiz*, and they have been working on that set for two years – they had a plan to do it, and then it didn't happen, and finally it was produced. So when I came on the scene the environment was pretty much established. My role was to create living, breathing characters in that space. The process is not usually that long, but typically the scene designer would meet with the director first. In England scene and costume design are normally done by one person. I have done that, and it is so much work that I cannot imagine what doing that job regularly is like!

I do not always know the cast in advance. You might know who the lead characters will be, but you are constantly adapting. I am always saying to the director, 'That isn't the type that you said you were going to cast. So now, I think that this might be a better choice.' I might do another sketch to show the director, or I might realize that a big, bold flower print isn't going to work, so we will buy another fabric.

On the whole I prefer period shows, although I like modern pieces if there is an element of fantasy. I don't care for modern pieces mainly because it provides the opportunity for everyone to have an opinion. Everyone has an opinion about what they wear daily, and about the people they see walking down the street, and it is so individual and specific that it makes my job that much more difficult. Everyone's connection to something that is as close as contemporary clothing is so varied. In doing research for a period piece, you become the authority.

When you are dealing with modern dress, you are really doing styling. You are servicing the actors and *then* the character, more than just the character. And the producer's wife, or director's lover, or anybody, can step in and say, 'Oh! I don't think that works.' Then everybody starts to question, 'Does it work, or not, and is it in support of what we are trying to do?' In point of fact if nothing had been said, it would have worked for some people and not for others, and that is what theater is, it is a point of view.

I spent a lot of time as a child people-watching. I would go to the mall, and sit on a bench, and watch people, to pass the time. I would stare at them, which is not very polite, but I found it really intriguing. I would try to figure out what sort of person they were from what they were wearing, how they cut their hair, and what make-up they wore. And I would wonder why they had decided to dress like that that day. And I made use of that, because now in the fitting room, I get an actor in, and you *must* have a dialogue with them. I don't feel comfortable just saying, 'Here. This is what you will be wearing,' and expecting them to put it on and think that I am done, because I know it will come back to bite me in the end.

I do a lot of emotional reading in the mirror as the actor looks at him- or herself. I try to think whether it feels right for the character and the person. I also look at their expression and how they are feeling about themselves in the garment. If an actor is really unhappy with something, I would try to find out what it is about it that they don't like and make changes. Sometimes I am better at it than others, but generally I have been able to release my idea so that I can be objective about it. Certain ideas I feel very attached to, but I have learnt that I have to be adaptable. I might ask the actor how we could make it better for them and still fulfill the idea that the director and I have come up with.

I also get involved with hair, and usually draw an idea of what it will be, and then discuss it with the hair designer. Being a hair or wig designer you need to be even closer to the actor than the costume designer in a way: it takes a special person who is very good at communicating. Some costume designers don't care how the actor feels, but I have a hard time compartmentalizing the knowledge that the actor doesn't feel good, and would rather just do the work to make something they are happy with.

That was the case when I did the costume for *Elaine Stritch at Liberty* in 2002 [a one-woman, Tony award-winning show, on Broadway, on tour and in the West End]. Elaine [a Broadway legend, born in 1925] is a marvel; she's great; she's a handful. She is everything that I think one would expect her to be. I saw a little too much of who she was in a way, but then she is just human. When you are dealing with anyone who is a celebrity, and especially with *Elaine Stritch at Liberty*, it is necessarily all about her. I wanted to make her look the best that she can, but I was not interested in recreating her, and she was not interested in being recreated, and if she was, I would be a little wary of that. She just needed to feel good about going out there. [Eventually she was dressed in a white shirt and black leggings.]

A lot of it was talking. We would have fittings, and she would bring in some outfits that she really liked, and that she liked performing in. I took a look at them and they felt kind of 70s and from a different era. So we tried a few different things, which I drew, and had made. She started off in a suit that was black, with a short skirt – kind of 'Armani-ish' style. But it was too much for what she was doing. It was too formal for the conversational style that both she and I wanted. And then an idea hit me. When she was rehearsing she wore a pair of black tights, or sometimes shorts, but her legs were always visible and she would have a T-shirt on. She was there to work, and it was completely no-nonsense. One day, she and George Wolfe and I were all there, and it was like we almost all said it together, that maybe she just needed to be in a shirt. Maybe it needed to be some very stripped-down shirt, because then it would be all about her legs, because she was very proud of her legs. So then we flipped from the suit to the shirt. We had to search for the perfect white shirt: the one that had just enough silk in it, but wasn't too flimsy.

I don't really feel I have a particular style, although there are stylistic choices that I lean towards. For instance, if someone wants to set a show in the 50s, and they want to have a big ball scene, then I know that most of my clothing will be modeled after Dior, Balenciaga, Charles James: it will have a sculptural, drape sense, with little pattern but a strong silhouette. That is what I gravitate to. There was a review of *The Wiz* in *Variety* where they talked about the clothes being stylish and witty, and that kind of wording is repeated about my work. Sometimes it is colorful, but not splashy or wildly innovative.

On the other hand, *Caroline or Change* [book and lyrics by Tony Kushner, directed by George C. Wolfe], had some quite unusual costumes. If you are faced with designing an inanimate object [apart from the people there are characters in the musical called The Washing Machine, The Dryer and The Radio] that needs to live in some way, and you don't want it to be a Disney walk-around, or a box, you have to figure out the spiritual embodi-ment of that idea. What was wonderful about that production, and why I have such a warm place for it in my creative soul, is that it was one of the times when the collaboration between the director and myself felt really right and strong.

I remember sitting in George's office at the Public Theater for hours, drawing as we were looking at research, and as he was describing what he thought it might need to be. I am not sure when, in his development of the piece, George started to incor-porate a collective history of African Americans, and with that, the direct tie to slavery. So with The Radio [embodied by three women, dressed in gold and flesh-toned evening wear, with gold chokers and bracelets] it is like a group of nude slaves. They are glamorous and showy, but they have gold shackling, and in some ways embody what the radio is for Caroline. Similarly I wanted to portray what The Washing Machine is for Caroline. [The Washing Machine wears a lovely dress with a tight, low-cut purple bodice, and skirt that appears to be made of large hand-kerchiefs: like loads of separate garments in one.] She is like a matron black figure of the Southern family, and she has real warmth.

I think the reason George and I work well together is that there is an unspoken communication. He does say when something is right, and I work at reading his mind until it is right. I am invested with the job of creating his idea visually, and work to make that happen. Tony Kushner was not descriptive at all in the script, ever, except in that the play was set in 1963. He did not get involved at all until we were in the theater, and then he was very happy with it. Most writers do not really have a lot of input. I worked on August Wilson's *Jitney* when he was around, and part of the production process: he was quiet, elegant, in a way. I think he was very reserved. It was rare that he spoke up to the creative team. He would talk to the director, and he would want a director that he approved of, often someone he had worked with before.

I do not really have a preference for working on straight plays, musicals or operas. I prefer pieces that are obviously poetic and are open to interpretation, because that makes my work more creative. I am not as drawn to pieces that are very straightfor-ward. Similarly, I enjoy working with directors who like to push the limits of whatever the image might be. But I believe that as a designer you always need to have a plan B, and that needs to be just as successful. It took a while for me to learn that, through working with different directors. I have worked with directors who, after a first preview, say that all of a certain character's clothes don't work. So you start to scramble around and make it right. Of course that is not the way you want it to happen, but you figure it out, and tap dance your way through it so that it all works out fine in the end.

All productions come with different challenges. *The Color Purple* on Broadway right now is probably the largest production I have ever done. And for that I am always redesigning something, because new cast members come in, and we are coming up to a tour in Chicago, which will mean some redesign as well. That was difficult more because of the quantity than the idea. For *The Wiz*, which I mention because it is so fresh in my mind, the challenge was to make something feel appealing for an audience today. It was first done in the mid-70s and much of the script and music is the same, but the hope was to have a production that was very contemporary looking. So the fantasy characters are inspired by things that you see today, as opposed to things that inspired the designs of the 70s.

What I enjoy most is creating different worlds, and telling stories with clothing. I actively try to set up an arc, which goes in parallel to the text. Much of the enjoyment, too, is seeing what I have created two-dimensionally come to life: there is a big thrill in that. I like the drawing and thinking. I do better when I think with my pencil, because it is clearer. I learnt to build [make] costumes when I was in school, so I have the knowledge of what it will take to have a garment do X, Y and Z. Some designers who do scenic work as well as costume, and actually some costume designers, do not necessarily have the building experience, and rely on the costume shop supervisor to engineer whatever is needed. One is trying to put a liquid geometric shape onto an organic form. So you need to understand what the shape has to do, and where the darts must go, so that it lives on the body the way you want it to.

At present I have a two-year leave of absence from teaching at Carnegie Mellon. I was there for three years, and both teaching and designing are full-time jobs, and I think that to be a really good professor you need to be present daily with your students. When I have done that I have seen the growth, but when I am not present I see the plateaux. But my love is designing and creating, and when my focus is teaching I am not able to do that. So I am going to go back to just doing freelance designing. As I get older I also want to slow down a little bit. I have been designing professionally since I was 24, and every season has been very charged. Somewhere along the way there is the fear that the next call isn't going to come, so you say, 'I'll do this while I am getting offered the work.' While I have the energy to run around the city of New York, or abroad, and get the show done, I'll do it. Nevertheless there is a certain wear and tear on relationships and family, so it is tough to be away a lot.

But I am proud of getting to where I have. I had talent, but you also have to stick to it to make it work. I wanted to be visible within the community of costume designers, and I am. I was up for a Tony Award for the second time for *The Color Purple*, and I think other designers appreciate my work, and that means a lot. In some ways it would be nice to design for film, because it would give me a simpler life. I would know that with the amount of money that I would make I would be able to take time off. I would also like to do more opera, either in Europe or in the States. I do some, for example, I did Washington Opera's latest production of *Porgy and Bess*, but I used to live in Washington for a huge amount of my early career and was never asked to do anything there. Then once they decided they were going to do a black show I was asked to do it.

You live it every day. Much of my job, especially if I am doing a modern show, is going into department stores and buying clothing. Well, I am not unlike any other black man that walks through Macy's or Bloomingdale's: you know their eyes are on you, and that they are sizing you up for what they think you might do – that you are going to steal something. I sometimes have assistants with me who have confirmed that that was going on, but some of that I am sure I am just wary of, and it is created in my head. But it is something which hovers. On the other hand, there is no other job that I can think of that puts together what my talents are and what my personality is so completely: my ability to draw, and my love of envisioning and creating beautiful things on women, and recreating period, and glamour, and shoes, and sparkly things and grit. It is all of those things wrapped up together, and also telling a story, and having a poetic voice, and working with people. What else would I do, given what I've got?

Deputy Stage Manager

Andy Hall

The title deputy stage manager implies that the job might involve similar duties to a stage manager, but at a lower level. In fact the duties of a DSM are quite distinct, and absolutely fascinating (and I say this not just because, many years ago, I used to be one). Deputy stage managers are 'on the book' in rehearsals and 'run the show' during performance – two phrases illuminated by Andy Hall, who is a DSM in one of England's most interesting theatres: the Stephen Joseph in Scarborough, Yorkshire, where playwright Sir Alan Ayckbourn has been artistic director since 1972.

The Stephen Joseph Theatre was the first theatre-in-the-round in Britain. Established in 1955, it started out as a tiny theatre on the first floor of the public library (with Ayckbourn as stage manager and actor). It later moved to the ground floor of the former Scarborough Boy's High School, but it was not until 1988 that it found a permanent home in what used to be the Odeon cinema. The new theatre comprises two auditoria: the Round, a 404–seat theatre and the McCarthy, a 165–seat endstage/ cinema. The Stephen Joseph Theatre runs with a relatively small back-stage staff, where, for example, the same person is responsible for light-ing and sound. It is a thriving theatre where Ayckbourn premiers the majority of his plays. He also directs their West End premiers: Ayckbourn is one of the world's most successful living playwrights, an internation-ally acclaimed director, and a life-long advocate of theatre-in-the-round. As DSM, Andy Hall is in the enviable position of watching his, and others', plays progress through every stage of rehearsal to last night.

Selected Production Credits

The Safari Party, Sugar Daddies, Fields of Gold, Miss Yesterday, Improbable Fiction, Intimate Exchanges (all at the Stephen Joseph Theatre).

* * *

This is my fifth year at the Stephen Joseph Theatre: I can remember being absolutely petrified on my first day. There is always a 'meet and greet' with each new company, when everyone in the building comes together and says who they are and what they do. There was a nice man sitting in the corner wearing really funky clothes and trainers, and I thought, 'That can't be Alan Ayckbourn!' But it was. He is just like any other person: I don't know what I was expecting – I suppose someone in a suit, being very authoritarian. He isn't that at all. He is very down to earth, and will sit and talk to you, and, for example, his character shows itself in his whole ethos about the Green Room.

The Green Room in every theatre is where everyone comes to relax, but in this building, absolutely everybody (except for the audience) has to go through it to get wherever they want to. So everyone from actors, to stage management, to cleaners, all use the Green Room to get anywhere. This means there is huge interaction within the building at all levels. Everyone is forced to talk to each other, whereas in other theatres, the artistic director or the people in admin tend to just stay in their corridor, and you might not see them for weeks on end. This is a very friendly place to work, and there is no one in the building who I don't know the name of, which is lovely.

I thought about working in the theatre from a very early age. While I was at school I did work experience at my local theatre, the Pavilion Theatre in Rhyl – a receiving house. It was totally different from where I am now, but I got to see a lot of diverse productions, from comedy, to musicals, to boy bands. That showed me that I wanted to work in theatre as a career. From there I went to the Arden School of Theatre in Manchester and got a degree in technical theatre arts. Personally I think the best way to get into theatre is to do a course like that, because it will give you a good grounding in all areas of theatre, but you don't have to come in from that background. I was particularly lucky:

while on the course I was taught by a stage manager, who asked me if I would like to go and work with her at the Royal Exchange Theatre, in Manchester, to work as her assistant stage manager! I graduated, joined her at the Royal Exchange, initially for an eight-week contract, but stayed two-and-a-half years, and progressed up to DSM.

After two years I felt I needed to work elsewhere. I didn't make a conscious decision to stay with theatre-in-the-round [like the Royal Exchange], it just happened that the next place was the Stephen Joseph Theatre, and when I was offered a job here, I jumped at the opportunity. At the Stephen Joseph we have our own in-house shows in the McCarthy, which is an end-on auditorium, and also the theatre in-the-round. Alan Ayckbourn directs his own plays, but we also have an associate director, who directs others. Additionally, we have links with various theatres around the country (such as the Orange Tree, Richmond, and the New Vic, Newcastle-under-Lyme) that send one of their shows to perform here, and we send one of our shows to perform in their theatre. When another company is performing they bring their own deputy stage manager. Backstage on our own shows we generally have a technician who operates lights and sound, a stage manager, deputy stage manager and assistant stage manager. We try to keep it to just those four per show, although there are times when it gets more complicated and we might need extra crewmembers or dressers.

I like working in-the-round: I think it is a much nicer way to work, because it is a much more intimate feel for the audience. You don't get the feeling of a black box where you sit and face forward and see just what is being presented to you. In-the-round, you never know where the audience is looking. Often a DSM sits in the wings during a performance in a conventional theatre. Here I am in a control room (with a glass window facing the stage), which is just behind the back row of the audience. At first it represented a bit of a challenge to me, having been taught very little about theatre-in-the-round at university. When you come to things like 'blocking', in rehearsals, there is no upstage and downstage. Blocking is part of being 'on the book' and involves following the script, and whenever an actor moves, sits down or picks anything up, the deputy stage manager makes a pencil note in the script, or draws a diagram of positions. When we come back to rehearse that scene again, and perhaps the actor has forgotten what they did, you can look at the blocking and reproduce the last time it was rehearsed.

The two parts of what a deputy stage manager does, in rehearsals and during the show, are very different: it is rather a strange job. In rehearsals, apart from blocking, being on the book involves prompting once the cast have come off script. The DSM follows the script, and if anyone calls for a line, or skips a line, or jumps a page, you interject with the correct line. Another part of the job is to provide substitute props, and sometimes, substitute sound effects during rehearsals. One of the first shows I did here was called *The Safari Party* [by Tim Firth, directed by Ayckbourn], which starts with two brothers running on stage and trying to put a flat-pack table together. Before anyone says anything, there is a doorbell. In rehearsals the DSM would usually say 'ding dong' to represent this. One day, I had been practising the cueing sequence in my head. In a show I would say to the technician, 'Sound cue one, go!' So instead of saying 'ding dong' I had silently thought 'Sound cue one' and I shouted out 'Go!' Everyone in the room collapsed!

Another very important part of a deputy stage manager's job is to be a communicator with the rest of the building. You take notes of everything that is happening in the rehearsal room to keep them up to date with anything that might affect them. For example, if someone decides they need a handkerchief, you would write a note to the wardrobe department. So any wardrobe, props, lighting or sound effects that you realize will be required, you make a note of. We have a separate rehearsal room here, because we tend to have shows on throughout the year, except in January when the company usually does a UK tour. So we often rehearse in the day and do a different show at night, with its set in place in the theatre.

Just before a performance my first job is to give backstage calls to tell the actors how long it is till curtain up. We have a half-hour call, a quarter-hour call, a five-minute call and a beginners call. These are all given five minutes ahead of time. So if a show starts at 7.30, the half-hour call is at 6.55. That has always been done in theatre to ensure actors are on stage on time. Then I give a front of house call to get the audience in. In performance, because in this theatre we are in a separate control room, we can't prompt, but sometimes that is one of the duties of a deputy stage manager. Most actors actually prefer to try to get out of it them-selves if they forget their lines in a performance.

During the show I follow the script and tell the lighting and sound operators when to do their cues. I also tell the actors when to come on stage: for example, if they are not on for 20 minutes, I can give them a five-minute warning, so they don't have to sit and listen to the whole show every night. As well as verbal cues backstage, and on headsets to the operators, I use a system a bit like traffic lights, with a red light to warn them and a green light to go. So I 'run the show', which is quite a scary position to be in – it is very responsible. I definitely get nervous, particularly on the first night of a performance, when everything is new. It is completely different when you get an audience in for the first time, and you don't know exactly how they will react. It can change an actor's performance, and the length of time of a show. Where in rehearsal there may not be laughs, suddenly there are minutes of laughter. I have had shows without an audience that lasted 55 minutes, but with an audience, it can change to one hour ten minutes!

Working with Alan Ayckbourn is an absolute dream. He knows exactly what he wants, which may come from the fact that he is both director and writer. He knows the show absolutely perfectly. The cast do a read-through first, but then they don't sit about for days on end analysing everything – which some directors encourage. Alan has a really nice way of working, because he trusts his actors. So he doesn't sit down and go through the play line by line, selecting each different thought pattern, which I, personally, don't feel is a very constructive way of approaching a script. That method is like holding the actor's hand and leading them through the script: Alan knows that his actors will go home and do all that work themselves. In rehearsal, if he doesn't like anything, he will say so.

Alan doesn't tend to give direct notes [verbal advice to actors on how to improve their performance]. He generally directs by anecdote. So he will start off on a story, and you think, 'Where is that going?', but by the end you see that it is perfectly directed at something he didn't like in someone's performance. For instance, if someone is trying a different accent, Alan might recall a time when he was working somewhere else, and someone tried a different accent, and it was a complete mistake. He won't directly say, 'No, I don't think you should use that accent. I think it's crap!' He will be very nice about it. And because he has done almost every job in theatre himself, he knows exactly what each of us do, and why we ask the random questions that we do. If someone says they can't do something, and Alan knows for sure that it can be done, he will push it and say, 'Well actually, I think you'll find that if you try it *this* way, it possibly would work.' But if he doesn't know, and someone tells him there is absolutely no way, then he will accept that and find a way of working round it.

Some of his plays, with a lot of multi-role playing by the actors, and quick changes of costume, are quite a challenge. But that is what makes working here so much fun. We have just done a play called *Improbable Fiction* [written and directed by Ayckbourn], which had 58 quick changes in Act 2 alone! There were seven people in the cast, and there was a costume change virtually every two minutes. It was a very, very challenging show, and a lot to get my head round, but I absolutely loved it. There was the stage manager, and assistant, working on that show with me, and a dresser. So three of them did all that on their own, as well as running around being in the right place at the right time.

When a play transfers from here to a theatre that is not in-the-round, everything has to change. First, the set design is completely different here, because there are no walls, because the audience wouldn't be able to see, and furniture tends to be minimal to aid sight lines. So when we go into a proscenium theatre, you have to add a whole new back wall. You tend to make a whole room, whereas before it was the floor, suggesting a room. That can take months to build, and then in January we usually go to Guildford, where we have a week-and-a-half rehearsal, with the same company, to change from in-the-round to end-on.

In-the-round we have three voms, which are the entrances onto the stage. 'Vom' is short for the word 'vomitory', which is Greek for 'to vomit'. So it is like the actors are thrown up onto the stage! You enter underneath the audience, almost like little tunnels in an amphitheatre. So when we change to end-on, the actors already know the script, but Alan will say, 'This door represents this vom; this door represents that vom.' And the actors work it out between themselves. In some senses you look at it as a completely different version of the play. Certainly, from my point of view, everything, including cues, totally changes.

By the end of a show, I know it word for word, and could follow it without a prompt copy. But going into end-on you have to be careful, because you can lapse into a familiar pattern, and think, 'This happens now', but actually it doesn't happen then any more, we have had to add on a few seconds, and the action has changed slightly. It is a challenge for me, so I am sure that for the actors it is an even bigger challenge. People often ask how I still find a comedy funny, when I have seen the show maybe 50 times. I say, 'Well actually, I have seen it a lot more than 50 times, because I have sat in rehearsals for four weeks as well. It is funny because it is ever-evolving.'

Usually we try to have the same company of actors for around a year. That is how Alan likes to work – with a repertory company. He might start with perhaps four actors to do the first play of the season at the end of April. Then he might bring in a few more people to add to the existing company – like he did for *Improbable Fiction*. Another show I particularly enjoyed working on was *Fields of Gold*, which was actually directed by Laurie Samson, who used to be associate director here. It was about a farming family stuck in the midst of 'mad cows disease', and there were various moments that I felt were so moving that in rehearsals I would have tears in my eyes. Judy Wilson, who played the grandmother, was so brilliant – her final death scene was heart wrenching. That will always be a performance that will stay in my mind.

Much as I enjoy being a deputy stage manager, I would like to be a stage manager, definitely within the next five years, although that is a completely different job. I saw that side a bit when I was an ASM, because the assistant tends to work quite closely with the stage manager, but with far less responsibility. In the long term, I would quite like to get into production management – just carry on up the ladder from where I am really. What I enjoy most is the satisfaction at the end of knowing you have entertained the audience. When I worked in Rhyl, it was a 1,000–seat house, and we put on variety shows with about 30 different acts each night. I helped organize all those people to get on stage at the right time, in the right place, with the right equipment, and it looked absolutely seamless from out front, and a lot of people enjoyed themselves, although for us it was probably blind panic. But the adrenalin that I got from that made me want to carry on doing it, and it still does.

Designer

Bob Crowley

Set and costume design can make a play more accessible and exciting, providing information about period and place as well as revealing character and social status. In addition, set design can create, among other things, a sense of claustrophobia, isolation, oppression, beauty or delight. Bob Crowley is currently one of the busiest artists working in theatre, designing for plays, musicals and opera, mostly in London and New York. Among his numerous awards are three Tonys and the Olivier Award for Designer of the Year.

Bob Crowley works from a large, light studio in London, where models of his sets adorn various surfaces. In England he usually designs both sets and costumes. In America these jobs are generally split between two people, and he has tended to do scenic design, which is what I concentrated on in my interview with him. Despite his potentially intimidating success, Crowley's lack of complacency soon became clear, as did his warmth and humour. Born in Cork he still speaks with a pronounced Irish accent.

Selected Production Credits

Hamlet (Royal Shakespeare Company, 1992), *Racing Demon, Carousel, Amy's View, The History Boys* (all National Theatre and Broadway), *The Invention of Love* (Lincoln Center), *Tarzan* (Broadway), *Mary Poppins* (West End and Broadway), *A Moon for the Misbegotten* (Old Vic), *The Coast of Utopia* (Lincoln Center).

*   *   *

I find defining the role of a stage designer a bit tricky. I would say it is someone who translates the play, which is a text, into something three-dimensional. But it is more complicated than that, because the text also needs visual interpretation. Depending on your style as a designer a director will come to you, knowing you do a certain kind of work, because each designer is different, and he may want a certain style for a particular play. Then you work with the director, because he too will have ideas.

What I do personally is to try to find a visual metaphor for the *lives* of the characters that exist in the play as much as the world in which the characters live. I like to express that as poetically as I can, rather than merely plonk down a realistic living room or a realistic house on stage. I try to find a world in which the audience's imagination is part of the event. I don't want to confuse an audience, or over-complicate things, since situations are often complicated already. I want the audience to feel at ease with what they are looking at, but I don't want to spoon-feed them either. I also think a design has to change in some way during a performance. For me the play is as much a journey that the set goes on, as it is a journey the characters go on.

But each project demands different things from you and different skills. Sometimes, for instance, you might use very little colour in your palette, to express very little colour in people's lives. Another time you might use colour to express different aspects of the psychological state of the characters, which will help an audience understand what is going on. I use colour to express joy, or fear, or a certain coolness, just the way a painter would. I have all these tools, so that, for example, in something like *Mourning Becomes Electra* at the National, it started with a very white/grey palette, and then for the interior scenes it became very hot and red, passionate and bloody. I don't want to be sledgehammer about this, but I think that if you are going to be abstract, as I usually am, an audience needs to be guided in terms of the temperature of where the piece is at, and colour is your greatest asset.

What I mean by abstract is not necessarily minimalism, but finding the essence of something, or its representation. For instance, I have just directed and designed *Tarzan* on Broadway:

that is obviously all set in a rainforest, but there isn't a leaf on stage. I have had angry theatre-goers write to me asking, 'Why are there no leaves on stage?' to which I reply, 'I have a stage 30–foot wide by 20–foot deep, so I can't begin to put a real rain forest on stage, any more than I can put real monkeys. You accept that an actor can play a monkey, but you are saying that you can't accept it if I put green, climbing ropes all over the stage, which represent the vines that they swing on.' It is a set entirely made up of these ropes – there are thousands and thousands of green vines on stage, which light *beautifully*. That is what I mean by abstraction. A child wouldn't question the *Tarzan* set.

Tarzan was an exception, because I directed it, and designed the set and costumes. In England I generally design sets and costume, in America it is 99 per cent divided. I love both, but when I haven't done costume it was because I physically couldn't, because I was working on too many projects at the same time. I would normally prefer to do both, because you have to create an entire visual picture on stage, and I suppose I am too much of a control freak to let that go. On the other hand, when I have just done the sets it is great fun, because there is another person in the room with you, and designing can be a pretty isolated existence during the creative process.

The first thing I get is a script, which I read, and it has to interest me in terms of what it has to say. Some plays aren't that interesting for me to design, because they might be set in somebody's kitchen or front living-room in Hampstead. Then all it takes is for you to research that, and reproduce it, and I probably wouldn't do it. There has to be something that I feel I can do with the play that takes it onto a different level. If I like the script I will meet with the director. At this stage in my life I tend to work with directors who I have worked with before. I sit down with the director and we talk quite openly about our reaction to the play, and what we think it should look like visually. I have got a pretty vast library of reference books, and I am very interested in art and painting, so I might reference a painter, or sculptor, or film that I have seen – it could be anything. One is a kind of visual magpie, so it could literally be a piece of paper that you find in the street and you take it to work with you.

It is a bit like plugging into a socket in the wall, when you plug into a play, because from then on, you are sort of wired about the world that you are now going to find out about. Sometimes you might even travel to the place where that world is, and completely absorb it. For instance, when I did *Carousel* with Nick Hytner, the play is set in New England, and neither of us had been there. So we went to New York and got on a plane, and went up to Portland, and drove around for three or four days, and it completely changed the way we saw that piece. I was very interested in the Shaker community and Shaker aesthetics, and I knew I wanted to apply that to the piece when it comes to the part when it is in heaven. Heaven is a really hard thing to portray on stage, because no one has come back and reported it! I couldn't talk to anyone about that, although I would have been prepared to have a séance if I needed to!

Anyway we visited a Shaker community, in fact the only one left in North America, called Sabbath Day Lake, and we walked into this little meeting hall. It was beautiful, and they had painted the walls an incredible blue, which I now call Carousel Blue. I said, 'My God, these walls are so beautiful. Why are they painted blue?' And they answered, 'Because this room is for dancing, and the room represents heaven.' So that was a metaphor for a musical if ever there was one! Nick and I looked at each other, and we put a blue room on the stage at the National Theatre, and eventually at the Lincoln Center.

Sometimes you have to do that sort of thing, and other times you don't. I have done an awful lot of Shakespeare, but didn't visit any castles in Scotland for *Macbeth*, or go to Denmark to design *Hamlet*. When it comes to Shakespeare, a lot of it is very strongly director-led, because it is very conceptual. You are dealing with literally no stage instructions at all, whereas if you are working with playwrights like David Hare, or Christopher

Hampton, they are very clued into the world they are writing about. That doesn't mean they are not flexible – they are, but they are steeped in it because they have been researching it themselves for two or three years. So you can plug into them, and they are your little instant Internet.

During all the early design process I am sketching away, with a pad, morning noon and night, on the bus, on the tube, on a train, on a plane. You have a little notebook with you all the time, and you start collecting things: postcards, things pulled out of magazines. You build up a little collection of reference things for whatever it is that you are doing. Then I tend to go pretty quickly into a model. You have a shape in your head of what you think this thing will be three-dimensionally, and you make a white-card model. That is a simple model with things slung together with glue and paste, made with white cardboard, just to get the physical dimensions. If anything has to move or do things, you can work it out very quickly that way.

Then the director comes in for another couple of hours. You open up a bottle of wine, and have a few glasses together in front of the model, usually late at night. I like looking at models at night rather than in the day. I work with them during the day, but at night I like to switch the lights off and work in a dark studio, because it simulates the theatre much more. You usually end up shoving a huge angle-poise lamp into the model, but it comes alive when you put light onto it, and it is the same thing with the set in the theatre. We are nothing without a lighting designer, who also comes in, usually after the white-card stage, when there is paint on the model and it is textured or whatever. The models get progressively more and more detailed, until by the end you have an absolute perfect reproduction of the final show. That is then signed off on by the director and the lighting designer.

If you are doing something at the National, for instance, at a certain point in that process, before you have completely finished the work, you do a presentation to the artistic director, and the heads of departments. So they physically get an idea of how much it might cost, how much work it might take to build and any inherent problems. Once you have finished the final model you are pretty far down the line, and usually you leave the model at the theatre. Then the production manager will start literally breaking it down into physical bits and pieces and start to cost it. You will have been given a budget at the beginning, but then they have to balance the books, which rarely happens. There is only one instance in my 30 years of designing in the theatre where I didn't go over budget. That was at the Metropolitan Opera in New York, where they took one look at the model, which was *huge*, the size of a small car, and actually asked me for more scenery! It was for *Falstaff* with Nick Hytner, and the production never saw the light of day. We say we got fired from it. But it is very rare that you are under-budget, because things always get more and more expensive.

You might have to compromise a bit, but I don't think any of the directors or writers that I have worked with have ever laid down the law to me. For example, when I worked on *The History Boys*, Nick and I and Alan Bennett went to sit in on some English and History classes in a school. We just watched the dynamic of the classroom to remind us of what it was like, since it was quite a while since we had been in it. But the play was set in the 80s, not in Alan's childhood, or now, so he didn't really know what the classroom should look like. I had gone to school in the 60s, and Nick in the 70s, so none of us really knew. We needed to decide whether it should be an old grammar school or a modern comprehensive, and we decided on a modern comprehensive. My school was kind of half and half – a bit of old and new, whereas I think both Nick and Alan went to old-fashioned grammar schools.

I referenced some books of city architecture built here after the war, and we just went from there. The only thing I did do was say to Alan that I was going to cover the walls with things that Hector [teacher in the play] loves – a bit like my studio is covered with things I like. I said, 'I am going to get a load of stuff together, and we will build it up during rehearsals, and the boys can start contributing as well.' So everybody in that show stuck things on that wall, and Alan had the final veto. I said to him, 'You go down the walls with me, and if there is anything which you think should not be there, then you get to take it off.' That is as interactive as Alan became on that set. And I don't think he did take anything off.

Often you have to change a show a bit if it transfers. For instance, *The History Boys* transferred to Broadway, where stages tend to be much smaller than in London. We had already shrunk the set down a bit for the British tour, and so that set fitted on Broadway. Conversely, with *Mary Poppins*, we actually ran out of space here in London, because the Prince Edward is a very small theatre, and there are certain magical things, which I wanted to do in London, but the New Amsterdam in New York is much bigger, and I am able to do two huge new scenes – but that is unusual.

Mary Poppins had been lurking in my head for about 12 years, since Cameron Mackintosh first mentioned to me that he was going to do a production of it, but then I never heard another word until about four years ago. Then I knew that Richard Eyre was going to direct it, and he had also become a friend. So Richard and I stepped into it with a kind of selective realism. The first thing we had to crack was how the Edwardian house would work. Richard and I had done a production of a Tony Harrison play at the Olivier, called *The Prince's Play*, based on the story of *Rigoletto*, where a large Victorian-like doll's house was flown onto the stage. So when Richard was talking about the house for *Mary Poppins*, I said, 'You know, we have done a kind of version of this.' I had the model nearby, and that became the beginning of that house.

It is like a giant doll's house, or like those Dorling Kindersley books where you get a *slice* through an entire house, and you see where all the plumbing is going. So we made up a rough model of that, and then we knew that the roof would have to lift off, and underneath that was the nursery. Then I knew I had to suspend the nursery, and take away the entire first and second floor so that just the nursery could fly in with a living nanny and children dancing inside it; it involves massive engineering. I didn't want it to be a big mechanical thing: I wanted it to almost float, so you couldn't see how it was done. So I needed to bring in the best person for that job, and that was a man called Mike Barnet. He had worked for Cameron for 25 years, and we got him out of retirement to do it.

I am lucky to work with such good people. I work repeatedly with just a few directors who I like. For example Howard Davies, who I worked with first on *Les Liaisons Dangereuses* for the RSC in 1985. Now we are doing *Moon for the Misbegotten* together, because we are both obsessed with Eugene O'Neill. Kevin Spacey [who stars in the production, and who is artistic director of the Old Vic] was away filming during the whole design process of that and just saw the finished product. That is rather unusual, and I felt a bit nervous about it, because I thought, 'We are doing it because of him', but he was absolutely fine.

When the play opens [after a couple more previews] I am expecting the set to be slightly controversial, because of the colours I have used. They are much more intense than you usually get in a Eugene O'Neill play. I have painted the earth an almost outback orange colour, and I know Americans are going to say, 'That's not Connecticut!' But my answer to them is, 'It is not a play about Connecticut, any more than *Hamlet* is a play about Denmark. It is about the human beings who exist on that earth, and it is universal.' I have to tell an audience a lot of information very quickly. In seconds they have to see that poor peasant farmers are living on the parched earth. And even though it doesn't look like it is worth anything, it is all they have got, and they will fight to the death to keep it. The house is pretty faithful to what O'Neill describes in the play, although I have slightly tilted it, and made it look as though it is falling over. But the isolation of the characters, emotionally and physically, is what I was trying to express in that set.

Another director I have worked with a lot is Nick Hytner, particularly on opera, and of course, *The History Boys*. Whether I do a play, or a musical, or an opera, it is all the same process. It is just that with musicals and opera, they tend to be more expensive to see, and have more money spent on them as a result. They also tend to hang around longer. For instance the production of *La Traviata* that I did for Covent Garden [Richard Eyre, 1994] could outlive me. That is why they invest in these huge shows and then run them into the ground. I also did lots of work with Richard Eyre at the National, including all the David Hare plays, which I loved doing. They were kind of state of the nation, up-to-date, contemporary plays.

Jack O'Brien is my latest addition to directors that I work with. He has become a dear friend, and we have been doing Tom Stoppard plays, not here, but in America, ironically. We did *Hapgood* about ten years ago, with Stockard Channing, which was a big hit, and then we did *The Invention of Love* there. I think Jack and I have a way of working with Stoppard's work that is different from the way that he gets produced here. I have never had the pleasure of working on a new play by him in England – they just haven't come my way. I have always seen them here though obviously. I have a theory that Stoppard is such an intellectual writer that sometimes he gets accused of not having an emotional heart, and I disagree. I also think there is a poetic side to Tom that I always emphasize when I do his work in New York. I tend to be a bit abstract with him rather than very literal.

Right now there is a company of 44 actors at the Lincoln Center, and it is as though they have been starved of something for years. They are jumping on Stoppard's trilogy *The Coast of Utopia*, like it is the last food on earth. It is thrilling to see these young kids getting completely fired up by one of the greatest brains working right now. He is pretty formidable actually, but he is great fun: he has a hilarious sense of humour. Actually

I think what connects all these people is a sense of humour. All the people I work with tend to be funny and witty, and God knows you need that. Don't even try to be a stage designer without a sense of humour!

I don't come from a theatrical background: my mother was a housewife and my father was a fireman, but they loved the theatre and musicals. I grew up knowing the soundtracks from LPs of *Oklahoma!*, *My Fair Lady* and all those classic shows. I lived in Cork city, which didn't have a professional theatre company, although English professional theatre companies toured regularly, so I was taken to see them. I saw all the local amateur dramatic society productions too. One of my earliest memories is when I think I was three, and I think I was sitting on my grandfather's knee, watching *Snow White and the Seven Dwarfs*. We had terrible seats, and I remember a pillar being in the way, so I couldn't see the whole stage properly, which may have been the deciding factor. Like, 'OK,' age three, 'I'm going to work in this bloody business, because I am going to get a better seat!' I have never thought of that before.

I was taken to the theatre a lot and I loved the lights going out, and a world being created in front of you that you believed. It was only ten feet away from you, with actors acting in it, and painted scenery, but you suspended your disbelief, and I was moved and touched by it. I could see there was stuff on stage, but I didn't know who did it: I didn't know that stage designers existed. As I grew older I wanted to do fine art and graphic art, and while I was still at school, I went to art school at night, two or three times a week, but theatre didn't really register with me as a profession. Then a touring production of *Oliver* came to Cork, which I saw. It was designed by a fellow Irishman, called Sean Kenny, and had a very famous set from the West End.

Sean Kenny was an architect, who used to work for Frank Lloyd Wright, so he didn't start out as a stage designer either. I think he was very influenced by the Berlin Ensemble, who had been to London in the 60s. He stripped everything away, and was rather Brechtian, even though I didn't really know who Brecht was at the time, but I knew that there was something new happening here, and that it was unlike anything I had seen locally. This was dealing with scenery sculpturally, and it wasn't just drops coming in and out. It wasn't realistic either. There was the whole of London, but it was all done with wooden planks, and he painted the back wall of the theatre and exposed the lights. I had never seen a lighting rig before, or the walls of the theatre, and I thought, 'God, this is really cool!' And that is when I thought that being a stage designer was also kind of cool. That is when the seed of the idea was planted that perhaps I could do this full-time, for a living.

I started doing amateur work in Cork, and got huge encouragement from some friends of mine who said I should think about getting training. They gave me a subscription to *Plays and Players*, and on the back page I saw an ad for Bristol Old Vic Theatre School. I applied, and went there with a tiny portfolio of amateur work I had done, and they gave me a scholarship there and then, and I have never looked back. I got a job within a year painting scenery, and then I got an Arts Council scholarship, and then a job at Leicester Haymarket. Ironically, my first job there was for a young, London producer coming up, called Cameron Mackintosh, who was reviving *Oliver* for the first time. My job was to go out to a warehouse in Loughborough, where they had stored the set from the West End, and take the set out. None of the designs or models existed, because Sean Kenny died very young, and I had to put the set back together and build a model of it – the show that I had first fallen in love with!

Then I went to the National, as an assistant. Next I went back to Bristol, and met Adrian Noble, who was the trainee director there. Then we went to the Royal Exchange to do *The Duchess of Malfi* with Helen Mirren and Bob Hoskins, which was a show that put both of us on the map. Trevor Nunn saw it, and invited us to the RSC, and I spent nearly 20 years there. Shakespeare is always a challenge, but eventually I had to stop doing it, which is why I went to the National. I had had enough. I needed to get away and reinvent myself as a designer of modern plays – do something to do with vicars and south London, like *Racing Demon*. But now I feel I haven't done Shakespeare for a long time, and I am getting needy again.

I was at the National for ten years, and now I am here, freelancing. A lot of it is luck, there is no question: it is being in the right place at the right time, and meeting the right people. I genuinely believe that you meet people who think similarly to you. Talent is a prerequisite, but it isn't enough. I have known lots of talented people in my time who have not been able to keep it together. Ninety per cent of what I do is just turning up! I am dependable; I won't disappear and I will meet deadlines.

I am personally thrilled that I am still being employed: that people still ask me to work. I am not being disingenuous. When my agent tells me that so and so has called and asked if I would like to do this, or that, I am always surprised and pleased. I swear to God that anybody who works in the theatre, especially actors, are programmed to think that every show we do will be our last one, and that we will be found out in some way, and no one will ever employ us again. That is why designers tend to do too much: you think you better do two or three things at the same time or you will never pay the bills. The theatre world is so precarious. You put every fibre of your being into doing your best, and on something like *Tarzan* I had about five days off in six months: it is a crazy working pattern. And then you wake up the next morning and some bloody critic has dumped on you from a great height and completely dismissed everything you have done. That is their prerogative, but it can be *really* hurtful.

The trouble with critics is that you can't believe them when they tell you you are a genius any more than when they say you are shit. So it is very hard, and, of course, you always remember your bad reviews: I could almost quote you my first bad review. But what keeps me going is exciting projects being offered to me, and thinking, 'Maybe I can do something with this that I haven't

done before.' I don't want to repeat things, or become compla-
cent and smug, and think, 'I've got three Tony Awards; a nice
apartment in London; I have worked for the RSC, the National,
the Lincoln Center, the Royal Opera House, the Royal Court and
the best fringe theatres like the Almeida – where is there left?' I
don't feel like that at all. If a play comes from the Bush next week,
and I think it is a great play, and I want to design it, then I will
design it. That is what I feel like. Are there any institutions
around the world that I want to work for? Not particularly. Even
though we got fired from the Met we are going back there with
Don Carlos in two years' time. What goes around comes around.

I have got the next six months completely planned out, and
then I have got another directing project in about a year, at the
National, if it works out. I loved doing *Tarzan*, being in control.
People are always saying, 'Why don't you do films?' and
although I have designed a few, my heart isn't there yet. But who
knows? That is the thing. You never know what is going to come
through the letterbox. It could all change with a phone call in half
an hour. That is what is thrilling and terrifying about the job. If
you have a nervous disposition, forget about it. I would like to
do more dance: the little I have done I absolutely loved. I go to
the opera quite a bit, but designing for it doesn't have any added
allure for me. I love the challenge of a new play. I love putting
something on stage that nobody has ever seen before. I am
going to do the set for a new, one-woman show, next spring on
Broadway, called *The Year of Magical Thinking*, which is based on
a book by Joan Didion. She has written this *amazing* book, and
Vanessa Redgrave is going to do it with David Hare directing, so
I am looking forward to that.

It is hard work and it is a religion: it becomes your life, for
good or for ill. But I am only as good as the work I produce
myself, like the model or the artwork. That has to get translated
to something three-dimensional on stage. So many incredibly
gifted people are involved in that process: scene painters, scene
builders, production managers, seamstresses, carpenters and

engineers. I have a huge back-up team behind me in order to make these things happen. You meet incredibly passionate people, who have equally devoted their entire lives to getting a show on stage every night. People in stage management, like Trish Montemuro – a genius woman: I love her. She is among the best, if not *the* best; amazing. So stage design is not like window dressing – it is much more complicated, and involves a huge body of people around you at any time. And they are never seen. But *you* are going to change all that!

Director

Sir Richard Eyre

Richard Eyre is one of the world's most respected theatre directors. Born in 1943, in Devon, he had an unhappy childhood. His father was a Naval officer turned farmer; a heavy drinker and womanizer. Eyre was sent to boarding school aged seven and later went to Cambridge University (where he was taught by Kingsley Amis). His career took shape, with hindsight, partly to attract the attention of his father. Starting at school, Eyre became an actor, performing in a play written for him by one of the teachers, 'to applause that intoxicated me and corrupted me irrevocably'. His acting after that was less success-ful, and when, in 1965, Clive Perry offered the young Eyre the chance to direct a play at the Phoenix Theatre in Leicester, he took the opportunity.

Later Richard Eyre was to run the Royal Lyceum Theatre, Edinburgh (where he met his wife, TV producer Sue Birtwistle) and Nottingham Playhouse, where he started his long-term collaboration with play-wright David Hare. Eyre became producer of the BBC TV Play for Today series, and then associate director of the National Theatre. He was the National's artistic director from 1987 to 1997, a period often described as a golden age. However, having to get 12,000 bums on seats every week, just to break even, was a mixed blessing for Eyre: fear, self-doubt, excitement, power and success mingled. Richard Eyre is the winner of very many awards and was knighted in 1997. He has directed TV (for example Tumbledown*), film (for instance* Iris *and* Notes on a Scandal*, both with Judi Dench) and has written (beautifully): a book of his diaries and an autobiography.*

I talked with Richard Eyre at his West London terraced house, which is large and elegant – the sitting-room has light sofas, modern paint-ings and book-lined walls. Eyre is charismatic, dressed in black with a white shock of hair. Perhaps not surprisingly, considering his job, he is extremely eloquent.

Selected Production Credits

Guys and Dolls (National Theatre), *Hamlet* (National Theatre, 1989), *Richard III* (National Theatre and world tour, 1990), *The David Hare Trilogy* (National Theatre), *Carousel* (National Theatre and Broadway), *La Traviata* (Royal Opera House, 1994), *The Crucible* (Broadway), *King Lear* (National Theatre, 1997), *Amy's View* (National Theatre and Broadway), *Hedda Gabler* (Almeida Theatre and West End), *Mary Poppins* (West End and Broadway).

*　　*　　*

It is very hard to define the role of a director of a play. The analogy with a conductor of an orchestra doesn't really hold up, because it is perfectly visible to the audience what a conductor is doing: he is in command, and driving the orchestra at the moment of the performance. You can argue the extent to which the orchestra are in charge and are an autonomous unit, and the extent to which conductors are, as James Galway [flautist] put it, 'masters of the grand wave', but at least they are there, at the centre, in the present. With a director it is much more elusive. What does a director do? One thing a director does is to gather together a group of people, and one of the reasons I am attracted to the theatre is because in some ways it replicates society, and is theoretically a utopian microcosm of society.

A director is hired to pursue a particular project. So you choose the project, or are chosen for the project, and the task is then to assemble the component parts of a small society and make that society function: make sure everyone has common aims and intentions, and that the sum of the enterprise is greater than the parts. So you are forming a successful society. The logistical part is seeing that through, seeing it mature, and seeing relations form, and the intentions of the project being realized. The art of it is that you are making a mass of decisions, based on your sensibility and your interpretation of the play you are working on, and every one of those choices is directing.

Before rehearsals even start, choices have to be made, and one is what period you are going to set the play in. These big decisions are made with the designer. A good example is a production of *Richard III* that I did with Ian McKellen [National Theatre, 1990], which was set in a mythical 1930s England. It is interesting because Shakespeare wrote the play in the 1590s, and it is set in the fifteenth century. So you have a sixteenth-century writer, writing about events of 150 years earlier, and then we did it 500 years later. What I wanted to do was to have the best of all worlds and offer a metaphor for a present-day audience, which was the fascist Britain of the 1930s. This was also, in a sense, what Shakespeare was writing about, taking the Richard III story and writing about his own time, because actually the play is simply about the rise of a tyrant. I wanted to express that as clearly as possible, and get the contemporary resonance for a British audience, and also give a sort of timeless quality to it.

The way that came about was not by me just picking a period, but by the designer, Bob Crowley, Ian McKellen and I, sitting, in fact, in this room, just reading the play. The three of us would ask, 'What is going on in this play and in this scene? What is this play about?' And we refused to make any commitment to period until we had reached the end of the play, and we felt we knew that the play had timeless archetypes which were about the way in which tyrants gain power.

Ian McKellen is a star. People think in today's celebrity culture that everybody is a star, but what I mean is that there are actors who have a charisma, and emanate a prodigious degree of energy, and they also consume it – in the sense that energy is constant. The energy is only fed by the actors they are with, and Ian is very challenging, and a strong personality, and he demands of the people he is with that they put in as much as he gives out. I think that is good, but it is what you get with most stars: they consume a great deal of energy as well as transmitting it. In some ways the job of a director, like perhaps that of a parent, is giving, but on the part of a director it is not disinterested, because you get it back.

A director exploits and encourages and incites the actors' talents. That is on a moment-to-moment basis, and again, you are making a number of choices. You are encouraging them to offer things up, and then saying, 'No, in fact *that* seems to work better than doing *that*.' It doesn't work if the director says, 'You do that!' and the actors are simply aping the director's command. You provide the territory by choosing the play. Then there is the drawing of the map – how do you cover this ground? You are the guide, and sometimes find that the map is faulty, and you re-write the map and lead the actors through this uncharted territory. Gradually the territory and topography becomes more and more familiar, until by the time the play opens – to pursue this metaphor to its bitter end – the actors become the inhabitors of the territory and the director is merely the spectator.

For any theatre director, I think, there is an endemic build up to a first night and anti-climax afterwards. It is a kind of bulimic cycle. You chose your project, assemble your cast and get into your rehearsal room that becomes this completely autonomous universe. You are sealed within this world, and it all works, unlike the world at large. Then if you are lucky, the audience say, 'This is absolutely wonderful!' So not only have you got paid for having this absolutely fascinating couple of months, but then you get applauded and complimented for it, and extravagant flattery. But for the director, there is nothing else; then you go home.

There is a wonderful moment in Mike Leigh's film about Gilbert and Sullivan when you see Gilbert, played by Jim Broadbent, sitting on his bed, after the first night of *The Mikado*, the greatest first night in the history of musical theatre, and he says, 'I feel so low.' It is a chemical reaction. You are emotionally and physically exhausted, and paper-thin skinned, generally with a hangover, and you pick up the newspapers, and someone says this gorgeous thing that you have created is actually just a lump of lead. So you do feel disproportionately angry and upset. I don't know a single theatre director who doesn't go through that sort of cycle. I have always been mildly manic-depressive, and occasionally clinically depressed, but I don't think I am unusual among theatre directors.

I continue because I love it. I really love the process of it. I have hugely enjoyed collaborating with David Hare. I have done a lot of new plays, and invariably enjoyed the collaboration with the writers: it is a wonderful conversation. And really, all good actors are incredibly stimulating. It is a dialectical process, because you suggest something, or they offer it up, and then you make an emendation, and then they build on that, and it is absolutely collaborative.

Here is a nice story: I was doing a television film called *Country*, written by Trevor Griffiths [1980], and it had an astonishing cast of Leo McKern, James Fox, Jill Bennett, Penelope Wilton, Alan Webb and Wendy Hiller. It was set in 1945, and Wendy Hiller was playing the aristocratic wife of Leo McKern. We were rehearsing before shooting, and when she started off she was way over the top: she was playing it almost like Lady Bracknell [in *The Importance of Being Ernest*]. She saw me frowning, and asked, 'Is there something wrong?' and I said, 'I just hadn't imagined the character like that. She is actually terribly matter-of-fact, and she wears her breeding very lightly.' And Wendy replied, 'Oh! I see what you mean. She is like . . .' and she mentioned a friend of hers. So she went back and did it again, and she said to me after, 'Thank you so much. You see, I do want to be good.' It is only a fantastically stupid actor who doesn't want to be good, and who doesn't want to be helped to be good. And almost by definition, very good actors are not stupid: they are not articulate, but they are very, very quick witted.

For example, I have worked a lot with Judi Dench, and she is incredibly smart, but not incredibly articulate, although she is pretty pithy. It is like Pavlova who said, 'If I could say it, why would I dance it?' Judi hates talking about what she is doing. She hates analysing, and tries to stop you discussing the character: she doesn't want to talk it out. She is fun and a really, really good friend, so working with her is just wonderful – and then you get paid for it. During the last few years I have been very lucky in that I have been going from films to theatre, so it has meant that neither has become routine, and I don't feel I am continually going from one show into another. I also enjoy doing opera. That is a unique world, not like the theatre, and slightly bonkers, but quite agreeably bonkers. I am going into very different territories and cultures. I would like to continue like this. I am doing *Mary Poppins* in New York in the autumn, and then I am doing a play at the National Theatre, and then I hope I am doing a film, and then a play after that.

With musicals, and films, there are an awful lot of other people involved, and producers are very much in charge of the process. The stakes are so high, and the investment so large, that although you are not oppressed, you don't have the same freedom as on a play. For instance, I was doing *Hedda Gabler* last year, and it was my translation, and I had an absolutely wonderful time. [The performance won Olivier awards in 2006 for Best Director, Best Revival, Best Actress and Best Set Design.] I was completely in my own world and there was nobody saying, 'You have got to do X, Y and Z,' or 'Why aren't you doing X, Y and Z?' But usually it is directly in proportion to the size of the budget. The film I am still working on [*Notes on a Scandal*, screenplay Patrick Marber, starring Cate Blanchett and Judi Dench] had a budget of 15 million dollars, which, in film terms, is talked of as a small budget, but 15 million dollars is a *huge* amount of money, and I don't blame anyone for being vigilant about how it is being spent.

In some ways it was a little bit like that at the National Theatre, too. It was also pretty wonderful; but I was there ten years, and I don't think anyone should stay in any job for more than ten years. This is one of the things that Tony Blair just can't get his head round. Everybody loved him in 1997, and now they say,

'Just get out! For God's sake get out!' He has been there long enough and someone else should have a go. Peter Hall, who was artistic director of the National for 15 years, said to me that he had done five years too long. Essentially it took me three years to get into my stride, and there were an awful lot of changes that I had to make in the theatre, and then the danger is that you just get bored by it. But I ran the National Theatre for ten years, and I am very proud I kept it open!

Being knighted was odd. I was mocked by some of my friends, one or two of them, incidentally, who have since taken knighthoods. It was a bit like a woman who has got married and changed her name. So for a while I was very self-conscious about it, and now, this probably sounds *incredibly* smug, I never think about it. Actually I am slightly shocked when somebody says, 'Sir Richard': I almost flinch and look behind me. Politics are important to me, and I never buy it when people say, 'I am a-political', because that in itself is a political position. I don't think people realize that if, for example, you see a classic West End drawing-room comedy, it has everything to do with politics. All the choices, in a sense, are political ones, starting with the choice the playwright has made of writing about one set of people rather than another, and how those people live and what they believe in. Party or partisan politics is a different thing.

Until I came to write about my life, and the process of that clarified my thoughts, it simply hadn't occurred to me that having an unhappy family background has been reflected in my work. Perhaps the apotheosis of plays about unhappy families is *King Lear*, and it is interesting that when I did my production of *King Lear* with Ian Holm [1997], my sister came to see it, and was profoundly shocked by it. She said, 'You do realize that you have made Ian play it exactly like Dad, don't you?' and I answered, 'I don't know what you're talking about!' And I said, 'I didn't tell Ian how to play it: I conducted the performance, and it is an interpretation.' But she said, 'Well, that is our father.' That was really quite shocking.

One might think something like *Mary Poppins* couldn't be more different. But when I first talked to Cameron Mackintosh about it, he said, 'Read the story.' I hardly knew the film, because it came out when I was a student, and we all thought it was ridiculous. It became a byword for bland children's entertainment. I feel slightly ashamed now, because having seen it, it is a sweet film, and rather touching. But when I read the stories, they are really marinaded in unhappiness. Then I got to know about P. L. Travers, and she had a very, very unhappy childhood in Australia: her father was an alcoholic. She came to live in London, and wrote these books in her 30s, and she thought of them as adult books, and they were clearly a form of wish-fulfilment. She was fantasizing about what she most wanted, which was to be brought up in a middle-class house in London and delivered from unhappiness by this sort of supernatural creature. In some ways she tapped into something that is at the heart of most children's experience, and I felt that healing the unhappy family was the story of the show. So I was always dogged about saying, 'That doesn't mean anything to me.' Or 'That does have meaning for me.' Because I always said that whatever we do with the fantasy, the thing that is going to grab the audience is if we try truthfully to show an unhappy family being redeemed.

When one wonders what of oneself is one putting into the work, you think it is little, because it is not autobiographical, but you are making all these choices – of material, of actor, of emphasis. So being attracted to plays about dysfunctional families, doing *Lear* as a play about my father, does not happen because you think about these things, but they are the bed on which you sit and make those choices. For instance, it is very hard to imagine how you could grow up in this country and be blind to class. Our class monitors are all very, very highly tuned. Admittedly the co-ordinates keep changing, and you can no longer say there is a clear class hierarchy, but class distinction is still very strong. So when you are working on a play you always have to think about how these characters live, and how they relate to other people in society. How much money do they have, and what do they spend it on and why? And what it feels like to be disenfranchised.

Another decision, of course, is how the actors speak, whether it be modern-day, or Shakespeare's verse. The point about writing in verse is that there is a rhythm to it. There is a pulse, which is the pulse of breathing – the iambic pentameter. If you ignore it, or treat it as contemporary naturalistic speech, it is absolutely unbearable; you simply can't listen to it, and it is completely daft. In today's world, why do people rap? People say things with a recurrent rhythm because it is more expressive. You would never say to a rapper, 'Do it how you feel it, and leave pauses.' It is just *terrible* when actors approach Shakespeare as though it were contemporary, naturalistic speech. The thing you have to master, and very few actors can, is the rhythm, and then you can play around with it. But you can't play around with it until you have mastered the score.

Often the way to discover the meaning is through the verse. Some actors will stress a word in order to make a line mean something which it doesn't, and you say, 'It cannot be like that. You can't write an iambic line that has the emphasis at that point.' In some sense that is a solace for a director, because you can almost say, 'Why don't you look at the score and see what the composer wrote.' You might say, 'You are taking three bars rest there, but there is no silence.' You don't have to be over-rigorous about it, but Shakespeare shows you where the pauses are, and if you go with the rhythm, the meaning will often follow.

I once said to John Gielgud that the reason I got interested in Shakespeare was that I heard him on the radio doing Prospero, and for the first time I understood everything. I said, 'You were so clear; it was wonderful.' And he said, [Eyre puts on Gielgud's voice] 'I never really understood a lot of it. I just followed the verse.' He would follow the rhythms and often allow the meaning to take care of itself, and it does. Although you have to be fantastically skilful to play the instrument. But when you hear the supremely skilful, like Judi Dench, or Michael Bryant, they make it sound like naturalistic speech while at the same time being incredibly expressive of the rhythms and the shapes of the verse.

I think one of the hardest things to understand about what a director does is that there are these large choices to make, and at the opposite end, there are tiny, microscopic decisions, and it is accumulation and a linear process. You aggregate from day to day, adding on detail. David Mamet [playwright] said that directing is all about actions and adjectives. It is things like, 'On that line, could you get up from that chair and cross the room slowly?' You try it and see if it works. People long to believe that directors are the autocrats and the actors are the glove puppets and it is just not the case. Even the most controlling directors simply can't, and don't, work like that. It is more like that in choreography, where you can't argue about a step. You also can't argue about a note of music: you can't say, 'Well, I feel that this should be a semi-quaver.' Some writers, like Beckett, would say that you can't argue about their words, either. He would say, 'That's what I wrote. Do what I wrote.' Then the room for interpretation is narrow, but I don't think that is a crushing thing at all. Part of the attraction of directing is the mechanics of the whole, and moving things around the stage. The lighting, scene changes – employing the toolbox in an expressive way is really enjoyable. That is actually the nearest it gets to the director playing God.

Dramaturg

Anne Cattaneo

The job of a dramaturg, though not widely known about, is immensely influential and interesting. The word comes from the Greek 'playwright' but is now synonymous with the term more often used in England, 'literary manager'. In England it is more common for either very large theatre companies, or small ones that concentrate on new plays, to employ a literary manager – in the US most theatres have one. Dramaturgs are concerned with texts: suggesting plays for performance, advising on interpretation and historical relevance. But as Cattaneo's anecdotes reveal, the job also entails a whole lot more.

Anne Cattaneo is the dramaturg of Lincoln Center Theater. This theatre observes the mandate of its founder, John D. Rockefeller III, 'The arts not for the privileged few, but for the many,' and is guided by the motto, 'Good plays, popular prices.' It is a not-for-profit company, which operates the Beaumont and Newhouse Theaters, producing a mixture of new and classic plays in these, as well as in a number of venues on and off Broadway. Recently the New York Times *called it 'the pre-eminent theater in the country'. As well as being dramaturg at this prestigious theatre, Cattaneo translates twentieth-century German plays, and is creator and head of the Lincoln Center Theater Directors' Lab. In her interview she was too modest to state that she is also the recipient of LMDA's first Lessing Award for lifetime achievement in dramaturgy.*

Selected Production Credits

Galileo (Goodman Theater), *Orchards* (Acting Company at Guthrie Theater and US tour), *Hamletmachine* (New York University), *Love's Fire* (Acting Company at Public Theater, US tour and Barbican), *Measure for Measure, Mulebone, The Sisters*

Rosenweig, The Orphan of Zhao, The Rivals, The Coast of Utopia (all Lincoln Center Theater).

*   *   *

There is no difference between a dramaturg and a literary manager: we use both terms. I have done the same job in many theaters for decades, and I have been called a dramaturg in some theaters and a literary manager in others. I think it is just a preference of the organization. The easiest way of defining what a dramaturg does is to say it is close to the job of an acquisitions editor in a publishing house. It is a job that deals with all things literary in the theater. Like an editor, we read incoming manuscripts, and may make sensitive editorial suggestions. We might also do some work in the press department, as I know happened in England, when Kenneth Tynan was literary manager at the National Theatre at the time that Olivier was artistic director. I, and John Guare, the playwright who wrote *Six Degrees of Separation*, are executive editors of the *Lincoln Center Theater Review*, a literary magazine we publish here. I am just doing the program insert for *The Coast of Utopia* by Tom Stoppard. It is all of the writing and literary surround of the theater.

John Guare says there are two kinds of people who go into the theater: the people who went to see *Auntie Mame* as a child, and the people who read Artaud, and I think I am the second. I went to the theater a lot, especially in my college years. It was a time when the theater mattered to me enormously – theater like the Living Theater, and some of the great Peter Brook productions. I had no interest in acting. There are also two more kinds of people in the theater – people who will do anything to get on a stage, and people who will do anything to get off it, and again, I am the second kind. So it was unclear what I would do in the theater, although I loved it, and knew quite a lot about it. I also had a very strong background in literature and I spoke a couple of languages.

To start with I worked as a critic in a small way, but I wasn't really interested in having opinions about other people's work, I wanted to be part of making something. The profession of dramaturg was unknown in this country in the 70s, but I realized it existed when I lived in Europe. I had the wonderful opportunity and experience of getting to know two of the great dramaturgs who were working in Berlin. Botho Strauss, a very important German playwright now, and Dieter Sturm, were dramaturgs at the Schaubühne am Halleschen Ufer [Theatre] with Peter Stein [director] and an amazing company of actors. I was doing some translating at that point, and I knew them, and have tried to do some of the things they did in my small way over the years.

Their work, which I consider to be the highest art of our little profession, was to figure out what plays might be of interest to the actors, director and designers. The interpretation of the play belongs to the director, but the dramaturg can add a different perspective and help define the interpretation. An example is a famous production of *Peer Gynt* that was done in the Schaubühne in the late 60s, which they saw as a story of the growth of capitalism. It was Botho's idea to cast a different actor as Peer in each act. In this way it stopped being the story of an interesting individual, and became a story of a new Peer in each generation, a sort of metaphor of the growth of capitalism because the play moves forward in time. So it was a very clever way of interpreting the play through casting, and that was the dramaturg's idea.

Dramaturgs had been around on the continent for some time: the first was Gotthold Lessing, who worked in Hamburg as early as 1767. But eventually in the States, particularly with the forming of regional theaters, there had to be someone on staff to read the pile of incoming manuscripts. Most American theaters were founded in the late 60s, which is when we got the first government support for theater, and all the major regional theaters, like Lincoln Center, the Arena, the Goodman, the Guthrie, were all founded then.

Shortly thereafter, when I started in the theater in the 70s, it was a very fertile time of new play writing: there was David Mamet, Sam Shepard, Wallace Shawn, Marsha Norman, Christopher Durang; a whole lot. At that point there was very little structure set up to filter those plays, so my first job in the theater was to read around 1,000 plays a year. I worked at the Phoenix Theater, one of the great old off-Broadway theaters – one of the first. We were doing American and international new plays. People sent scripts from everywhere, in many languages. There were young people we brought over, who no one had ever heard of, like Philip Prowse, Robert David McDonald, Ron Hutchinson and Mustapha Matura, who now lives in London, but was originally from Trinidad. We began to put on those people's plays in context with some new American plays, by Wendy Wasserstein, or Chris Durang, who we were just discovering. The theaters were new, the writing was exciting, and we were trying to do something internationally – and all those things seemed to create a job which we now know as dramaturg or literary manager.

With new plays we don't give advice to writers unless we are asked, but for all of us who have been in the theater for a long time, we have many friends in the business who are writers, and we will often respond to work they have done, or offer suggestions. I had a very long-standing and happy association with Wendy Wasserstein, who unfortunately passed away last year at a very young age. My first day of a professional job was on the second day of rehearsal of her first play, *Uncommon Women and Others* [1977]. It was a play we did at the Phoenix with a wonderful company: Jill Eikenberry, Swoosie Kurtz and Glenn Close in a small supporting performance. I commissioned Wendy's second play, *Isn't It Romantic*, which we produced at the Phoenix.

The choice of plays in any theater is made by the artistic director. Each theater receives many, many plays to read, but nowadays we don't get many unsolicited manuscripts. I mostly get submissions from agents, or perhaps professors on play-writing programs. What I do here, with André Bishop, the artistic director, is read a lot of material, go see a lot of things, and try to know what is out there in the field. We are following a whole community of writers. It is not necessarily a thumbs up, or down, on a particular script: you will see a growth in a writer, or see something they haven't done before. It is basically preparing the ground for work that might be performed here in the next couple of years. I have a colleague here, Ira Weitzman, who does the same thing as I do, but strictly with musicals.

An example of something that is particular to a dramaturg's work is two evenings that I created for the Acting Company. I had the great pleasure of being asked to commission a project which allowed me to read Chekhov's short stories: there are hundreds of them, and they are all amazing. I chose some, and sent individual stories to a number of contemporary playwrights, and asked them to make a stage adaptation. The evening was called *Orchards* and consisted of seven stories adapted by Maria Irene Fornes, Spalding Fray, John Guare, David Mamet, Wendy Wasserstein, Michael Weller and Samm-Art Williams. That evening was presented here in New York, then toured the United States, and went to the Barbican too. The other evening I did was called *Love's Fire*, which was devoted to responses to Shakespeare's sonnets. I chose seven sonnets, which are not set in any particular place or time, but each embodies a particular, powerful emotional situation. Again the writers included Wendy and John, and also Tony Kushner, Eric Bogosian, William Finn, Marsha Norman and Ntozake Shange. So that was a case of taking an idea that involved working with writers, who I knew and loved, and creating an evening that was later realized.

Another example of my work, on a classical front, was a wonderful production that we did here called *Mulebone*, by Langston Hughes and Zora Neale Hurston. It was a play they wrote together and had a famous falling-out over in Harlem Renaissance history. They didn't speak after the argument, and the play was never produced and was basically lost to archives. It was rediscovered, and I read it in manuscript when I first came to Lincoln Center, and thought it was absolutely wonderful. We made a production, which ran on Broadway for a couple of months, with music by Taj Mahal. My part in that involved advocating for it, and then working with the Hughes and Hurston Estates, families and biographers, to get this belated world premier 'right'. It is a simple folk tale of two friends who are both in love with the same girl: it is a light-hearted, comic play. The music in the original play was traditional folk songs, with rather silly lyrics, as some folk songs tend to have. I suggested to the director to substitute those with some of Langston Hughes' poetry that was appropriate to rural life, and is very lyrical. Then we commissioned Taj Mahal to write music to that poetry. It changed the play in a way, because the music and lyrics were so incredible that it gave the two young men in the small town a sense that there was some potential there or some sense of greatness.

Similarly, I did historical research in 1993, when we did *In The Summer House* by Jane Bowles, wife of Paul Bowles [composer and writer]. That was a play written in the height of the avant-garde, in the middle of the last century, but the play was originally produced on Broadway [in 1953] with Judith Anderson in the leading role. She had required certain rewrites, which Jane Bowles made reluctantly. The play was a huge flop and then disappeared, so I had the interesting task of tracking down all the early versions of that play, which I think our director, JoAnne Akalaitis, felt were more true to the author's intentions. Everything I do goes through the director. It is always important to have one person in charge, but I am often asked to edit or cut plays a little bit. For example we did a wonderful production of *The Rivals* [Sheridan], which the director wanted to shorten slightly, so I proposed the cuts for that.

The Coast of Utopia [Stoppard] is about to open here now, and several months ago I spent quite a bit of time with all the leading actors in our company, giving them all the historical material [the play is set in mid-nineteenth-century Russia] on the characters they are playing, and got them prepared. So when they jumped into rehearsal they were totally at home with Alexander Herzen [played by Brian F. O'Byrne] and Michael Bakunin [played by Ethan Hawke], and all the scenes, which are complicated, but very playable. They did a tremendous amount of work, and all got very excited, to the extent that they bought plane tickets and went to Russia. Our production will be very different from the one in London, so it will be interesting to see how it goes.

Dramaturgs have to be useful people, able to communicate with writers, directors and actors. They need to be theater people, rather than academics, but with a background in literature and languages, and they have to be able to do research. That is our specialty, in the same way that designers are theater people who are visually very gifted. If someone wants to be a dramaturg, there are now training programs in many colleges. It is also important to go to the theater a lot, and perhaps find a small theater with a company who thinks like you do. If their work speaks to you, I would present yourself and try to get involved. You could say, 'Look, you have this amazing actor; have you ever thought about doing *this* play? It would be a great part for this person.' In European theater the dramaturgs on staff spend a lot of time doing that, because they have permanent companies of actors, and part of their job is to say, 'Actor X has only been playing certain kinds of parts, let's find a play that would stretch them in a certain way.'

Part of my job is to meet with actors and ask what they have always wanted to do. I was very close to Jack Weston, who has now passed away, who was one of the great comic actors of the American stage and screen. When he died the Academy Awards included a little tribute to him. He was in the original company of *South Pacific*, and had done a lot of Neil Simon and was a great clown. He played Pompey for us in *Measure for Measure*. It was his first Shakespearean role, and of course, he was just brilliant. He really wanted to do some more Shakespeare, so I was trying to get him ready to play Falstaff in *Merry Wives of Windsor* when he died, because I thought he would have been absolutely amazing.

What is nice is that a dramaturg is a bit of a mystery job, but it has some crossovers with casting and directing. I directed in the old days, and would find myself at 1.00 a.m. on the phone with some actor, reassuring them, saying, 'But you're *wonderful*,' and I thought, 'I want someone else to have to do this.' I like the idea of doing all this other interesting stuff and letting the director deal with the actors. When you are working with a director who is really gifted, the experience can be wonderful. For example, I translated *Galileo*, by Brecht, for Brian Dennehey [actor], and it was directed by Robert Falls, who runs the Goodman Theatre in Chicago. He is one of my favorite directors, and he has worked a lot with Brian.

Bob had the idea of working the play through the lens of Brecht's HUAC [the House of Un-American Activities Committee] experience [Brecht was called before the committee in 1947 and denied being a member of the Communist party]. He started the play in a very period setting, but as the Copernicus theory goes out the door, and the center of the universe cracks open, the clothes gradually became more modern. As Galileo has to recant his teachings, there was a slightly 1940s look, which is when Brecht was called before HUAC. It is interesting to thread some of those things through with a director. And there are many other directors I have worked with and really admired: Mark Lamos, Garland Wright, Adrian Hall, Robert Wilson, Jack O'Brien – I have had a wonderful time investigating the plays alongside them.

I am also involved with the Director's Lab, a project I created 12 years ago. It is for young, working directors – not students, but directors in the early part of their career. It has brought a very large number of directors here: the Lab is free of charge, and now about a third of the directors are from other countries. We work very intensively for about three weeks each year, in the kind of way that you get tired, and boundaries break down and you bond together. We investigate whatever seems to be of interest at the time. For example, before 9/11 was very different than after. We had just finished a very interesting Lab a few months before 9/11 on the question of style in the theater – in play writing, acting, design. After 9/11 that seemed awfully aesthetic and removed from reality, so to heal ourselves, we pushed up our sleeves and produced 25 short new plays.

Last year we posed the question, 'Is it true that all great theaters were created artistically by young people with a unique way of looking at the world, who banded together with actors and designers to make a new theater; not by penetrating existing institutions, but by creating their own?' So we looked at the Moscow Art Theatre, The Group Theatre, Joint Stock, Steppenwolf and many others, across the board. This led us to consider whether there was a particular aesthetic that young people are working in today. It is an unusual chance for directors to share insights together.

Co-editing *Lincoln Center Theater Review* is another part of my job that I enjoy. The magazine comes out three times a year, and investigates the power of theater in the modern world – not just the entertainment industry. So, for example, in the latest issue we interview writers from other fields who reflect on *The Coast of Utopia*: it is as though you went to the production, and then came out into the lobby with the most ideal companion on your arm. We interviewed Margaret Atwood, who wrote about the quest for utopia in her novel *The Handmaid's Tale*. We talked to the Russian fiction writer Tatyana Tolstaya, a descendent of Tolstoy's, to see if the characters in *The Coast of Utopia* mean anything to Russians today. It is a chance for us to place the plays in a discourse.

I enjoy the fact that my job calls on so many skills and that it is so completely different from year to year. Right now I am deep in nineteenth-century Russian socialists, but I could be deep in the Harlem Renaissance. Or to get a salary for reading Chekhov stories – what could be better in the world than that? It is a changing job depending on the project. I am always keen on keeping things as challenging and ambitious as they can possibly be. I don't like to know what is going to happen when I go into a theater, but you are always dealing with the climate. At the moment people like musicals and things which are familiar to them, but I am interested in pushing theater into the realm that is more mysterious. Sometimes I worry that I am a little out of sync with American reality!

There have been many plays that I have loved working on, and mostly it has to do with the collaboration with the director, designers and actors. I had a very good experience years ago [1982], when I was very young, working with James Lapine on a production of *A Midsummer Night's Dream* at the Delacorte, which is our outdoor, Shakespeare in the Park Theater. In fact the eventual production was rather mixed: some things I thought were amazing and some things were not. James had never done any Shakespeare before, and he would come over to my apartment every morning and we would just read the play to each other, discuss it and ask questions. Years later in the Directors Lab, Richard Eyre was speaking to the directors, and to my surprise, he told the group he had done exactly this with Ian McKellen and Bob Crowley as they began to explore *Richard III* for a production at the National.

In my apartment, I remember saying to James Lapine that the social class of the playwrights of the Elizabethan era was actually closer to the mechanicals than it was to the lords of the play. He was surprised to hear that, and in a way, it affected our casting choices: I was in the casting sessions with him. Our mechanicals were not played as buffoons at all, but as regular guys. And *Pyramus and Thisbe*, the play within a play, was played totally straight and worked really well. That is an example of how research can have an effect on what you see on the stage later. It remains one of my favorite productions of the play, in part because of the happy collaboration.

I am having a similarly wonderful time just now on *Utopia*. I love this company – they are amazing actors; I have had a marvelous time working with Jack O'Brien [director]; I love Bob Crowley and Scott Pask, our set designers – what is better than sitting down and hashing out ideas about the period with these people? It is absolutely wonderful. Jack, Bob, Scott and I also met in my office a year ago. We all read the play to each other and would keep stopping and asking, 'What is this about?' I had found some interesting population statistics. At the time of the play, in 1830, there were 60 million people in Russia. One per cent were gentry – that is the people in the play; one per cent were clergy; about eight per cent were merchants and professional classes; and 90 per cent were serfs, basically slaves. That idea became very resonant in our production. Actually when Tsar Alexander II freed the serfs in 1861, he freed 12 times as many people as Abraham Lincoln did. So the young noblemen's lives were really propped up by a legion of serfs, and one of the opening images in the play that Bob and Scott created is this mass of people who are a constant presence on stage, as they were in real life then in Russia.

I have found this to be a very interesting and creative job. If you had told me that I would be working at Lincoln Center for close to 20 years, I would never have believed you, because I worked at many theaters before I came here. There is a very small staff here, and we get along very well: we are like the Indianapolis 500 pit stop crew. The show comes in and we all work together on it. It is hard to imagine better working conditions, and we continue to do interesting work, so I am happy here. I have done quite a lot of teaching over the years, and I suppose I could go into academia. At present I just teach the Theater History course at Juilliard, created by Michel Saint-Denis. The course teaches how to investigate historical material and style for contemporary stage production. But I like actors, I like being in production, and there is nothing as exciting as a night like tonight, when we will see what happens when our first audience comes to this amazing play [*The Coast of Utopia*]. I just can't wait, and we are taking all the actors out to dinner afterwards. It doesn't get much better than that. There are so many interesting aspects to this, kind of secret, job.

Dresser

Kate Slocombe

Kate Slocombe has worked as a part-time dresser and masseuse at the Royal Shakespeare Company in Stratford-upon-Avon for over 20 years. She is another example of somebody who is crucial to the success of any large theatrical performance, but whose work is never seen by the audience. She needs to be efficient, trustworthy and caring in a job that is intimate, responsible and fun.

The Royal Shakespeare Company employs over 500 people. It is one of the best-known theatre companies in the world, attracting and inspiring a highly talented ensemble of actors and core of associate artists. The original Shakespeare Memorial Theatre, built on a site donated by a Stratford brewer, was opened in 1875. It was destroyed by fire in 1926 and a new theatre opened in 1932. Established actors, such as John Gielgud, Laurence Olivier and Peggy Ashcroft, as well as new ones, such as Richard Burton, won the Company critical acclaim, and in 1960, under the direction of Peter Hall, the repertoire widened to take in modern work and renaissance classics as well as Shakespeare. Now under the artistic directorship of Michael Boyd, the RSC has three theatres in Stratford: the Royal Shakespeare Theatre, the Swan and the Courtyard. The company also performs a season in Newcastle and throughout the year in various venues in London. The collaborative nature of the company, its ideals and high standards remain at the forefront of its work.

Selected Production Credits

Nicholas Nickleby, Macbeth (1986), *Romeo and Juliet* (1986), *The Plantagenets* (1988), *King Lear* (1993), *A Midsummer Night's Dream* (1996), *Othello* (1999) (all at the Royal Shakespeare Company).

*   *   *

Although I wasn't interested in the theatre at a young age, my family were theatrical people. My parents were heavily involved with the Birmingham Rep and my great-grandmother was a dresser. I was a nurse, and had two children, when my ex-husband, who was a sound engineer, came to work at the RSC in Stratford. It so happened that they needed some dressers on *Nicholas Nickleby*. He came home and said, 'It is a huge show and they are desperate for people to help,' and I said, 'Ooh, I'd love to do that. That would be a bit of fun!'

I still did my nursing, a couple of shifts a week, juggling it with the children, and I worked part-time at the RSC, and then just carried on. Actually, I don't think it is unusual for a dresser to have stayed in the same job for 20 years. To start with I deputized for an elderly dresser, who had a day job as well. In those days we always did a Thursday and Saturday matinee, so I always did his Thursday matinee, and covered for him whenever he was unavailable. At that time things were a lot freer; now they are a lot more rigid about hours, and everything is contracted. But I think it is still the sort of job that you get through people you know.

You don't really need any training to be a dresser; you just need to be a certain kind of person. You can't be star-struck, and a lot of people are – we live in a celebrity-worshipping society. You have to know when to shut up, and when you can chat, and be quite sensitive to other people's needs. Gradually people got to know I was a nurse, and I saw there was a need for massage, too, so I did a course, and started doing that as well. It is really quite separate from being a dresser, and unusual to do the two, but has worked out well for me. I built up a little business in massage for injury and relaxation, but mainly for therapy. The actors already knew and trusted me, because once they knew I was a nurse they would come and ask me about all their medical problems! I have a treatment room at home, and the actors make appointments to come. I have been on tour as a massage therapist, but I only do dressing in Stratford.

There are about nine dressers in Stratford; four full-time, core dressers in the main house, and depending on the show, they will use more. We start at 6.30 p.m., an hour before the show, and go and collect the laundry for the actors that we are dressing. The rest of the costumes are set out in the actors' rooms by the maintenance wardrobe mistress, but I collect things like socks and pants and add those. Any quick changes that are not done in the dressing room also have to be set out. The place where they change will be pre-arranged during the technical rehearsals before the show opens. It could be downstairs, or in the back dock area by the side of the stage. So I would set those costumes in a particular order so the change is done as quickly as possible.

The actors usually come to the theatre half an hour before the performance. I check to see that the ones I am dressing are OK, and then make myself scarce until they call me. There is a sort of hierarchy; so if you are dressing the principal actor, you do a lot more for them than you might if you have two rooms of lads who are each playing several parts. If you are dressing the person who is playing King Lear, you might get them a cup of tea, and look after them generally. The more experienced a dresser you are, the more likely you are to be dressing the principals. You also have to do more for period plays than modern ones. If you have rooms full of girls wearing laced corsets, you work it out with them how it will work, who will be helping who, and sometimes hurry them along a bit.

At the RSC every show has about six dressers working on it. Women dress women and men, but men dressers normally just dress men, although they might help on a woman's quick change if it is something they can do, if you understand me! I have had lovely experiences with men and women who I have dressed. I have had rooms full of women where we have had a riot of a time, and the same with men. On the other hand, you might get a room full of men straight out of drama school and they throw their clothes on the floor, and you are having to go round after them, saying, 'Hey, come on, get your act together; pick it up!'

Because I have always done relief work it has been lovely. I could be dressing the principal actor for a couple of weeks while his dresser has a holiday, or I might have a room full of 'spear carriers' as we call them. It is a great, fun job, although I have never wanted to do it full-time. I don't really like working six nights a week, although there have been times, when they have needed me, when I have done that. Funnily enough the most demanding show I have ever worked on was *Nicholas Nickleby*, and it was the first one I ever did. It was extremely difficult because with such a large cast, and with so many of them doubling up playing several parts, there were hundreds of costumes. It was quite taxing, because I didn't really know the score, or what I was doing, and the actors were stressed, playing all these different parts, and wanted you there, with the next costume, ready to help all the time.

We all have everything written down, so during a show we might have three changes in the actor's dressing room, then run downstairs to do a change, then help another dresser with a change. Some costume changes are extremely fast: the fastest I have had to do was about 15 seconds. In cases like that you might have three dressers helping with the change. It is often quite frenetic. You have to have everything ready so what they put on first is laid out on top. Sometimes the actors under-dress, so we are helping them take something off, rather than put something new on. This is all worked out at the technical rehearsal, when we find out exactly what there is time to do. It might be that the maintenance wardrobe has to take the costume to pieces and put Velcro on it to make things easier. Occasionally an actor has walked on stage slightly late, or with the costume half on, or half falling off!

When you do a show from the beginning you know the routine, but doing relief, working from someone else's notes, it can be quite difficult, and I have had my share of disasters! For example, when Alex Jennings was playing Richard II, he had a quick change where he wore a big coat and top hat, and it was a very dark scene with dark clothing except for a pair of red gloves. He came running off stage, and I had to give him the hat and gloves, which I set inside the top hat. But one night the gloves got stuck inside the top hat, and as he put the hat on, the gloves went on his head. He realized he hadn't got the gloves, and wondered where they were, but luckily they fell off onto the stage during the scene. But when he came off he said to me, 'You are not going to tell me that my gloves have been on top of my head?' So I apologized, and told him what had happened.

Once I was dressing a very tall actor and a very short actor, and I got the jackets mixed up. So one of them had his sleeves half way up his arms, and the other had his sleeves covering his hands. That sort of thing can happen when you have about four men coming off to quickly get into costumes that look the same. You have got it all laid out on chairs at the side of the stage, but for some reason, one of them might go to the wrong chair, and end up in the wrong thing. It might be a hat which is too small, or whatever. I am pretty sure that for the most part it is only someone like me that would notice, although the actors obviously make rather a song and dance about it, saying, 'I must have looked terrible!' and you would like to say, although, of course you can't, 'I'm sure no one noticed, and if they did, there is something wrong with the play!'

Another thing that went wrong once was that I fell over backstage and knocked an entire quick-change room over during a very quiet scene of *King Lear* [directed by Nicholas Hytner, 1991]. It was John Wood's last big, quiet, speech, and I went flying over a sword that had been left on the floor. I grabbed hold of the quick-change room and it concertinaed on top of me with an almighty crash. John Wood wasn't very happy, as you can imagine! I was actually dressing David Troughton [Earl of Kent], and he was a lovely man and had witnessed my fall, so when John Wood came off and asked, 'What the bloody hell has happened?' David Troughton replied, 'Don't shout at her; she has really hurt herself and it was an accident.'

David Troughton isn't at all 'actorish' – he is really down to earth, and yet he had this superstition. He had to have his socks put on in a particular order. He had to put his left sock on before the right one, or he felt it might be bad luck. Of course no actor will ever let you mention *Macbeth* backstage for fear of bad luck: I think it is a 'sackable' offence! They have their little rituals. Ladies, too, will have certain things, like trinkets, on their dressing tables, which they have always had, and wouldn't dream of not having. Actors used to have their own little cloth on a dressing table, with their things laid out in a particular way, but that is quite old-fashioned and dying out now. Some of the young ones don't have any sort of order at all!

I have dressed all sorts of actors: Charles Dance, Ralph Fiennes, Joseph Fiennes, Jeremy Irons – they were lovely. To be honest, there are very few awkward people; though they sometimes have their little ways. For example, some actors need complete quiet when they are in their dressing rooms, and so you learn not to disturb them. Michael Kitchen is one of those. As soon as he came into the building he would be in his part, and you couldn't have a laugh or a joke with him, because he was very much in his own head. But in a nice way: he was an extremely nice man. Actually *Romeo and Juliet* [directed by Michael Bogdanov, 1986] with Michael Kitchen as Mercutio was one of my favourite productions. I did a lot of dressing for Hugh Quarshie [Tybalt] on that too, in all his leather gear.

Another, quite different, actor I really liked working with was Robert Stephens. He was the most amazing storyteller. On *King Lear* I was actually dressing Owen Teale and Simon Russell Beale, big mates of his, in a dressing room next door to his, but he used to come in during the interval and chat. He was a very interesting, very lovely man, although he was very, very ill when he did *King Lear*, but no one would have known it, really. I knew it because of my nursing background. I thought, 'This is a very sick man,' and it was just before he had his liver transplant.

Over a whole season you can get very close to people, seeing them every day, and it can be quite sad when they leave. Actors often say that the theatre is like a big family, and at Stratford, it really is. It is lovely when actors that you have been really close to come back after three or four years. I have also made loads of friends with wig girls and wardrobe girls. It is a really fun job.

The director can make quite a difference to the atmosphere of a production too: whether it is happy, or fraught. Greg Doran is always lovely to work with. Terry Hands was pretty scary! There was always a very serious feeling backstage during a Terry Hands show. Ian Judge was very disliked – his were not happy shows. In those cases particularly, mine is quite a caring role. Particularly now that I am older, I feel a bit like a mother figure a lot of the time. But what I enjoy is the buzz of being involved with a good production, and the banter and camaraderie. I always think of it as an extremely enjoyable job, even though it is not my only job, and my nursing is very important to me. It has been a gorgeous job to do as a secondary job.

I am going to make this my last season. I have had a great load of fun with it, but I miss nursing. So I have gone back to doing three days a week of palliative care nursing for the Shakespeare Hospice in Stratford, and the other two or three days of the week I do my massage therapy. I still do a little dressing, but I am cutting right back. It was lovely to get my Long Service Award from Prince Charles, who is president of the RSC, and came to Stratford for the AGM. He handed me a cheque for £300 (which I spent on a painting) and we had a little chat. He was more interested in my massage actually, than the dressing. He wanted to know how it worked with actors, and what alternative therapies I was into. Then we were all given tea. I remarried last year, so my husband came with me for the occasion, and we had tea and cakes and it was all very nice.

Fight Arranger

Terry King

Look at the list of credits in any theatre programme in England, and if there is a fight arranger, it will probably be Terry King. He does not deny that he is at the forefront of his profession, but he is realistic and unromantic about himself and his job (his conversation peppered with expletives). Theatre is not his sole interest in life, nor does he crave a sense of community, of 'family', enjoyed by most who work in the theatre: Terry delights in the fact that he is a freelancer, constantly moving from one venue, and one set of people, to another. I met him in the distinctly unglamorous rehearsal rooms of the Royal Shakespeare Company in South London.

The cream and green entrance hall was plastered with notices. Among the call sheets scheduling that day's rehearsals for Romeo and Juliet, Julius Caesar, Much Ado About Nothing *and* Anthony and Cleopatra, *were other announcements stating, for example, 'Fruit and biscuit fund come to end. Pay DSM or ASM £2 and supplies will be restored.' Another read, 'One bedroom flat wanted.' The central heating was not working and there was an unfortunate smell of drains. Although wonderful work emerges from 35 Clapham High Street, I could not help contrasting this setting with the usual comfort in film studios.*

Another difference between film and theatre is that in the former, fights can be achieved by using specialist stunt doubles, camera angles and effects – in the theatre everything is seen for real. In a recent production of Sam Shepard's The Late Henry Moss *at the Almeida Theatre, every time Brendan Coyle fought and kicked Andrew Lincoln, the woman in the seat beside me jumped, put her hands to her face, and gave a sharp intake of breath. Terry King directed this fight, making sure that the actors felt confident and safe, while the action appeared totally real and fulfilled its function in the script. It was a contemporary two-man fight, but King is equally adept at arranging complicated battles with period weaponry.*

Selected Production Credits

Richard III (1988), *Macbeth* (2003) (both Royal Shakespeare Company), *Jerry Springer: The Opera, Elmina's Kitchen, His Dark Materials* (all National Theatre), *Richard II* (Old Vic, 2005), *Private Lives* (West End and Broadway), *Olleana* (Royal Court), *Fool for Love* (Donmar Warehouse), *Porgy and Bess* (Glyndebourne), *Otello* (Welsh National Opera).

*   *   *

I don't give a fuck whether I am credited as fight director or fight arranger – I am credited as all sorts of things and it doesn't bother me. My work is completely freelance, and I have been very lucky: over the last few years I have worked a lot at the RSC, the National, in opera, West End musicals and shows, the Royal Court, the Almeida, the Donmar, fringe theatres and regional reps. I work across a huge range, and for me, that is the interesting part about it. On some jobs, like *Henry VI* here, at the RSC, I will have a big involvement, over several months in rehearsal, and attending the technical period; and yet yesterday I went for one session at the Royal Court and that was finished. There is always a different requirement and commitment.

Basically, what I do is arrange a fight. The director will say, 'There is a fight here, between this person and that person, or between these people.' Some directors might say, 'We need to stage the Battle of Waterloo. Come back in three weeks and show me what you have got.' In doing that, they give you the rope to hang yourself if you don't do a good job. The other end of the extreme is that the director will want to be there, doing everything, and using me just as a guide to make sure it is safe, or because there is a legal requirement. Either way suits me just fine. I prefer that it is always different. I would get a bit bored if I was never given any responsibility or opportunity to imagine what I think will work best, but equally, I relish the jobs where I come in, and the director wants to do it all. Then I do what I am asked, and if it is crap, it is not entirely my fault. It is my job to fit in with what the director wants.

I also like the variety of fights in different times and genres, from battles to an unarmed scrap. The only thing I don't do is when they have a battle in slow motion, as in the current National Theatre production of *The Royal Hunt of the Sun*, which Trevor Nunn is directing, and the battle is arranged by a choreographer. Slow motion can be fantastically effective, but on the whole, it doesn't engage *me*. What I do is naturalistic, real. Sometimes there might be a period of three or four weeks when you seem to be doing the same kinds of fight all the time, and at the end of it you feel, 'Surely there must be something *nicer* to be doing with your days!' Then something might come along, like, say, a sword fight with a different dimension, or a bit of humour. I get the story from the director, and have to understand what he wants. I am always much more persuaded by the dramatic integrity of the moment, than by the historical accuracy. And if something works as a piece of drama at that moment, and it is not historically correct, I personally find that more important than exactly how the sword would have been held: there are so few people in the audience who know, that I don't feel it matters.

In a sword fight, pretending to kill someone by thrusting your sword between your opponent's arm and body is obviously a bit clichéd, so I would try to avoid it. If you place the blade on the person's tummy, you can pull it quite hard across their body, so it looks as though you are slicing them open. You can also give the appearance of slitting a character's throat, particularly if you are standing in front of him so he is partially concealed. At that point you can activate some sort of blood effect.

Some directors feel it is better to leave it to the audience's imagination, and indeed it is true to say that you often raise more questions by having blood when someone has their throat slit, than if there is none. For instance, the audience starts thinking, 'It is the wrong colour; it is not gushing enough; it has stopped gushing.' On the other hand, if you don't use it at all, the audience will accept that that is the theatrical convention. No one is right. Sometimes the most effective use of blood is to not have blood at all, and sometimes it is best to have gallons of it. It depends on how well it is done, and on the overall view. Someone like Michael Boyd, director of the RSC, loves blood. Michael Boyd wants blood even if no one is being cut! But Nick Hytner, director of the National, doesn't like blood. He is much keener to use some sort of metaphor, or to leave it to the imagination of the audience. Both can be fantastically successful.

In a fight, noise is incredibly important: it is the cement between the bricks, and covers a multitude of sins. Some actors are instinctively good at this, which is the best; some you have to say, 'Groan a lot!' I do everything incredibly carefully, and when you make noise, it tends to release energy, and that is the raw material of a fight. In the early days you should positively resist making noise, so that by the time you are making noise and you are releasing energy into the equation, the mechanics of the fight are secure and the actors are following the same routine subconsciously, and the acting is only a veneer over the top.

There is an old cliché among fight directors where they say, 'I could have arranged a better fight over the phone.' It is very difficult to describe something that is essentially very visual and tactile, in words. But I will try. If you are doing a punch, you don't hit the person's face, you hit the air. But you do it in a place where the audience can't see. Where you place the punch in relation to the audience is crucial. You then need the victim's reaction, and this is actually more persuasive than the action itself. Then the most convincing thing of all is if you generate a good noise. Whether the noise is exactly accurate is less important than whether it is loud.

The ways of making noises are: hitting your chest with the flat of your palm; hitting your two hands together; a third party can, surprisingly, sometimes make the noise; you might even have the noise as a sound effect made by someone off stage. In something like *The Late Henry Moss* where an actor appears to be being kicked, it was generally his hand that was being kicked. For instance, one character is told to clean the house up, and is thrown to the floor by the other one, and given a rag and made to mop the floor. I had to find a way to use the story to get the two actors into a position where they can do a bit of trickery without it looking contrived. In this case I told Andrew Lincoln to be in a position on the floor where he was across stage (rather than up and down). Then I would say, instead of mopping the floor with your right hand, mop with your left hand, and tuck your right hand underneath you, so your right palm is sticking out from your body upstage where the audience can't see it. Then I would ask Brendan Coyle to kick his hand. That noise would make the audience think he is being kicked in the ribs.

You can actually kick a hand quite hard without it hurting, but there are rules and regulations for the person being kicked. For instance, you must not have your hand floppy: you have to hold it quite firmly, so the hand is not kicked away, or up into your face, or so that it flips your wrist back. But if audiences applaud, they clap till their hands sting. Hands are quite resilient, although it varies a lot from actor to actor. Safety is of paramount importance, and I hope that I have a reputation for being safe. I categorically believe that it is not worth hurting yourself: it is only a play. I also believe that if you make actors feel safe with the choreography you give them, and if in the process they subconsciously glean that you are concerned about their safety, and that ultimately they do feel safe, they will do the rest. At the end of the day, fights are just a bit of coarse acting.

Fights are only ever as good as the actors doing them, and as good as the actors want them to be. Some actors are particularly keen, and want the fights to be good, and are prepared to commit to them, work at them and cooperate with me in order to hit that pinnacle. The fights in *The Late Henry Moss* were good, partly because of the way they were constructed, but overwhelmingly because of the way that those actors took them on board. You could say the same about watching a play. At the end of the day, a play is only as good as the actors doing it.

You would never deny that Shakespeare is a fantastic play-wright, but how many productions of Shakespeare have you seen that have actually been rather tedious? Either the actors may not have been quite good enough, or they didn't quite come together and ignite in the way that the basic material is capable of. Fights are exactly the same. Fights only work if you believe the moment when words fail and violence begins. If you believe the first three seconds of the fight, you are on your way. If in doubt, I would go for brief and brutal. You are much more likely to get a good fight if you stop it before you are found out to be a fraud. But it depends on the function of the fight within the drama. There are fights in Shakespeare where they are struc-turally part of the show: they give it a bit of a lift, or form a big finale.

In the course of a year, you only get two or three fights, if you are lucky, that are really good, and hit that gold standard, where people jump in the audience, or where you get really strong feed-back of people saying, 'The fights in that were fantastic!' Those are the jobs that earn your reputation and keep getting you work. There are other occasions where the actors are either not capable of hitting that standard, physically and emotionally, or not willing to aspire to it. They might be frightened of aspiring and failing somehow, so they are prepared to settle for second best, and where you earn your money is in making those fights look per-fectly OK. Then instead of the audience saying, 'Oh, that's shit!' they would just not make any comment at all. And if they came out at the end, and you asked, 'What was the fight like?' They might say, 'Was there a fight? I didn't notice a fight.' There, you have done your job, and that is how you earn your money.

Again it is variety. Some actors are simply not good at it. It is the same if you ask a group of actors to sing, or dance: few of them would be scintillatingly good. There are all sorts of skills an actor is required to have, and doing a fight is one of them, but not many actors are really good at creating the illusion of conflict. All actors *can* do a fantastic fight if they choose to really, really commit to it and work at it and go for it.

Somewhere along the line in a fight, when the fight director isn't there, actors subconsciously, or consciously, come to an agreement as to what level they will aspire to. And this is based on whether they feel safe, whether they feel comfortable, and whether the fight makes them look good, in that it makes the moment feel real and true. The two actors in *The Late Henry Moss*, for example, undoubtedly subconsciously decided that they could make it look fucking good. They were really going to hit that gold mark. If they feel really safe they will act the anger, the danger, the emotion, the energy, because they don't feel compromised by the possibility of hurting each other.

Another performance where I think the fight achieved that high was *Henry IV Part 1* at the National in 2005. I think the choreography was part of it, and I was proud of the fight, and the way it fitted together, but the way they did it was just fucking brilliant. I thought the whole battle was good, but the fight between Hal and Hotspur (Matthew MacFadyen and David Harewood) was outstanding. Another production that I particularly remember was *The Murderers* at the National, directed by Peter Gill, because it was through that that I really got a lot of work. *Porgy and Bess*, at Glyndebourne, had a very good fight in a fucking amazing show. The production of *Macbeth* with Iain Glen, in Scotland, was also memorable. It was the first job I did with Michael Boyd, and that has been a very fruitful relationship for me, as he has used me a lot ever since then.

Iain is fantastic. It is hard to put your finger on exactly what it is. It is being able to pretend to hit someone, and have exactly the right physical and mental aura about you as you do it. Or, thrusting a sword at someone, knowing damn well that you are aiming to miss, and sticking to the safety parameters, but looking exactly like you are a savage who is intent on killing somebody. On stage there are limited options in the moves that build up into a fight, and you could probably write down the tricks pertaining to stage fighting on the back of a cigarette packet. They have been around since actors started performing plays. However, as a fight arranger, the way you apply and adapt those principles is limited only by your imagination. The thing about having a reputation that goes before you, and having worked with most people before, is that people feel comfortable with you. I make an effort to work around people's capability and their preference. I try to make the fight fit the story that they want to tell.

Having a good reputation means that most people will cooperate. And during that period they will feel able to say, 'I can see how to do that.' Or, 'I didn't like that: it didn't feel right.' I am always at pains to say, 'If it doesn't feel right, tell me'. People like Iain Glen are great in that way, because they contribute a fantastic amount, in terms of their understanding of what works for them. Many people can understand what works when they see it, but one of the real skills of a fight director is being able to put it into words, and problem solving. I need to be able to spot what someone is doing wrong, and be able to put it into words. I also need to be able to say, 'Try it like this.' I have to be able to demonstrate it, so that someone who is not necessarily good at it has a model to copy. Once you copy something it becomes your own.

Many first fight calls will be with the director in the main rehearsal room, while he or she talks about what they want, and how they see the story. Then many of the rehearsals will be at a separate time or place where you are simply drilling the fight. You demonstrate with one person, and then the other. But there is only a certain amount of demonstrating that you should do, because it is more important for you to stand back and look, and be able to say what you want. Someone like Iain is able to articulate what is wrong. Toby Stephens [son of Maggie Smith and Robert Stephens] is also excellent. He did a very good *Hamlet* at the RSC, and he was exceptionally good as Coriolanus, also at the RSC [in 1994, when Stephens was only 25], in the production directed by David Thacker, as indeed was Barry Lynch, who was Aufidius in that production of *Coriolanus*.

Like some actors, some directors are good with violence: Michael Boyd, for instance, is fantastic. He is interested, which not everybody is. Some directors just see it as an interlude between their bits, and the quicker it is over the better. That is also fine by me. Basically the director requires three things from you: first he or she wants you to be quick, because every minute you take is a minute out of their rehearsal period; second they want you to be effective – they want the fights to look good in context, whether funny, savage or whatever; and third they want you to be safe, so the actors can go on to fight another show the next night! The actors require exactly the same things, but in exactly the reverse order.

I think I am rather lucky in that I don't have an angle. I didn't ever intend to be a fight director, and had no ambition to be one – it came about by pure chance and bullshit. I happened to be at the right place at the right time, and I got one job, and it snowballed from there. But it is really peculiar that I have become a fight arranger. I would like to think of myself as someone who is completely anti-violence. I think fighting is just stupid; the last resort of the incompetent. I have been in one fight in my life when I was ten years old, and even then I remember thinking how stupid it was. I would regard myself as something of an old hippy!

But I like my job, and I think I am immensely suited to it, not so much because it is arranging fights, but because of the nature of the work – I am a peripheral member on a lot of different projects. I am here for an afternoon, and gone: there for a few hours and gone. That suits me perfectly. Most people in this business are attracted to the family atmosphere, but I am not. I enormously respect and admire and like the people I work with, and genuinely enjoy seeing them again when it has been a while, but I am an outsider.

The passion of my life was climbing mountains. That is what I cared about, and had to do to be me. For most people who work in *this* business, *this* is what they have to do, and if you took it away, there would be a huge void, but there wouldn't be for me. It is a great job, but it is not something I have to do as part of my identity. But climbing was something I really needed. Actually my only interface with violence was that the climbing world in the 60s and 70s was full of fights. Where I climbed, round Sheffield, coal miners and steel workers would go out to Derbyshire and get into terrible fights with the quarry workers. The stories that went around the climbing world were all about who was dobbing who. I was only tolerated within that world and by the people I climbed with because I could get them up good routes.

I have climbed the north face of the Matterhorn and of the Eiger; I've climbed in the Alps, the Himalayas and all over the world, and for me, that was a driving force. I don't do it any more. The trite reason would be to say I got married and had children. But for me, climbing was a bit like a drug. I wish I could go climbing like some people play golf, on the odd afternoon; or like alcoholics wish they could pop down to the pub and have one pint. I just couldn't do it: I had tunnel vision. For years I feared that if I went out for a day climbing, it would be a bit like offering an ex-junkie a recreational hit, and I would be back on it. Actually I could go climbing now, because I wouldn't be able to compete, so it wouldn't be so intense. But I suppose the truth nowadays is that I haven't got time. My work is a constant commitment and it is hard to ever get a week off. In September it is my twenty-fifth wedding anniversary, and I have been told that I am having a week off or we are getting divorced! We go away for long weekends, but we haven't had a week together for as long as I can remember.

I got into this business by teaching in drama schools. I had been to drama school myself, to study acting, at the same time climbing like crazy. I came out at 23 and worked a bit as an actor, and decided very quickly that if I didn't go away and do the kind of climbing I wanted to do, I would end up as a bitter old man.

So I spent the next five or six years climbing, earning money to go on the trips doing anything. If I got an acting job, fantastic, but I also drove delivery vans and worked on building sites. When I was 28 I went to see an agent I used to know, and he handled a guy who used to teach stage fighting and tumbling and acrobatics at RADA, and had indeed taught me while I was at LAMDA. While I was in the office this guy phoned to say he couldn't get to RADA, and I said to the agent, 'I'll do it!' He asked, 'Can you?' and I replied, 'Of course! I'm brilliant at that kind of thing.' So he rang the principal at RADA, and told him that Barry couldn't come, and a bloke called Terry King would come instead.

Then I thought, 'Oh shit, why did I say that?' But I thought, 'It's money, and I'll do it, and I'll enjoy it, and if they don't, that's their problem!' I had the odd seed of information from having been taught myself, and because the students were keen and highly motivated, I got tenfold back, and learnt on my feet, running five steps ahead of the students. At the end of the first day the principal told me it had gone extremely well, and asked me to cover until Barry could return. I did about three weeks, and because Barry was starting to work mainly in America, I was asked to come back for the following term. I said I couldn't, because I was going to the Himalayas for the next six months, but I said I would phone them when I got back.

That is exactly what I did. I taught at RADA, and at other drama schools, and then someone I had taught recommended me for a job at the National Theatre, and I thought, 'I'll see if I can get away with it.' You wouldn't be able to do all this now. You would have to get onto the Equity Register of Fight Directors and get qualifications which I haven't got! To get on the register you need an Equity card, which you might get as an actor. You would also need qualifications in martial arts, British amateur fencing and first aid. Then you would have to do a weekend course where you are observed choreographing fights, and you would probably serve an apprenticeship working with a fight director, travelling about with him, or her – there is a woman who does some work as a fight director. In theatre, to be truthful, there are only really two fight directors who make a proper living out of it, without doing anything else.

It has been hugely fortuitous that I have been able to find a job that suits me so well. What I find satisfying is seeing my work coming to a successful conclusion. And a couple of times a year, just occasionally, I will watch a performance and think, 'That is fucking great, and I contributed to making that as good as it is.' But how many times, during, say, the span of a director's career, can they really say, 'That's sublime!' If you hit a mean average which you don't often drop below, people keep employing you. I think it is the same if you are a designer, a choreographer or an actor – how many times can they say, 'Wow! That was breathtaking!' There are many obscure and noble conditions that link together to make any one bit of a show sensational.

I hesitate to say I am good at what I do, but I obviously do something right because I have got so much work. But I honestly don't know what it is. It may be a combination of being able to look at something and see how it would work, being able to work with actors, being able to persuade them that it is a good way of doing it. You become more confident as you go along to go with something that may not work immediately. You do get some people who are just no good at it, and can't remember their moves, and you have to push and push, and at the end of the day you know that they are never going to be good at it. That is the biggest challenge, and it is often those people who are the most appreciative. I get great satisfaction when an actor who just didn't think they could do it, and was terribly worried, perhaps feels that what I did enabled them to cope with it. Whether they say it or not, you get the feeling that they were glad you were there and got them through it.

I am probably most proud of making a good living in a very difficult industry. I do a job that I find interesting, stimulating, challenging and demanding, and I have got through it, and brought up my children. The children are leaving home now, and my wife and I feel like we are in a hot air balloon discarding ballast. We are lifting into the sky, saying, 'Fuck me! We have a life coming up. Whoopee!' That is what I look forward to. I don't want to do this forever. I can't complain, because I had my early retirement between 24 and 30, when I travelled round the world climbing. And when our youngest daughter was little I had a lot of time with her, and I really valued that. But recently I don't even get a whole weekend off. It has been particularly compounded lately by having to go backwards and forwards to Canada to work on *The Lord of the Rings: the Musical*. It has been a brilliant job, but all the travelling was a strain. But I am very lucky. My mum always used to say that, and I have always felt it.

My mortgage has got three more years to run, and we have one child left at home. I would like to stay on the crest of this wave, and work at this level for another four or five years. Eventually I think the wave will just swallow me anyway, but I am hugely looking forward to saying, 'Right, I am going to be away for the whole of September.' We want to travel. I want to watch whales, and go on a journey with huskies. That will signal the start of the slippery slope. But because this has grown quite slowly, I think it will also decline quite slowly. So during that time I shall continue to earn some kind of income, which we won't need to pay for anything in particular. So it is a great fucking sunset to look forward to.

Flying Director

Ben Haynes

Ben Haynes' stock-in-trade is Peter Pan *and Christmas pantomimes. But in the show* Mary Poppins *there is a line, 'Anything can happen if you let it', and to some extent this is true of Haynes' work. He can create the illusion of magic. When I saw* Mary Poppins *two effects blew me away, and Ben Haynes created them. One was spectacular, when Bert, the sweep, tap-dances up a wall (at right angles to it), upside down along the ceiling, and down the other side. The other effect was moving and impressive: at the end, Mary Poppins flies away, out into the auditorium, over half the stalls, and up until she disappears through the top of the theatre. Unlike in a film, where the audience is removed from the action – here it was part of it. Yet although the show works so well now, it was one of Ben Haynes' worst experiences.*

Haynes set up Freedom Flying 'in order to continue his work within the performer flying industry, while pursuing the quest for greater and more spectacular flying effects'. He operates from a unit on an industrial estate in Epsom, Surrey. There is an office, and a warehouse filled with tracks, cables, ropes, wires, a flying carpet and a basket for a hot air balloon. There are rows of different-sized leather harnesses, made by a saddler. These generally have to fit under a costume, so when Tara Fitzgerald wore one recently, under a very flimsy costume, in And Then There Were None, *she had a special, very fine harness. The front of the harness normally forms a cross over the front of the body – although depending on the build of certain women, this is not always possible! The harness also goes between the legs, which for a man is more complicated!*

Selected Production Credits

The Producers, Mary Poppins (both West End), 1984, *La Sylphide, The Tempest* (all Royal Opera House, Covent Garden), *The Magic*

Flute (Glyndebourne, 2004 and 2005), *The Wizard of Oz* (Theatre Royal, Norwich, 2005), *Guys and Dolls, Wicked* (both West End).

*   *   *

Mary Poppins was one of the most frustrating jobs I have ever done in my life. There was a combination of different people providing flying effects, which is not how we would normally work. The automation system was provided by Stage Technologies, whereas usually we would provide all the equipment, rig it and instruct the performers and the operating crew on the correct and safe way to use it. We get the performers to look like they are flying, and not hanging, because there is a very fine line between the two. But on that show, the systems doing the lifting and travelling are not ours, and the way that came about was quite strange.

We were involved to a certain point, but because another company was already providing a lot of automation in that show [for instance the roof of the house flies up to reveal the attic, and park benches slide in and out], Cameron Mackintosh wanted to use their automation for the flying. It was bad financially, but it also meant we had a lot less control over what was happening. It was a trying time, and it very much tested my relationship with Richard Eyre, the director, and it is the only time I have worked with him. The only other time we have not provided a package was on *Chitty Chitty Bang Bang*. I had only just started my own company then, and we needed the work, but didn't have all the automated equipment yet. That was a stepping-stone, but to get involved with *Mary Poppins* in the same capacity was a big step backwards.

It happened because at an early meeting, I was asked by Richard Eyre and the choreographers, Stephen Mear and Matthew Bourne, if it might be possible to get Bert to tap dance along the stage, up the wall, along the proscenium arch and back down the other side. They said, 'It is a bit of a strange request, so tell us if you don't think it is possible.' I said, 'Nothing is impossible, we just need to have a bit of time to play around with it.' Lee, my business partner, and myself were working with a really good aerialist on *The Tempest* at the Royal Opera House at the time. An aerialist is someone who might have a circus background; someone like a trapeze artist, or who does silk or rope routines. Anyway, we took her down to the set of *Jumpers* at the Piccadilly Theatre, where we had our own equipment.

Jumpers had two side walls for the trapeze part, so we lowered the borders, and set a camera up in the stalls, and attached the aerialist to wires, and got her to walk along the stage, up the walls, and walk along something that wasn't there – but from the camera angle it looked as though she was walking upside down along the bottom of the border, and down the other side, and we filmed it. We worked out how she could keep her body straight while she was at right angles to the wall and upside down, and how to make those transitions. We did it several times, but within two days of them asking, I took a video tape back to *Mary Poppins*, and said that was the sort of thing we could do.

In *Mary Poppins* it is very similar. There is a lift and travel truss system that comes down from the side – and an up/down, left/right track. Then there is a little tap board with the wires that support Bert on the side of the track, attached to the moving carrier, rigged within the proscenium arch. The actor has two wires attached from his hips, and as he walks the wires pull him straight in the system, which travels with him. As he gets to the wall it starts lifting him, and the wires hold him from a straight vertical position to a straight horizontal, so he is walking along with his feet on a tap board that goes along with him, till he gets to the top, where he will revolve so he is upside down, and then do the reverse down the other side, and then he carries on walking along the stage.

They wanted to use the effect, but not our equipment. My biggest regret now, is that I ever got involved with the show. At that point it was a question of whether we got out, because it was not that beneficial for us, or whether we would be more frustrated watching someone else doing it, so we stayed involved. On that particular show it was a motorized system operated by a computer, so you have complete repeatability. Bert's transitions from stage to wall, wall to pros [proscenium] and pros to wall have to be exactly the same. If you are an inch out, he is an inch closer to the wall and his steps won't look right. There are different paths plotted for the understudies, because they have different leg lengths! Gavin Lee, who plays Bert, put in hours of work to make that as good as it is. He is fantastic, and once he did it, the pressure was on the understudies to make it as good. Gavin was very dedicated. He was frightened, most definitely, as I think a lot of people would be. He was taken higher than any typical Peter Pan flying, but also upside down, singing and dancing!

It was challenging for us too, to our mental states! The director just wants to go to someone and say, 'This is what I want.' And if it is not right, 'This is what needs to be done about it.' Unfortunately for us, Richard would tell me it wasn't right, but rather than be able to do anything about it personally, I had to go to the automation team from Stage Technologies and explain to them what was needed. They were under a lot of time pressure, and we might come back to that effect three days later, and it would be the same. Then Richard would say, 'Ben, this is exactly the same as it was the last time!' And I would just have to say, 'I'm sorry.' I apologized for months, but there was nothing I could do about it. We wanted to build relationships with people like Richard Eyre, and I can't help but think it had the opposite effect. I don't think he was ever aware of exactly what the situation was. I didn't want to bleat about it, but I did feel like a spare part. Richard must have wondered what I was doing there.

But as to challenging in terms of effects, when we are creating the illusion that someone is flying, usually, the novelty is when their feet take off the ground. In a couple of productions, it has been the reverse. For example we did a show last year, at the

Donmar Warehouse, called *A Cosmonaut's Last Message to the Woman He Once Loved in the Former Soviet Union*, where the characters are in a space station. So every time you see them they are in the air, and it was challenging for us because there was so much of it – they are always floating.

It was also challenging for the actors. Normally it is the technical period, whether it be three days on a panto, or three weeks on a big London show, which is the hardest time for someone who flies. Their body is only just getting used to the harness, and they will be asked to wear it for 20–times longer than they would do in the show. The sequence in the show may last two minutes, but to get that right, with, perhaps, Peter, Wendy, Michael and John – four people in the air, with eight operators in the wings, and the director, choreographer and ourselves watching, all with an opinion, might mean they are in the harnesses for four or five hours in a day. We take it upon ourselves to monitor that, and try and make sure they don't overdo it. If they do too much on the first day of the tech, and are a bit bruised and sore, you are not going to get an awful lot out of them the next day. And that is not their fault; it is because you are applying pressure to a part of their body that normally wouldn't have that sort of pressure.

The Cosmonaut show lasted about an hour and a half. There was a scene above where they were always floating, and also action going on on the stage; so we would always land them behind a black screen and they would have a few minutes' rest before they went up again. That was probably the most challenging for us, and for them, because there was so much of it, and the novelty was not when they took off, but when they landed. I did another show, many years ago, where the whole thing was set underwater and it was the same, and also the more time in the air, the harder it is to get consistency.

People are probably right to expect more and more from flying effects, but I believe there is no need to over-complicate things. Some of the most wonderful effects can be created simply. For instance, there is always a wow factor in auditorium flights, like at the end of *Mary Poppins*. You are breaking a line that you never normally break. As soon as someone comes out through that proscenium arch, and breaks that line, there is a different feeling for everyone out there; suddenly it is with you and you are part of it. We quite often do auditorium flights for pantos and *Peter Pan*. At some point during the show, Peter would fly out over the audience's heads and disappear out the back. But you can have too much of a good thing, and an effect like that is best kept to once or twice only. The exit in *Mary Poppins* is quite spectacular because the Prince Edward Theatre is so high. There is a gallery right at the top, and there are two people to see her in, and put a bar across, and then she gets unclipped and walks downstairs.

In a stage with a proscenium arch you can hide everything in the ceiling, and the only things that need to come down to the person are very fine wires. When you are in an area where there is no masking and nothing to hide behind, you have to make your systems as discreet as possible. Otherwise you would get people who walk in, sit down, look up, and say, 'Right! He is going to fly out there.' Then there is no magic. In some situations it is very hard to disguise, but we go out of our way to make everything the same colour as the ceiling and put borders around the truss. We make the wires as thin as possible within safety standards. You need to know the weight of the person, and what they are doing on the wires, and that determines what kind of wire you would use. The wires attached to a person are blackened because unless it is against a white background, black is the easiest colour to hide.

Something like the boys in *The Magic Flute* was quite simple. [This was a Glyndebourne production, directed by Adrian Noble in 2004, where three boys floated in and out on balloons, or humorously flew across the stage riding a three-seater bicycle – which I loved!] There was no up and down movement, which I think was a shame, because it would have looked nicer with more fluidity. There was a rigid track system, and there were platforms either side to load and unload the boys. It would have been better with a more complicated system, but the turnaround time and budget didn't allow it. The boys in that, who were different on various nights, didn't need to change anything except belt sizes, because they were just passengers, whereas Bert makes his effect what it is.

If we are doing a big show at the Royal Opera House, where they work in repertory, the turnaround time is so short that we operate the shows. All the gear comes down when a show is finished, then we test everything, and put it all back up for the next show, and operate it. I am not really built for flying, but if Lee and I are at the Opera House, and put the rig back for a show that night, we will run the moves with one of us on it, probably in a different, sit-harness, to make sure it is all OK. More often I would be on the buttons and let Lee do it! But I would never put anyone on something I wouldn't go on myself, so I have to be able to do it. If there is quite a lot of flying, for instance in a show like *The Cunning Little Vixen*, we would bring in a couple more guys to help with the flying.

We could actually do with three or four more of me and Lee, but people don't present themselves very often. We both have a passion for it, but we have not often found that in others. We get quite a lot of CVs sent in, but we mainly find people who have worked as operators. Sometimes there is a guy in a theatre who shows a lot more interest than anyone else, and is keen to help you. They also need to have good relationships with performers, because some can be quite testing. And although somewhere like the Opera House has been a very good customer, it is a huge place with a lot of different people, and it is a job on its own to make everyone happy there. So you need technical and people-dealing skills. And we haven't yet found someone who we would let go out and do a job on their own.

Then there is also a second, creative side to our work. You have to forget the nuts and bolts. Someone might play you some music and say, 'There are four people to fly, eight operators, two minutes of music – fill it!' It is two totally different jobs. You could teach anyone to do up nuts and bolts and make it safe, but you need the technical knowledge and the imagination to make it work and look really good. A lot of big shows will have a very firm idea of what they want beforehand, but on something like a six-week run of a panto over Christmas, they don't know what they want. So you listen to the music and that might give you ideas.

The most important thing is not the most comprehensive motorized system, or the newest bit of kit: the starting point is talking to the director. It is nicest to work with a director who is happy to give you a certain amount of freedom. But when we know what the director wants we work out how best to achieve that effect, whether it be a manually operated system – which is a man pulling ropes which are heavily counter-weighted, or if it is a motorized lift with manual travel. That is the third part of our job – to make sure the operators are competent, confident and consistent. Depending on the production, we might stay a few days. Travelling someone through the air without making it look jerky requires a special technique, which is usually easier manually than with a motor. If a little Peter Pan is hopping from the bed, to the floor, to the chair, to the mantelpiece, with a wire on, a motor is not responsive enough to do that; you would need someone giving and taking slack on a rope, so the wire always stays tight and the audience don't see it.

Funny things do happen sometimes. If one of the children hasn't got clipped up, he might have to walk to Neverland! So Peter might be teaching the children to fly, and the dialogue will change to, 'We'll fly out of the window, and Michael, you run behind!' You only get one go at it, and Michael, who might be a little child, is looking around frantically, trying to get clipped up. Actually, if I sat and watched that happen I would be distraught, but it doesn't really matter, so long as no one is in danger. Occasionally, too, an operator doesn't pay attention and instead of them flying towards the window, they fly the other way and Peter might say, 'Well we will get some practice flying round the room first, and then fly out the window!' The audience love those sorts of things. They get a story from it: 'The night *we* went, Michael didn't get into his harness, and then a pair of hands came out from the wings . . .'

I would be foolish to say that accidents never happen, although no serious accidents have happened with our company. With every *Peter Pan*, the first time you fly him through the window, or back to land on the mantelpiece, which might only be 10 inches wide, the performer might get a bit bruised. Occasionally we have had actors in a show who just didn't want to do it. It amazes me sometimes, because you would think that when the actor is being cast, they would be told that they need to fly! One thing that might happen is that an actor has said, 'Yes, I'll be fine with that,' and really they are not fine, so you have to take a lot of time.

You might have just finished rigging everything. You get covered in grease and crap in the roof, because no one ever cleans up there. You have to get everything safe, deaded off and secure. You may do that till four or five o'clock, and you walk downstairs all filthy, and you have people turning up for a five thirty flying rehearsal, when it is the first time they have been in the air, and the first time the operators have seen it. So you try to wash, change your T-shirt, and present yourself as this other person who needs to gain their trust.

The first time I fly anyone I have the minimum number of people there, particularly with children. In *Peter Pan* or *Chitty Chitty Bang Bang*, if there are a lot of other children sitting watching in the auditorium, the chances of the kid who is flying for the first time really telling you how they feel is very slim. They will either be showing off, or won't want to look silly. Adults, to a degree, do the same thing; some of them are just big kids anyway! So I try to talk to them on their own. Then I always walk along underneath them, if they are nervous, holding their hand, and am right next to them when we first do it.

We might travel them along the stage at a relatively low height, and then go back and do it a bit higher. If they are happy with that, you take your hand away, and just walk along with them and ask the operator to go a little higher each time. Then they might say, 'That's enough', and you bring them down and start the process again. If the performer is not confident they will never, ever look like they are flying. They will look like they are hanging. But with the right time, equipment and personalities, flying people is not rocket science.

My great-uncle was Peter Foy. He was born in London [in 1925] and worked for Kirby's Flying Ballets, and went to New York to stage the flying sequences in *Peter Pan* starring Jean Arthur. Later [in 1957] he started up his own company, Flying by Foy, based in Las Vegas, which became a world leader in what it did. From about 1982 they started to do some shows over here. When I was about seven, I was taken to see *Peter Pan* with Bonnie Langford in Wimbledon, and because the family were involved, I went backstage, and Garry, Peter Foy's son, flew me. I decided then that it was a really cool job! When I was at school, and the careers people said, 'What are you going to do?' I said, 'I'm going to fly people!' I was a bit naughty at school, and they would say, 'Yeah, yeah, come back when you've got a serious answer.' They didn't understand, and I wasn't going to elaborate on it if they weren't going to listen. But that is what I did. I left school, and *Peter Pan* was on in Horsham at Christmas, and because flying is not the sort of thing you can learn from a book, I got in at the deep end.

I was 15 or 16, and a guy who was working for my uncle's company came and rigged the show with me in Horsham. It was the first time I had seen any of this equipment, but we rehearsed it, and I stayed on and operated it for five or six weeks. I probably pretended I was 20 and had been doing it for five years – there were about four people on the end of wires who I was totally responsible for. So it was sink or swim. I would like to think I swam, or doggy-paddled for a little while, and then we went out on tour. All the equipment would come down on a Saturday night and get loaded on lorries, and we would travel through the night, and the next morning, set it all up again. You wouldn't be able to get the tracks spaced exactly the same distance apart, because of different roof structures, so there were always challenges. That is the way to learn, and I did that for about six months, and then got taken on full-time.

The company grew, and moved to Boreham Wood, and eventually I ended up running the company for two years – Peter was in Las Vegas, phoning regularly to hear what was going on. But things were changing quite quickly over here in terms of health and safety. I was getting involved with the British Standards Institution, because they were trying to make rules that would stifle what we were trying to achieve. I understand that there needs to be legislation – there was remarkably little, and you would think there would be more in the States, because of litigation, but there wasn't much – the name Foy seemed to be enough. But I had to keep dealing with this, and trying to come up with an acceptable standard here, and Peter felt that it wasn't necessary, and we fell out over it.

It was much the same as when he had left Kirby's, 40 years before, because he saw that things needed to be done slightly differently, but ironically, he failed to see that in my case. I couldn't do what I needed to do in that company with the restraints that were put on me. I was being told to work to various standards, and wanted to negotiate, but because I didn't have the backing of the man who owned the company, I felt very isolated. I didn't have the freedom to do what I needed to do – hence my company, Freedom Flying!

I had worked for Foys for about 12 years, and had never done anything else, and we were just moving house with our first child on the way. It was the middle of the Christmas season, when the schedule was crazy. You are under pressure to take on too many shows, working day and night to get everything open on time, and Peter FedExed me a letter telling me all these things that I was doing wrong, and I resigned. I didn't leave to set up my own flying company; that was never my intention. I was fed up with it. I had worked very hard and felt quite low about it all: I knew I needed to do something, but I didn't know what, so I renovated the house and took some months off.

The next year, coming up to Christmas, people started phoning me, asking me to do shows for them. I thought, 'I could do it, but I haven't got any gear.' All the equipment is custom-made, and I didn't have any money, so I borrowed enough to have five or six flying systems made. When I was with Flying by Foy, everything was made in the States, or manufactured to their design. So I had all sorts of patent issues, because I couldn't just copy their equipment. The worst thing I could do would have been to take on a show and have some lawyer come and tell me I was infringing a patent law. I needed to have connection points on the harnesses that had to be very quick release. Peter Foy had been working on them for 50 years, but they were his. So I couldn't come up with anything bigger, bulkier or slower. When Peter Pan flies through the window, and the kids go off and hide when Nana comes in, they have to be clipped up in less than 10 seconds, walk back out with the wires on, and when Peter teaches them to fly, they go up.

Anyway, I got my harnesses made, and I got through the first season, and then it just carried on. The thing I enjoy most is going to see something we have done and thinking, 'I don't think we could have done it any better.' I very rarely say that, because you always pick on things. I think the best *Peter Pan* I have ever done was at West Yorkshire Playhouse, about eight years ago. It was very different because it was a thrust stage [no proscenium arch, the stage extending forward into the auditorium]. Normally we would hang a track system across the pros on the house bars. You can fly someone backwards and forwards slightly, by moving them off that line, lifting them and then swinging. You can't travel towards the audience in that situation because you would swing back. In West Yorkshire we had four tracks upstage, about a metre apart, running up and down, and a bridge where the operators were, with gauze in front, hiding them. As a result we were able to fly people back and forth as well as sideways. I sat and watched that show and felt very happy.

That production was directed by Matthew Warchus; someone I very much enjoyed working with. He wouldn't accept anything if it wasn't right, but would give you the time to do it. Another director who I liked working with is Tom Cairns, who designed and directed *The Tempest* at the Royal Opera House in 2004, which was a very rewarding show to work on. Tom Cairns is a fantastic guy because he listens to you, and tries to help solve problems with you. Doing a new opera or ballet is always nice. I think you have always got to try to come up with something different. Sometimes I dream of people flying! I would really like to come up with a really good underwater sequence for a show – something very carefully choreographed, where you would have people really believing that there were people swimming. I would also like to do more ice shows.

Expanding is difficult because of finding the people. We are already completely booked for next Christmas, and last year we turned down about 50 shows. We felt we couldn't do any more and do them justice. If we expanded we would have to buy a lot more equipment and have more people. There would be more work and more grief. Selecting the right shows to do is always hard. There are people who you feel loyal to, and people whose shows sound really good. I would rather have quality than quantity. You spend a long time building a good reputation, and if the wrong person goes out to do a show, it could be ruined, so I don't want that to happen.

When I meet people socially, and they ask what I do, I say, 'I make people fly.' They often ask, 'Are you a pilot?' Then I say, 'I make people fly in the theatre,' and I tell them about wires and harnesses. A lot of people want to find out what performers are like, but I feel there has to be some sort of code of conduct where I don't reveal too much. I am in a lot of situations where I am putting a harness on someone, and it has got to go pretty close to their skin, and be fitted correctly, but you do it to as many guys as girls, and it is like working under a car bonnet at the end of the day! You are only concentrating on the harness, and that the person is safe.

I feel quite lucky to do what I do, although if you asked me in the middle of December, when I was a bit jaded, I would probably say it was not the best job in the world! But I have done shows in Dubai and Marrakech, Copenhagen and Strasbourg and it has been good. I don't want to be away for too long now, because I have two young children. Molly is four and Megan is two. Molly came to see *Chitty*, and I took her for a fly in the car afterwards. She knows I make people fly, but I would like to hear a conversation at her school when they ask 'What does your Daddy do?' It is probably a bit like when I was at school; they probably think she is making it up, because she has got quite a good imagination, and I think she is a little too young to understand completely. I took her to see *Santa Claus* in Southampton this Christmas. When Anita Dobson flew in, as the Ice Queen, Molly turned to me and said, 'Daddy, how can she be flying, when you are sitting here next to me?'

Footwear and Stock Co-ordinator

Sara Wan

Shoes and boots play a more important role in a play than one might think. Of course, they have to suit the period, costume and style of the production, and be comfortable to wear. But shoes can also reflect the character the actor is playing, and affect the way they walk.

If you have a shoe fetish combined with organizational and people skills, working in a theatre can be a dream come true, although you may not easily find employment, since only major companies have the luxury of someone who deals specifically with footwear. The Royal National Theatre in London is such a company, and it is where Sara Wan works. The theatre houses a store of 5,000 pairs of boots and shoes, arranged according to style and colour, on shelves in sliding cupboards more normally used for archive material. Sara's office is a floor below. Its walls and door are covered with pictures of shoes, some humorous, such as a cartoon of a woman sitting disdainfully in a shoe shop, surrounded by dozens of open boxes of shoes, while the assistant delves into yet another, to take out a gun.

Sara herself was wearing smart leather boots in a rather unusual shade of mushroom, which matched her top. She is charming. Interestingly, her father is Hong Kong Chinese, and only two generations ago, one of her relatives by marriage had concubines, with bound feet. Girls' toes were broken and bound down towards the heel so that the foot fitted tiny shoes. Considered beautiful, it prohibited walking.

Selected Production Credits

Oklahoma!, *My Fair Lady*, *Mother Clap's Molly House*, *The Birds*, *His Dark Materials I & II* (all National Theatre), *Cinderella* (Royal Ballet, Covent Garden 2004), *Once in a Lifetime* (National Theatre).

*   *   *

I have always had a bit of a shoe fetish, in that I have always loved shoes. I have a blanket-chest full of shoes myself. It is very difficult for me to go to a show that I haven't worked on, and not look at footwear all the time: that is my world, my job. I do it outside, too. I could go out now, and look at stranger's shoes, and say, 'They're from Clarks; they're from John Lewis.' It is quite obsessive, really. I am funny about my own shoes, too, because I see so many, and part of my job is being paid to be critical. If I see a pair that I fall in love with, I know I have to buy them.

I sort of fell into my job here. I trained as a theatrical costume-cutter, at the London College of Fashion. At that time it was called a Theatrical Interpretation course, which was only about pattern-cutting and costume-making, whereas now it is a degree course which includes a lot more design. The course lasted three years, and then I worked freelance, working with various freelance makers in their studios, doing work they were given by costume supervisors in different theatres. I also did a lot for 'Kingmaker' through Madame Tussauds, for the animatronics figures in Warwick Castle.

Next I got a full-time job at Cos Prop, the theatrical costumier, and when I left that I did 'running wardrobe', which is maintaining the costumes for a show. For example I laundered, dry cleaned and repaired the costumes on *Kiss of the Spiderwoman* and *She Loves Me* in the West End. But each show only has a limited lifespan, unless it is something like *The Mousetrap*, which I would never want to work on for long, because it would be too monotonous. And I wanted to broaden my horizons a little bit, so I started putting feelers out. It is all about contacts really. My job is very much a people job, and it is the same people that you come across over and over again. A friend of mine got me an alteration-hand job, which got my foot in the door here, at the National.

Because I am a bit of an all-rounder, they kept me on, creating a position for me as a general assistant. So I went to work with whoever needed an extra pair of hands. I did quite a long stint with the dyers, with costume props, buying, making and administration. Then I started getting interested in footwear – which is boots, shoes, gaiters and spats. Socks and stockings aren't part of footwear; they are hosiery and are a finished good. There was a guy here, Tony, who needed a helping hand, so I stepped into that, and then he got a promotion to a managerial position, and I took over the job, and changed it quite a lot, so that I became much more involved. For example, I go out and buy the footwear as well as having it made. There are only a few large companies who have someone specifically dealing with footwear. In the West End, the costume supervisor would deal with shoes. I love it now, when people call me and ask if I can help them with something, especially when I am able to come up with the goods.

My official title here is footwear and stock co-ordinator, which are two quite separate things, which for some reason have come together in one job. I'll take you through the footwear side first, as we would run a show. On average, we have a month to get ready for a show before it is on stage. It would be nice to say that we did 12 shows a year, but we usually do 16 or 17, in the three theatres here, so they all overlap, and I get pulled in various directions because naturally people think their show is the most important. When the actors are rehearsing, they will find some time to come up here, to the costume department, and the workroom will measure them. Rehearsal time is so precious that it is very rare that I would go with the actor to choose shoes.

The designer comes in with his or her designs, and then the costume supervisor, who holds all the strings within the department, sits down with me and goes through how many people are in the show, the designs and what each character requires. If there are 12 actors, it might still entail 50 pairs of shoes. Then I have to start thinking about what the designer wants. If it is a period show, I know that I have a store upstairs with about 5,000 pairs of shoes, which I pull on all the time. I will bring down different shapes, and heels, to show the designer what I think might be good. The designer might not like it so we have to go down a different route. Some designers find it quite difficult to understand what I am saying unless they have a 3–D object in front of them.

Anthony Ward, who happens to be working on a show here now, is a very accomplished designer. He did *My Fair Lady* here, and lots of big West End shows, but he is always interested in what you think, too. He will always ask, 'Do *you* think it is right?' which is lovely, because it makes you feel special, and that your input is important. Some designers leave more up to me than others, and sometimes I'll be called into fittings to give my opinion on whether the footwear works, or to suggest a style. If I am already in the fitting, I have to know when I can offer my opinion and when to keep shtum! Sometimes, though, there are designers where you think, 'That's not going to work' and they are adamant that it will, and then you see it on set, and think, 'Bloody hell, they were so right! I couldn't see that.' I learn things every day, and I think that it is very sad if you think that you know everything.

From my experience in the job, I *will* know whether we can buy something in and adapt it. Then I would go to the West End and purchase pairs of shoes. Usually these are for modern plays, although sometimes they can be adapted for period pieces, by painting or dyeing, or, for example, for *Once In A Lifetime* I bought new shoes, but had the heels changed. L.K. Bennett are probably still rubbing their hands from my purchases from them: we must have bought about 50 pairs of ladies' shoes. The style was perfect except for the heels, which were too stiletto, so I sent them to a theatrical footwear company, who matched the leather, and put chunkier heels on to look late 1920s.

More often if the play is set in the past we will use something from stock, if it fits the actor or actress, or I will advise that we have the shoes specially made. If they are being made, I send the measurements away, and the maker or I will source the leather or the fabric, or the suede, that the designer likes. They will send back a fitting stage, which I fit on the actor or actress in rehearsal, and mark up alterations, and send it back. Most of these shoemakers work specifically for theatres because regular bespoke shoemakers don't understand the rapid turnover that we need. I have had a pair of shoes made in a day!

We have all our shoes 'rubbered'. A special rubber sole is put on, made up of tiny pyramids, which is non-slip, and it also deadens the sound – if you have a leather sole, you don't want a clumping sound across a wooden stage. However, we have had shows where they want them to make a lot of noise, so I have had leather soles put on rubber shoes. It is not just the look of shoes; they make you walk differently. For instance, you wouldn't walk in the same way in flat ballet pumps, or Wellington boots, or high heels. The technical week before a show opens is very important. If a director or designer doesn't like the way someone is walking, or the noise they are making, we have to reassess the shoes.

The other thing that most people don't think about is that if we buy a brand new pair of shoes, and the brief for the character is that they have been sleeping rough, we can't give them a new pair of trainers. If you give someone a new white T-shirt, or a new pair of trainers, they actually look fluorescent on stage. So a T-shirt will be dipped down by the dye room, and a pair of trainers will have to be aged with different paints and sprays, and we crease and batter them. Sometimes we use sandpaper on shoes. The dye girls usually do that, but if I am not too busy we do them together.

About 42 per cent of shoes per year are used again – even if it is six months or two years later, but if shoes are looked after, they last. But if an actor really falls in love with a pair of shoes they can buy them from us. Occasionally an actor or actress doesn't want to wear a stock pair of shoes, but a lot of time the shoes have been *made* to look old and scruffy, 'broken down'. We explain this and usually the artist then understands. I try not to keep old smelly shoes in stock, as my motto is, 'If I don't want to put them on my feet, then why should I expect someone else to?' When we recycle footwear I clean them up and spray them with an anti-bacterial spray.

If an actor hates the style, it is my job to persuade them into it, because that is what the designer wants, and has been employed for his or her designs. Women actors are generally fussier than men. Obviously, I cannot say, 'You have got to wear them.' You know that if your feet are uncomfortable, the rest of you is uncomfortable. I have to assess *how* they are uncomfortable and whether I can do something about it, like stretch or soften them, or change the heel, or pad them out with a cushioned insole. Sometimes someone might say, 'I can't wear those shoes because I have to climb a ladder, or run up a flight of stairs,' and it is a valid point. In some ways I am the middleman, and I will relay problems to the supervisor or the designer. You have to look after people and want to get it right. I might buy a pair of shoes that a designer is totally in love with, but no size in the shop fits the actor, and we might get them made in exactly the same style. In one year we have to find about 500 pairs of shoes, of which about 300 pairs are purchased.

I enjoy going out shopping, but also going sampling different fabrics and leathers, getting the design together with the right heel height and toe shape. I also have to be good with money, organized, computer literate and good with people. I used to get really excited about working with famous actors and actresses, but I don't really any more. My parents have always said to me that at the end of the day, they are all only humans and you have got to treat everybody the same. I won't kowtow to people if they are shouting at me because they are not getting what they want, because I have to look after the designers as well. But my worst nightmare would be to go on stage and have everybody look at me, so I think, 'They have got their job to do, and I have got mine.' Actually my job doesn't end with getting the shoes. While the show is on, shoes come back up to me for maintenance, if, for example, they need re-soling, or a strap breaks.

The other side of my job, stock co-ordinator, is connected with maintenance too, but of stock fabric. By stock fabric I mean 'basic' fabrics, for example linens, silks, cottons, tailoring canvas and interfacings. These are used as the base of a garment, giving it its structure. We call this stock 'saleable stock' as it is charged to each production as and when it is used. Because we buy in bulk we are usually charged a lower price. This saving is then passed directly to each production. Each bolt of fabric is labelled with a stock code and is recorded in a book. At least once a fortnight I charge each show accordingly for the meterage utilized. This system saves a lot of time for the costume supervisors, the cutter and our buyers. A good knowledge of fabric type is essential, and I have to keep my ear to the ground for new supplies as some of the traditional fabrics are no longer being made. For example, the mill in Ireland, which makes a huge variety of tailoring canvas (which holds its shape better than modern alternatives when washed frequently), is closing down.

I also keep stock levels constant in the Laundry. This isn't one of the more interesting aspects of my job but is still important! I take advantage of the Internet here, and use 'Home Shopping' from a supermarket. We tend to stick to the same products that we know and trust, seeing as skin allergies are not desirable for anyone! We also have to be careful not to wash out all the 'breaking down' the dye department has worked so hard on. It is important I keep on top of all this, as it would have a knock-on effect through the department if stock levels were not kept constant, and alternative fabrics were not sourced. So there is some satisfaction in having an organized stockroom, and I can be quite anal about these things sometimes! However, this part of my job is not at the forefront of my day when I'm busy with footwear.

One of the most challenging things in my job is when someone comes in with a shoe and says, 'This is what I want!' but they don't know where it was bought from, or if it is still made. Also, designers don't design to seasons. For example, in the middle of summer, a show will call for a fur-lined boot, or in winter they will want strappy sandals. That's when you really have to do research and call people. It is very important to have a good relationship with shops, because often you need to ask someone over the phone to go into a stockroom and check that they have a particular style in a certain size and colour. If you just say, 'Well I need it now!' it doesn't work. I always try to remember people's names and write them in my address book.

But I enjoy the challenge. I worked on *Oklahoma!*, directed by Trevor Nunn and designed by Anthony Ward. In that there was a character, Ali Hakim, a peddler, who was a bit of a wide-boy. The actor Peter Polycarpou wanted a secret compartment on his body, whether it be in his hat, or wherever, to keep his money. In the end, we decided to have a secret compartment in the heel of his shoe. We had to work very closely with the makers to get that right. *My Fair Lady* was also designed by Anthony Ward and was absolutely beautiful to look at. I would say 90 per cent of the shoes for that show were made, so it was a big project.

Mother Clap's Molly House, directed by Nicholas Hytner, and designed by Nicky Gillibrand, was unusual too. A Molly House is where men in the eighteenth century used to go to dress up as women! I think people think cross-dressing is a new thing, but actually, it isn't. So I had to get a lot of tongue-and-tie, and tongue-and-bow shoes made in women's styles, but for men's feet! They were big, pretty shoes, if such a thing exists – you know they always put the smallest size on display in the shops, so they look the prettiest. I also did part of the Transformation Season, actually as assistant costume supervisor, and in *A Prayer for Owen Meany*, we had to make everything look big on Owen Meany because he is a tiny character. It is a story adapted by Simon Bent from one of my favourite novels, by John Irving. I was petrified that it was going to spoil the whole book for me, but it didn't: I sat in the audience every night and cried!

The Birds [by Aristophanes in a new verse version by Sean O'Brien] was another interesting production I worked on, because it was a collaboration with circus artists who had to climb ropes and go on a trampoline. Some of the cast who were climbing the ropes requested shoes like Japanese Tabi socks, but with a sole on them. These are called Matsuri boots, and are worn at one particular festival in Japan, so I couldn't buy them anywhere here. In the end I had to call the Japanese Embassy and they were fabulous! They gave me a website name, and I contacted a place in Japan and got them.

Of course, sometimes mistakes happen: once a label was left on the bottom of a shoe. The actor knelt down in the middle of the stage, and my heart was in my mouth, because it was a show, not a rehearsal, and I had to wait till the interval and dash backstage and pull it off. But in the main I have been very lucky. In 2003 I got a sabbatical for six months to work at the Royal Ballet, Covent Garden, which added another string to my bow. I did a lot more dyeing and spraying of shoes there, because there is only so much variation in shoes you can give a ballet dancer, and I didn't work so closely with designers there. But I did get the chance to work on a newly designed Cinderella [starring Alina Cojocaru, Wayne Sleep and Anthony Dowell], where I got all the shoes made in Italy.

Another pair of shoes that was interesting recently was for *Coram Boy*, where Melly Still, the director, wanted one of the characters [Meshak Gardiner] to look clumsy and odd, and a bit geeky. The designer, Ti Green, suggested clogs, but we wanted to keep them within period. So I managed to find a master clog-maker, called Jeremy Atkinson, who was so enthusiastic it was wonderful. He actually went out and chopped down a tree! It had to be an interpretation of shoes from the eighteenth century, but our feet have changed, and we need to be able to do different things in them now. So years ago they were probably uncomfortable, but hardwearing and cheap. The ones for the play were a little lighter, and hand-lasted from inside to fit Jack Tariton's foot. That was lovely to do.

I have worked with all sorts of interesting people. The designer Mark Thompson always has an edge on designs. Everything has a twist, so it looks both period and modern at the same time, like his designs recently for *Henry IV parts 1 and 2*. There are so many designers I have worked with, and actually, I don't think there is one that I wouldn't want to work with again. On *Anything Goes* I worked with Anthony Powell, who had worked with people like Greta Garbo! He was such a gentleman. He was a lovely old pro, and I could have sat with him for hours listening to the stories of people he had worked with. He wasn't bigheaded about it at all, and it was a *real* pleasure to work with him. He gave me the nickname 'Shoe Empress', which people call me now.

When people ask what I do I usually say I work in the costume department in the theatre, and that I am a shoe-buyer, because they don't really understand the concept of what I actually do. I hate it when people say to me, 'Oh, my wife would love your job!' They have no idea of the stress that we all go through. It is not just going out with a credit card that my work has provided for me, and going on a jolly. People think my job is glamorous, but it is hard work. Sometimes I see women looking fabulous in the street, in beautiful suits, and immaculate hair, and high-heeled shoes, and I think it would be wonderful to go to work like that. But I can't. I am crawling under desks, looking in dusty stockrooms. I have to have flat, comfortable shoes on every day. I try to look reasonable, because I am representing the National Theatre. If you have baggy old jeans on, and you go into a shop, you don't get good service. So if at least my handbag matches, it makes me feel confident.

I like the fact that I come in every morning and don't know what is going to hit me. I have never had two days the same in this building. Very occasionally, when everyone is pulling their hair out, I say, 'I'm going to leave and open a cake shop!' But I wouldn't be here if I didn't enjoy it, and I would like to stay. I enjoy specializing in shoes, I enjoy my relationships outside, and that I am working with a huge team whose sole aim is to work together to put a production on stage. When people come out and I hear them say, 'God! That was fantastic,' it is a reward in itself. Ironically, I know I have done my job properly when people don't notice the shoes. People only notice the shoes when they are wrong, so if people don't mention them, I am happy, because I know I have got it right.

Head of Sound

Ian Dickinson

Ian Dickinson is relaxed and unassuming, but his job is fascinating and he works for an important theatre. As head of sound at the Royal Court, he is in charge of sound throughout the building, and designs the sound for most productions. Working on plays, rather than musicals, his job is less concerned with amplifying, balancing and mixing live singers and musicians, than with decisions as to the placement of speakers, volume levels of playback, and sourcing or creating music and sound effects. His office is filled with computers; a video used to archive the shows; a mixing desk; a patch bed consisting of input and output cables and plugs reminiscent of an old-fashioned telephone exchange; and a large library of sound effects stored on cassettes.

Sound can make a huge difference to a play, enriching the audience's experience: the spoken word is just one aspect of sound, which informs, warns and communicates. Sound can suggest location, season, time, weather and atmosphere. From the simplest sounds of a cockerel, a clock or crickets, the listener is influenced almost unawares. Sound can also be used to link scenes, and to act as a powerful emotional stimulus. In the past decade sound in the theatre has undergone a radical change. Digital technology has increased the range of possibilities for sound designers, and directors are increasingly turning to them to provide an added dimension to their shows.

The sound designer is one of the members of the creative team that includes the director, designer and lighting designer. It is their names that are often on posters and advertising material along with the principal actors', and they can be compared with members of a film crew who are listed before the title rather than only with the end credits. It is clear that Ian Dickinson is proud of his position, and of the theatre he works in.

The Royal Court opened in 1956, and its first artistic director was George Devine, who aimed to create a theatre where the writer was of paramount importance. His policy inspired a new generation of British playwrights, among them John Osborne, Arnold Wesker, John Arden and Ann Jellicoe. The theatre has had a long and successful history of innovation built by gifted individuals. The 2005 Evening Standard Special Award was given to the Royal Court 'for making and changing theatrical history this last half century'.

Selected Production Credits

Fast Food, As You Like It (2000) (both Royal Exchange, Manchester), *Night of the Soul* (RSC/Barbican), *Push Up, Caryl Churchill Shorts, Alice Trilogy, Rainbow Kiss,* (all at the Royal Court), *Pillars of the Community* (National Theatre), *A Few Good Men* (West End), *Rock 'n' Roll* (Royal Court and West End).

*   *   *

When I was about 16, I remember being *dragged* by my English lit teacher at school to see a play at the Royal Exchange Theatre in Manchester, where I lived. It was *Twelfth Night* and I remember thinking, 'I really don't want to go and see this.' I had been to some musicals before, but not to a straight play, but I quite enjoyed it. I come from quite a working-class background, and I used to have a bit of a chip on my shoulder about the middle classes, and I think I was kicking against that a bit really: I didn't want to be part of that scene.

I got into sound because I used to play in bands when I was younger – I was a drummer, but I was very interested in the recording side of it, so I wanted to be a music producer or a studio engineer originally. I used to record our band all the time in rehearsals. It sounds a bit conceited, but I was quite bright at school, so I knew I could do a degree, and I decided to combine a business and media course at Manchester. Most of the tutors there were from a radio background, and they had a purpose-built sound studio, which at the time not many universities had.

That was 1989, just before all these drama courses at university started up. There are now lots of sound courses, for example, Central School of Speech and Drama, although that teaches more sound design.

The way I learnt was by making everything. If we needed a headphone amplifier we would make one, so I got really good at soldering and working problems out. I meet so many youngsters now who have just graduated and don't know one end of a mixing desk from another. They know how to talk to a director, and how to create sounds, but you also need to know the basics. The people who taught me really knew what they were doing, and wanted to pass that information on – and I am like that now.

As part of my course we had to do a work placement, and I got four weeks at GMR – the main radio station in Manchester – but at that time they never gave more than four weeks, and I needed five weeks somewhere else as well. Time was running out, and I had nowhere to go when one of the girls on the course dropped out of a nine-week work placement at the Royal Exchange, and my course tutor said, 'You don't really have any options: why don't you go for it?' But I thought, 'Oh God! I don't want to go and work in a theatre.' I still had a bit of a phobia about the middle classes and theatre, but I went for an interview. I was sitting in the green room waiting, and a guy walked in and said to the man sitting next to me, 'Oh Casper, darling, how are you?' [Ian puts on a very posh accent] and I just thought, 'What the hell am I doing here? Get me out!'

At the interview I met three of the loveliest people I have met in my life, and felt I could do the five weeks there. I did that before the four weeks at GMR, and within a week I decided I wanted to stay at the Exchange. I loved the lifestyle: it was very suited to the sort of person I was. Then, fortuitously for me, the guy who was operating the sound bust his back, and the head of sound, a man called Phil Clifford, who went on to co-found the big sound company Autograph, took me under his wing. He discussed the matter with his deputy at the time, and he must have seen some potential in me, because when she said, 'Shall I run the show?' he looked up from his paperwork, and said, 'No. I think we should let Ian do it.' At that point I thought, 'Oh my God!' I had never worked in theatre or done anything like that.

Phil taught me how to operate sound for a show, and I found I had quite an aptitude for it. It has totally changed now, because you press a button and everything happens, whereas then you had lots of cartridges, like big cassettes, with a loop of tape with the sound effect on. There was quite a lot of skill involved, because you were constantly taking the cartridges in and out, and mixing, and I loved the adrenaline rush of operating shows. That was still during my placement, but they were doing a big musical in the summer for which they needed another person, and asked me if I would stay. So I did that and then went back to finish my final year at university, absolutely knowing what I wanted to do when I left.

I graduated and kept my foot in the door at the Exchange, and Phil would ring me up from time to time to help with Sunday jazz concerts. I remember he rang me one time and it was George Melly. Usually I helped someone, but this time I was doing it! I think he just knew it was the right time to throw me in at that point, so I did it, and it was good. I did bits and pieces at the Exchange and at the Library Theatre in Manchester, and then Phil's deputy left, and I applied for the job and got it. I worked with him for about a year till he left to go to South Africa, so then I worked as deputy to Steve Brown for about five years. He designed most of the shows, and I did the day-to-day maintenance and running of the shows. I would wire-up props, run the fit-ups, organize the rigging crew for new shows on the Saturday night, and have a plotting session on the Sunday to set new sound levels.

When I had been in Manchester for about six years I began to think about leaving. But I was a bit of a 'Professional Northerner' and it used to really rankle with me that theatre was so London-centric, and if you weren't working in London you were seen to be inferior. So I was still kicking against London, and went to Edinburgh, and worked at the Royal Lyceum for a year. I didn't especially like that theatre or how it was operated. I went back to the Exchange to do a freelance show and wrote my letter of resignation on my way back to Edinburgh. We weren't doing the work I enjoy, and I knew I had to leave.

Then I wrote to people I knew a bit, asking for work. I wrote to Paul Arditti here, and to Rob Barnard, head of sound at the National. Rob invited me down and offered me a job at the National, which I accepted. Then the very same day, Paul rang me from here and said that he thought his deputy might be leaving, although he didn't know when, and he couldn't promise me anything. Straight away I knew what I wanted to do. The Royal Court is *the* place to work and always has been, I think, because it does new writing. So I had the embarrassment of phoning Rob Barnard at the National and saying, 'I am really sorry, but I don't want your job any more.' He was very understanding, even though I was turning him down without any firm alternative, but I did get it.

I have worked at the Royal Court for six years. I came as sound deputy to Paul Arditti, which I did for about two years. Then Paul decided to go freelance, and worked on *Billy Elliott*, and I was acting head here for about six months, and then I got the job of head of sound. I do most of the sound design now. Sound design involves helping to create an atmosphere and mood, and is there to *support* the play, in a similar way to lighting. If I am doing the sound design, the first thing I will do is to read the script, and mark any obvious sounds that are scripted. For example, in the recent production of *Rock 'n' Roll* pretty much all the music was stipulated by Tom Stoppard, and it was clear that I would need a flushing toilet sound, birdsong in the garden and various obvious things. But then you might think, 'Where are we? What sounds might there be in a garden at midnight?' and you try to recreate that.

But to some extent *Rock 'n' Roll* did not allow for an awful lot of input. I love music, so the joy of sound design for me is partly when you get a script where there is no music stipulated, and you have to listen to a lot of stuff to get something that fits and is interesting. But I enjoyed getting the music for *Rock 'n' Roll* and listening to it, and occasionally editing it a little bit. *Rock 'n' Roll* was quite a big show for the Royal Court, but Trevor Nunn was absolutely fantastic to work with. I think everyone was quite nervous of 'Sir Trevor' and 'Sir Tom', and I had to have a meeting with Trevor because I had never worked with him before. People come with certain reputations, so I was a bit, not in awe, but wary of meeting him, because it was a bit like an interview for the job. But he was really nice: likewise Tom Stoppard – he is a really generous, lovely person. So the whole thing suddenly became much less pressurized. We were all pulling in the same direction, and I don't think anyone ever lost their temper during the ten previews and the technical week. It was great.

In effect I was facilitating *Rock 'n' Roll*, but Trevor always made me feel involved, and I spent a lot of time with Tom Stoppard, talking about why he had chosen certain things. He just loves that music. There were some bits of music that we were not sure about using: some are in reference to year, but not all of them, but he said, 'I just really like that song and so I want to use it.' Then when I came to discuss the music with Trevor, and what might possibly be changed, I said, 'It is quite difficult for me, because Tom has stipulated all the music, and it is music he really likes.' Trevor was quite indignant about that and said, 'Tom has obviously chosen the music for a significant reason.' I think he felt even if this was not conscious, it might have been the case subliminally. Anyway, Tom didn't say anything and I just started smirking a bit. Then Tom and I got a taxi back here, and he said to me [Ian now puts on a good imitation of Tom Stoppard's voice] 'I really should tell Trevor that I chose some of the music just because I like it.' I thought that was really sweet.

It reminds me of a play I did called *Shining City* with Colin McPherson, who is another great playwright, and again, a lovely fellow. There is a lot of country-style music, and Gene Clark, who used to be in the Byrds. There was one particular song called 'Polly' which was integral to the play, and from which we took our lead for the rest of the music in the play. In the first dress rehearsal, the whole upper-management for this theatre were saying, 'You can't use this music; it's too turgid and depressing, and it's ruining the play.' I was getting quite upset about it, because Colin was saying what he wanted to use, so I was caught in the middle between what the playwright wanted and what everyone else said they wanted. So I had a chat with Colin and he said, 'Ian, if it wasn't for these songs, this play would not exist. When I was writing the play, this is what I was listening to, and this is why it is so important.' As soon as he said that, I thought, 'Right! I'm sold; it's fine.' Then the play opened with five-star reviews, and everyone loved the music and suddenly no one had a problem with it. So with that, even though Colin was very much leading it, there was a pleasure in designing it, because I got to listen to a whole world of music that I would never normally listen to.

Each play is different. For instance, I am going to do a show in a few months which will be a much more abstract piece, and I have been talking to the director about trying to find pure sounds. The set is quite simple, with lots of colourful lighting in certain scenes, and we are going to try to attach a pure sound to those pure lights, and have a different one for each scene. Sound design can be very basic – 'We need an owl, we need a car'; but the other side of that is, 'We need something, but we don't know what it is, and we won't know until we are in the rehearsal room.' Once you are in the rehearsal room you can start playing around with different sounds and making up your own sounds.

Some shows have no specific music stipulated, and often a big part of my job is to find music that will help the play along and service the play. It might evoke feelings, or it might just be to give it energy between scene changes. Sometimes you will work with a director who absolutely knows what they want to use, and that scenario might be quite difficult to work in, because you feel you are just facilitating someone rather than designing. But often I will suggest different things, and also not just use a chunk of music. I might try to find instrumental bits of a track and then loop it, or chop it around, so it is less obvious and more interesting. I have worked quite a lot with a director called Marianne Elliott, who says, 'I kind of want this . . .' We have a shorthand now because we have worked together so often, and I will go away knowing what 'this' means.

I did *As You Like It* with Marianne Elliott at the Royal Exchange, and being set in a forest, there was a sound track going virtually the whole time. In addition I was recording a guy singing and playing a guitar, and then he started tapping his guitar, and I carried on recording, and I ended up making up some sequences that were like drum beats, but done on the guitar. The director heard it, and she thought it was fantastic for a recurrent theme in the play as one person would run into the forest and another would leave. It was a big job, which all came together and all worked well, and remains one of my favourites as sound designer.

As a sound designer now, you are always referred to as part of the creative team, and that is when you can come into your own. It is a growing field, and has developed, I suspect, because of technology. Years ago the assistant stage manager would do some sound effects off-stage, or they might play something on a cassette. Then it progressed a bit more, and it might be the assistant electrician who would do sound – not because they wanted to, but because they were the most junior. It was never really given much time or thought. Now, a large theatre like the National might have about ten people in the sound department: we have three here. But since technology forged ahead so much in a relatively short time, it has opened up a whole world of possibilities. I think cinema has helped too. Directors will go and see a film and they will be more aware of sound being used in unusual ways, and will say, 'I want to do this; I want to do that.' And it is up to people like me to try to make that work.

In rehearsals sound designers now use laptops. I use a program called 'Audition' and can play back music, cut the introduction, and play about with it, all from my laptop. That is another reason why sound is being used a lot more. You can sit in a rehearsal room and a director will say, 'That's not quite what I wanted. Have you got . . .?' And invariably you can say, 'Yes,' or 'Just give me two minutes and I will have.' Whereas when I first started out, if you wanted to change something you needed half an hour to go to the studio and edit it on tape.

But a sound designer is still quite a poor relation. You still work with some directors who are very 'old school' and sound is last on their list of priorities. In many theatres lighting is still given much more precedence. For instance, in time allotted for focusing sessions – which might be all day, whereas the sound people might have a lunch hour to plot the sound. Plotting sound is setting levels within the space when the set is in place, with the doors opened or closed, walls in or out, as they would be in the show. You try to locate every sound, so if music is meant to be coming from a record player over in the corner, then that is where it should come from. You make a lot of choices as to where you are going to put the speakers, and why.

Before getting onto the set in the theatre I may have played some sound to the director through the two speakers in my office. But in my design I know a certain sound will be played from a certain speaker, and a different sound from a different speaker, and altogether it will make up this sound montage which will depend on which speakers it is coming out of. So you can give the director the building blocks of what you are going to do, and show him or her your pallet of sound, but when you actually get in the space you can start changing it and being creative with it.

I think a musical background can help. A lot of people would debate whether I was ever a musician, because I was a drummer. I *wish* I could play the piano, but in a way, it has made me go in a different direction, because I have to. Some sound designers

who are stuck will just play something, and create it musically. I
have to find samples, or cut bits of music up to make it into what
I hear in my head. I think having a good ear, and a sense of timing
also helps with being an operator.

In the theatre here, the operator sits at the back of the balcony.
In the old days, the sound operator would sit tucked away in a
little sealed control room where he couldn't actually hear what
the audience was hearing, which was ridiculous. We use a hard-
disk-based recording system, which can be on a PC or an Apple
Mac. Our system is called Pro Tools, which is an industry standard for multitrack recording. It is basically playback from the
computer, which means you can store lots and lots of information on sound files, whether music or sound effects. In the old
days, you might have had two-track tape and 24 inputs, but
because it is all done on computer now, editing is a lot easier and
everything is more precise. It can be programmed to play what
we want at whatever level at whatever time. It has become very
much like lighting in that you can press a button and everything
happens.

Our first port of call for a sound effect, like, say, shattering
glass, would be a sound library, and we are blessed here in
having a big one. But often it is not exactly what you want, so
you go out and make it yourself. Because I mainly do new plays
at the Royal Court, almost every play has a mobile phone ringing
in it somewhere. So as a new ring comes out we will record it.
That is another part of the job I love: if you can't find the effect
you want you end up making it yourself. For a show I did
recently, I needed the sounds of an auctioneer at a cattle market.
I ended up in Sussex with my big, fluffy microphone and my
headphones on, and these 60– and 70–year-old farmers looking
at me with *deep* suspicion as they were trying to buy their sheep
and I was pointing a microphone at the proceedings. Another
thing you cannot get on a sound effect CD is ice cream van
chimes. But I met a man who has hundreds and hundreds of
them! The joy he got from being able to talk to someone about it

was fantastic. He had a little workshop and he kept getting out more and more of these chimes, like little music boxes, for me to listen to.

Once I had to go and record a woman in Belfast. She was 75, and had been a club singer, and I had to teach her all these songs and record it in a day. It was a really big event for her because she hadn't sung for ages. She was dressed to the nines – all in black with gold lamé shoes and a little gold handbag, and she had got herself all made up. That was for a play called *Loyal Women* [2003] and the horrible thing was that we didn't end up using it! It was a play about the women's UDA in Northern Ireland, and the obvious thing would have been to use loyalist paramilitary fife and drums, but we didn't want to do that. It was about strong women, so we wanted a strong woman's voice that had seen life, singing these kind of torch songs. It took me ages to track her down, but in the end someone in one of the clubs, which are still quite a big part of life in Northern Ireland, suggested Maisy. And we did it all, and it sounded fantastic in the theatre, but then the playwright [Gary Mitchell] came, and he didn't like it. So we ended up using fife and drums, which was rather upsetting! I had to write to Maisy and say I was really sorry but we couldn't use it. The Royal Court is a playwright's theatre, so in theory, they have ultimate say.

Another thing that is different about working here is the fact that virtually everything is a new play. So you read the play, and straight away you think 'Wow!' and you get ideas of what you could do. It can get very pedestrian doing old plays all the time with period music and a little door chime. As soon as you start reading new work the scope is phenomenal, and directors also tend to be a bit more imaginative, because it has never been done before, so there are no parameters to work within. It is not like Shakespeare, or Oscar Wilde, or whatever, where there are certain set ideas: you can have your set design, and lighting and sound as wacky as you want. There is nothing really enforced on me. It is exciting in itself to know that you are going to be working on the next big show that happens. The next play that drops in the door might be fantastic.

I feel very privileged in that I have worked with all these legends of British theatre, like Caryl Churchill. You get nervous beforehand, but more often than not, like Caryl, they are so unassuming. It was very good fun working with her on some of her short plays, where there was very little décor and so sound and light made the sets. I also worked with Caryl on *A Number*, which I get the Mickey taken out of me about; that it was my best sound design ever, because it ended up with no sound in it! It was directed by Stephen Daldry, and when I first met him to discuss the play he said, 'To be honest with you, I don't think I want any sound.' And I said, 'OK! Fair enough.' It is a play about cloning, and had a very simple set. We did try different pieces of music, but Caryl was fairly sure that the play could just stand on its own, and she was right. It didn't need anything, because it was just fantastically written. But it is nice to go through the process. With any art, you have to be allowed to fail, or you would never try anything new.

Last year I did *Stoning Mary* with Debbie Tucker Green, which is also a fantastic piece of writing. Debbie told me she would like me to do loads of stuff for this play, and I read it, and then I went to watch a rehearsal, and I was quite convinced we didn't need anything for it, but during the rehearsals we did try different things, and in the end there was quite a lot in it, but it was all very subliminal. There were none of the usual time locators where sound can indicate the time of day and year, and whether it is hot or cold. Sometimes you do need one sound, like an owl, or the rush-hour, to trigger the audience's psyche. But part of the fun is trying to evoke those moods in a very simple way. Ideally, you would sit in rehearsals and see the play evolve from day one, but it is a luxury I don't have, because I do a lot of shows, and also run a department, and look after all the communications systems in the building. When I was in rehearsals for *Rock 'n' Roll*, I thought, 'This is the bit I really love.' If you are in rehearsals, you are more at ease with the director, the actors know who you are, and it is much more enjoyable. Actually, I also occasionally like operating, too, because then you feel a bond with the show that you often miss once you have finished the design.

Sometimes I think, 'I can't do this for the rest of my life,' because it is such hard work and long hours with no real let up. But the thing about theatre is that it is a real team thing, and a real family thing, and I have been really blessed in working in two fabulous places. When I was at the Exchange I felt it couldn't get any better – everyone got on so well. And everyone who works here loves it and no one wants to leave. But I am toying with the idea of going freelance. We will be getting a new artistic director and a lot of people will be leaving – although actually I am quite excited by the idea of working with Dominic Cooke, so sometimes I feel I should stay around and see how it goes. And I do love the fact that it is different every day. I hate press nights, because I find them anti-climactic, and you never really know if people are telling you the truth when they come and say, 'You've done a great job.' But I love first previews, because you know then. There is such a fantastic buzz, and you feel, 'Wow! It really worked.' You know how to change it to make it better, but it is the first time you see the play with an audience, and you have all been striving to get to that place.

If I went freelance I would have to do old plays again and that doesn't really excite me. Doing musicals is a whole different field: about understanding microphones. When people come out of drama school now, they seem to go either the straight drama route, or the musical route, which is much more lucrative. The only way you get good at musicals is by doing them, and I never have. Paul Arditti, my predecessor here, has managed the shift, and I do miss the concerts we did at the Exchange, because mixing the music, you feel you are just as involved as the musicians. I think our venue here would be fantastic for a small musical: not all bells and whistles, but something quite low-key, in this great little space. Because I still feel this is really where it's at.

Lighting Designer

Paule Constable

Paule (known as Paulie) Constable is a likeable, remarkable woman who combines being a mother, living in Brighton and working long hours in London, Glyndebourne, Leeds and elsewhere. She is also currently writing a book about stage lighting, is the recipient of several awards, and is at the top of a profession dominated by men.

Paule got into her job through pretence. While studying for an English degree at university she shared a flat with a drama student who got a job as a follow-spot operator in a theatre. The day before the flatmate was meant to start she went to Spain, forgetting to tell the theatre. When the theatre rang up asking for her, they were answered by Paule – who, without money or work, pretended to be her flatmate and did the job. Now, some 20 years later, as Matt Wolf wrote recently in The Sunday Times:

> *Paule Constable is one of the great talents of the British theatre industry, though only those who pore over their programmes are likely to know her name. Why is that? . . . As long as you can see what's on stage, that's all you need, isn't it? Except that Constable helps you see better than you ever knew you could.*

I met Paule during the preview week of A Moon For the Misbegotten *at the Old Vic. She was kind and helpful. When arranging a time over the phone she said, 'I am still very busy – there is still a lot to get right.' I told her that I had already seen the production (which later received wide critical acclaim) and thought everything about it worked wonderfully well. She was genuinely surprised, grateful and pleased.*

Selected Production Credits

Amadeus (Old Vic and Broadway, 1998), *Uncle Vanya* (RSC, 1998), *Proof* (Donmar Warehouse), *Les Contes D'Hoffman* (Salzburg

Festival, 2003), *His Dark Materials* (National Theatre), *Jumpers* (National, West End and Broadway, 2004), *Don Carlos* (Sheffield Crucible and West End), *Giulio Cesere*, *Cosi Fan Tutte* (Glyndebourne, 2005, 2006), *Faust* (Royal Opera House, 2006), *Evita* (West End, 2006).

*   *   *

If people at a party ask what you do, and you say you are a lighting designer, they always go, 'Oh, that's nice . . .?' in a rather bewildered voice. It is one of those things that nobody quite understands. I think it is not only people outside the industry, but also a lot of people within it, don't really know what a lighting designer does.

In its most basic form you put light on stage. You make decisions what the light should look like on the stage. But I also feel that as a lighting designer, your dialogue with the audience is about how you are looking at something, and how you are feeling about it. Is it warm or cold? Is it outside or inside? Is it colourful, pictorial, something you feel close to, or distant from?

In a way, the thing I think it is most similar to, which I think more people would understand and recognize, is being a film editor. It is the rhythm of how you look at an image: if things change on stage it often relates to changes in lighting, and how that change happens. It might be fast or slow – you could snap the lights off in one place and put them on in another, or it could be very gradual and almost unnoticed. It is a whole language of how people are looking, and what visual material they are receiving. Is it a big image in a small space, or a small one in a big space? You are also a little like the cameraman in that you are framing the picture that the audience is seeing, sometimes bringing something into close-up by giving it prominence. The big difference is that you are lighting for the naked eye, not for a camera, and I adore the fact that it is live, and never quite the same twice.

If someone asks me to do the lighting design for something, it depends what it is, and what the idea and reason behind doing it is. A lot of my work is about very long-term collaborations, so I tend to be brought in as part of a team. It is very much about the director, designer and choreographer that I will be working with, as well as what the actual piece is – whether it is a play or opera that I am interested in. My relationship with it starts right at the beginning, because I really need to decide if it is the right thing for me to do. I would say no if the style and the idea of doing the piece didn't relate to what I do and what I am interested in. So I will have read the play, know who is doing it and where. Then the director and designer will go through a process with a model, talking about how they want to do this particular piece. I tend not to get too involved with that too early on because any triangular relationship can become confusing.

Usually, when they have a rough idea of what they are doing, and have a white card model, they will say, 'Why don't you pop in and see where we are with it?' So I will come in and have a conversation, either with them both, or just the designer, who might say something like, 'We are thinking of having lots of windows, or spare space where light is going to tell the story.' So you know what the function of light is going to be in that piece. Next I try and get there for a few early days of rehearsals, and then an intensive week in the rehearsal room towards the end of the rehearsal process, before they come into the theatre. I sit and watch, thinking about my ideas, but now in terms of three dimensions, because the actors are up on their feet rehearsing. Then of course I have the technical time in the theatre, and stay all the way through till opening night.

Once you step out of being an electrician you have a team that you work with who do all the physical work of rigging for you. Actually, I sometimes miss being a technician. Now I spend time in the sea to get my kicks rather than hanging from ladders! In opera houses you have a lighting crew of up to 20. In the Cottesloe [the smallest stage of the National Theatre] there are four or five. I work most closely with two people – my production electrician, who sorts out all the logistics of achieving what I want, budgeting it and realizing it, and a programmer who inputs all the information I give them into the computer, which is then manned by an operator during the show. Subsidized theatres have their own staff, but with commercial theatre you can often hand pick your team.

Lighting rigs usually involve placing lamps on bars in horizontal rows above the stage, and attached to the front of the circle; they are also sometimes in the side boxes, and in the wings. A small space like the Soho Theatre, or Lyric Studio, might have between 50 and 100 lamps for a show. At the Opera House, or the Olivier Theatre, there are 300 or so in the air. You hire additional special equipment for each show as the budget allows. With a non-subsidized venture, like *Evita*, you hire everything from the bars, to the cables, to the lights.

It is my job to draw a big technical plan showing which lights go where, and what colour they are. If it is wrong it is very easy to change colour gels or think, 'That is too cold, or that is too blue.' You are constantly looking at what you are doing. And for me, the wonderful thing about being a lighting designer is that it is incredibly creative and it is very technical: it is one of the few jobs which combines these two aspects. Another is architecture, and in both you also need to know about your materials and what is available, but not be too restricted by them.

In something like *Moon For the Misbegotten* Howard [Davies, director] and Bob [Crowley, set designer] had had lots of meetings about the play in New York where they both happened to be. When they came back Bob phoned me and asked me to come in and see where he was with it. So I went in on a day when he was literally cutting out bits of blue, which became the sky, and he said, 'Do you think I am completely mad? I am really interested in this language.' As soon as I saw it I knew it was so right for the piece and what we were doing, and the sort of CinemaScope pictorial sense of landscape. [The set is fairly bare apart from an isolated, falling-down shack. There is a vast expanse of blue sky, inky at the top in Act 1. In Act 2, although there is a lot of talk about the moon in the play there is no moon visible. The sky is a dark bluey green with a pinkish/white light on the ground. As day dawns clouds in the sky turn pink and then take on a yellow hue. The set is bleak, but the lighting gives it a beauty, which echoes the play.] But it is an absolute nightmare to light! It is bigger than just literally showing a sun or moon projected onto a backdrop. As soon as you see it, it is a completely lyrical space.

The play and the set do that amazing thing of being incredibly human and real, but absolutely abstract as well. It has been interesting for me, because it is my third show with Howard, and his tendency with O'Neill is to find that abstract and lyrical side. My muscle tends to be much more about the real, and quite often finding an ugly brutality, but a lyricism in that reality as well. So whenever we work together it is always Howard pulling me away from my tendency, and me pulling him away from his. So with O'Neill he has pushed me to be much more painterly with things like the moonlit scene than I would normally be. In my head that would have been much bleaker, but of course he is right to release the imagery of the play: it needs to be bluer and richer and 'silveryer', and more of an extraordinary sense of what night time is. It is a heightened version of reality: the moonlight bluer, the sunlight more orange.

A Moon For the Misbegotten is previewing now, and previews vary with each project. I work a huge amount with Katie Mitchell [director] and we tend to develop the language of light through the previews. One of the things that is really frustrating about being a lighting designer is that in a conventional theatre or opera situation, you will get a couple of days to put the set up, and put the lights up, and point them all where you want them. Actually the time you get to put on an opera is always tighter than with plays, so working in opera has made me much more time efficient. The next phase is the technical rehearsal, when the actors or singers are on stage and you work very slowly through the play or the opera. But while the actors have had five weeks in a rehearsal room, and the designer has had a model box that he or she has worked on for months beforehand, as a lighting designer, your process is incredibly public, and is in that crisis period of opening to an audience.

So you can use previews to sketch things in and really get a sense of the language of it, and finesse it, and make it better. And you can really look at whether the audience are engaging. Are they not engaging because, very simply, it is too dark? Are they not engaging because it is not telling the right story? I tighten up the details through previews, but with something like *Moon*, the long preview period is much more for the actors to really get used to everything. For example Eve [Best] spends a huge amount of time on stage – it is like training to run a marathon.

Some actors, who might have 30 years' experience, might, when you put one light on stage, stand 2 metres upstage of it, because they are not aware of it. Other actors, when you slowly fade down to one light on stage, even if they are 20 metres away from it, by the time that cue is complete, will be right in the middle of it, and lit perfectly.

One of the most common problems you get is working with low angles of light that go in the actor's eyes, so it is very difficult for them to engage with other people on stage because they are being blinded. Sometimes I might talk to the actor and try to tell them not to look into the light, but try to look beyond it. But if people have a real problem being able to perform in the light then you really do need to help to solve the problem for them. It is weird, but if you get put into very bright light from lots of sides and you can't see the floor, it is like being in a sensory deprivation tank: you can't see anything. In some ways this is even harder in opera where the singers have to be able to see the conductor, although fortunately you can light the conductor, so at least he or she gives them a fixed point if they have bright light in their eyes.

I think because of the nature of opera, and the emotional level it is working on, you can necessarily be visually bolder. I am very interested in key lights and directional lighting. So with something like *Cosi Fan Tutte* [Glyndebourne, 2005], which was set in a room in front of a garden, all the lights came from upstage. The idea was to show the girls living in a hot climate, and when they could be outside and when they couldn't be. And all the action takes place in one day, so you have to tell that story. It is like Shakespeare or Chekhov: the story of time, or season, is very important. And Mozart did this so much – the story of where the light is becomes very important, almost a performer in the piece. You can't do *Don Giovanni* and ignore the fact that so much of it relies on not recognizing people, as it does too in the last act of *Figaro*, so you have got to get that right.

Another challenge was *Krapp's Last Tape* [Royal Court, 2006], which I did recently with Harold Pinter in the title role. That was an exercise in pretending there was no lighting. It meant creating a version of darkness within which you can see by using very dim diffuse grey light with very concentrated light on the table. I wanted it to feel as though the light came from one light above the table – Krapp's own light.

I love logistical thinking and problem solving. I like that part of my brain being taxed. But at the same time I love looking at images and visual information, and a sense of object and person in a space, and how the simplest change can make something that might appear the same, absolutely different. Most of the time when I am doing a show well, I think I am painting. That is really thrilling. In a way, I am not changing what people are seeing, but heightening it. I think 99 per cent of the audience wouldn't notice: but I feel I have a contribution to make it more.

Sometimes I walk away from a show and think, 'That was a really good piece of work.' I think Schiller's *Don Carlos* that I did with Michael Grandage [director] was a really good piece of work from all of us. I don't think there is ever a piece where you can go, 'Oh, I lit that really well, but it wasn't very good.' I think it is only ever a good piece of work if everything works. It is not just about what you do, but how you collaborate and communicate with everybody. From the moment we looked at that play we knew it was Velázquez: figures in darkness. It is also epic, political and heightened – the play is like an opera. Everything is incredibly elevated and of extraordinary importance, and you never want the audience to feel passive.

On the other hand *His Dark Materials* [for which Constable also won an Olivier award, as she had done one year earlier for *Don Carlos*] was quite different. It was about getting through six-and-a-half hours of bloody madness, and pulling rabbits out of hats. 'Oh and now you have got two minutes to create the entire Aurora Borealis, and then two minutes for the Land of the Dead.' It was mayhem, and the speed with which you have to convey information isn't something I am particularly good at. I think my sensibilities are more towards something sustained. When there are less dramatic changes in the light the audience can look at something for long enough to see slight shifts and changes in the way that the world shifts and changes. Something like *His Dark Materials* or musical theatre don't usually give the audience that time.

That said, I have just done *Evita*, and the thing I am most proud of is the fact that I feel it looks like I lit it: it doesn't look like a piece of musical theatre, it looks like an opera. There is no colour in it. We wanted to tell the whole story in an iconic, film noir, sensual way, rather than sit back and we will flash bang entertain you. It is a very restricted palette with just one moment of saturated colour, and it might not even be the colour you were expecting. I think it delivers as a musical, but in my terms. Michael [Grandage, director], Christopher [Oram, designer] and Rob [Ashford, choreographer] created the world of it, and I keyed into that. Michael was the person who had the dialogue with Andrew [Lloyd Webber]. I think it is quite important that as a creative team you need to be strong in what you are doing, and if you start to get information from all around you it can start to get very difficult. You need to have an idea and put it on stage in the best and strongest and most extraordinary way you can.

Occasionally you walk away from something and think, 'Somebody else might have done a better job of that than me.' The shows that I have walked away from in my life that I thought were good I could probably count on one hand. There is an awful chicken and egg situation where nobody wants to be too categorized, but at the same time, I know there is a kind of preconceived idea of my work – as we were saying, maybe big directional sunlight, and quite a painterly approach. That is my natural home, and sometimes when you are doing a show where that is not needed, you think, 'Why am I doing this?' But also it is good to be pushed.

For me, becoming a lighting designer makes a lot of sense about who I was when I was younger, but then I had no idea what career to choose. I was very arts and science orientated, so even when I chose my 'A' levels there was a lot of unhappiness, because my school system seemed to make me one thing or another. So eventually, after a lot of u-turns, and thinking about architecture, and engineering, I eventually did an English degree. Fortunately I did it at Goldsmiths College, and after a year I changed to doing English and Drama, because I had always been very interested in theatre. I started working in lighting as a way of making some money as a student. My flatmate had done some follow-spot operating, and I did that. I had done a lot of climbing when I was younger, so I had no fear of heights, and enjoyed it.

Then I discovered this thing called lighting design, and met people who were doing it, who were really interested in technical things, and how things worked, but could also sit and talk about text. For me, that was incredible, and I realized that was what I always wanted to be, but I never knew that it even existed. But I am really pleased I didn't go and do a degree in lighting design: I am very glad my degree is in English. I am fascinated by texts, and scripts, and scores, and watching people rehearse, and the whole process of making theatre of any sort. Nowadays you can do a degree course in lighting design in this country – when I was studying you could only do it in America.

Even now in America there is more of a system. If you train to be a lighting designer at university there, when you come out you will probably be an assistant, then an associate, and then become a lighting designer. In this country we don't usually have assistants and associates. Also, 90 per cent of my life has been in the government-subsidized world, where there is a support network, while in America, a person is often brought in on one project on a commercial basis. In England it is certainly more usual to start out by being attached to a theatre or a company.

Quite early on in my career I worked with the designer Rae Smith, who is one of a number of people with whom I have had quite long-term work relationships. Rae has an incredible ability to talk about, and look at, space. From my point of view, being quite young then, it was thrilling to meet someone who was willing to talk about the things I was feeling. It helps you build a language and makes you confident that the language you have is valid. Then both she and I worked with the company Complicite. I was working as an electrician, but often I would be working with a designer on something that would go on tour, and so I would look after that show when it was touring, and make decisions for it in different spaces. So I was developing a creative dialogue, but quite a hands-on one. It also gave me the opportunity to make things better and change things, so they weren't static. That taught me a huge amount about constantly looking and changing.

I also met Vicki Mortimer [designer] at Complicite. Vicki and I have grown up and developed our language together, and I realize that more and more when I do shows without her. I know that I can go further when I am working with her because we work in a mutually sympathetic way. I think working with a lot of women also made me confident to be who I am, and also we do have a shared understanding. You read a Jane Austen novel, or see *The Piano* [film written and directed by Jane Campion] or go to a Georgia O'Keefe [painter] exhibition, and you realize there is an articulation of something that is essentially female there: not that that precludes half the world from appreciating it. I have a daughter and a son, and they are so different: our whole way of seeing the world is different. What I do, I do as a woman. Whether that means I see colour in a different way, or not, I don't know, but I am sensitive to different things.

I believe very strongly in enjoying my work. But because the moment when the lighting designer gets really involved with putting on a show is when everyone is at their worst crisis moment, it is easy for tempers to get frayed and people to get cross. I *won't* do it – I won't get angry. It is such a waste of energy. So I tell terrible jokes and jolly everybody along. I think that may be a bit about being female, and reading the situation that everybody is in, and trying to help everyone get through it, including myself. I am very calm. I always wanted to be Lieutenant Uhura in *Star Trek*, because when a bridge is blowing up she is sitting there keeping her cool and being the head of communications.

I don't think the lack of women lighting designers in England has anything to do with the fact that you usually start as an electrician, and it is physically quite demanding. In America there are more women lighting designers because in terms of sexual politics we are way behind them in the work place. Also, because there are more role models, even subconsciously, people find it less unusual. It is a hard thing to articulate, but there is absolute rampant sexism in this industry, and it is hideous.

Winning awards is a box that I had to tick because of that sexism. I was really lucky because I had been nominated three or four times before I won an Olivier, and the really important thing for me was that I was being seen in that group. In fact the first Olivier I won was quite funny. I went to the ceremony with my partner, and when the nominations were read out a cameraman filmed the other nominees, but there was no one filming me.

Then a cameraman moved towards where I was sitting, but filmed my partner, next to me, and so all you saw on TV was him pointing to me, saying, 'It's her, it's her!' When I won, I just felt it was something else that couldn't be held against me!

They weren't expecting a woman winner, but also, some people do think that Paule is a man's name. Actually it is my middle name. I wish there was an intelligent answer as to why my parents chose to give it to me, but there isn't. My first name is Amanda, which I always hated, and the day I left school I dropped it, and introduced myself as Paule from then on. I didn't adopt it because it was a male name and I was going into a male industry, because I didn't know that at the time. But there are people who haven't met me who think I am a bloke.

I got a lovely letter from a man who had been to Glyndebourne and seen *Cosi*. He had obviously loved it, bless him, and had a lovely time. He wrote that it was so sumptuous, and that it reminded him of his trips to Amalfi, but then he said there was a terrible point in Act 2 where the sky was brighter at the bottom than at the top, 'and I would really like to point out to Mr Paule Constable that it slightly marred my pleasure in an extraordinary experience'. So I wrote back to him and said, 'It is so nice to know that someone is looking. Love, Ms Paule Constable.' He was mortified!

Now my partner is at home full-time, but when my two children were babies, I just had to bring them to work with me. There were women around in the industry who had children, but I don't think there was anyone at my level, and I just had to learn to deal with it as I went along. My biggest challenge was probably having two children! I am proud of being a mum, and being where I am in my profession.

Producer

David Ian

David Ian was named most influential person in British theatre in The
Stage newspaper in January 2006 (long before the BBC TV programme
How Do You Solve a Problem Like Maria?). He replaced Andrew
Lloyd Webber, who had previously claimed top position, and came
ahead of the likes of Cameron Mackintosh, Harold Pinter, Kevin Spacey
and Ian McKellen. This is because David Ian, Chairman of Global
Theatre, at Live Nation (a US-based company), is one of the most successful, prolific and powerful producers in the UK. He runs more than
20 theatres in Britain alone, and his smash hits include productions of
some of the best-known, and best-loved, musicals. But Ian, born in 1961
in Essex, started his career as a singer before becoming a jobbing actor,
understudying for Cliff Richard, and starring in roles such as Rocky in
The Rocky Horror Picture Show, and Joseph and the Amazing
Technicolour Dreamcoat. Then in 1993 he took out a second mortgage to finance the West End production of Grease, and he has never
looked back.

Liz Hoggard of the Independent noted: 'It is difficult to imagine
anything ruffling his well-coiffed hair.' And I admit that this is the
impression gained from seeing him on TV, and his many broadly
smiling photographs on the Internet. Yet when I met him this is not how
he struck me. He was wearing the same dark grey trousers and fine-
wool, dark grey, roll-neck sweater as on TV, but his short grey hair
seemed natural, as did his genial manner and welcome frankness.

David Ian is different from everyone else in this book in several ways.
He is unashamedly commercial, but then that is part of the job of a successful producer. The place where I interviewed him was the most up-
market: his office is located off Grosvenor Square, next to government
embassies, in London's Mayfair. Moreover, he is no unsung, backstage
worker, but a TV celebrity, having played a major role, as one of the
judges, in the immensely popular reality elimination show to find a

new talent to play Maria in The Sound of Music *at the London Palladium.*

The TV show (8 million people watched the final) cleverly guaranteed the success of the musical. When I tried to book I was told Saturdays were sold out for the next six months. I eventually got tickets for a public preview. Andrew Lloyd Webber was hovering nervously around the sound desk at the back of the stalls at the start; an understudy (Christopher Dickens) played the part of Captain von Trapp, Simon Shepherd having suddenly 'withdrawn' from the part; and the performance stopped for around five minutes due to a technical problem towards the end of Act 1. But Connie Fisher ('the people's Maria') was applauded after every song, and there was a standing ovation at the end. David has recently repeated the process to find a Danny and Sandy for Grease.

Selected Production Credits

Grease (West End and UK tour, 1993), *Evita* (UK tour), *Saturday Night Fever* (West End), *Defending the Caveman* (West End), *The King and I* (West End and UK tour), *The Producers* (West End), *The Lion King* (both Broadway and West End), *Guys and Dolls* (West End UK tour and Broadway), *The Sound of Music* (West End).

*   *   *

From a professional perspective I think I am most proud of the fact that I was an unknown actor, born in Ilford, Essex, and have become a successful, world-wide theatre producer, currently producing a show at Drury Lane and the Palladium at the same time. That is a pretty stiff climb in 15 years. I wasn't given anything: I don't come from a theatrical background, there was no silver-spoon element to me at all. I could be working in a bank, lucky to be working at all, or struggling to get an acting job at the moment. I took a gamble, and it paid off.

When I was an actor, primarily in musical theatre, I had done a series of shows before I was in *The Pirates of Penzance* at the

London Palladium, and the star of the show was the actor Paul Nicholas. Paul and I became good friends, and on one occasion he asked me if I knew what I was doing next, and I said, 'No, and that is the problem.' When he asked why, I told him that I loved the actor's life, but at the end of the day you are very dependant on other people deciding they are going to produce something, and even more dependant on them deciding they are going to cast you in it. I liked the business side as much as I liked the show side, and I felt I had an opinion on what the advertising was like; which theatre was chosen; who the other actors were; what the product was; and I would quite like to produce. Thankfully, Paul said to me, 'Well! If you think of anything that would be good for me to be in, and we can work on it together, let me know.'

Paul was a very big name, and very successful, and I thought this was a huge opportunity. So I thought back to what Paul had done in the past, and it happened to be 20 years since he had starred as Jesus Christ in the original *Jesus Christ Superstar*. I thought it might be a good idea commercially to do a commemorative anniversary concert, and have Paul starring, recreating the role of Jesus, but in a concert form, with the musicians on stage, and the actors in dinner jackets. And that is what we did, and I produced it. To cut a long story short, it was very successful, and Paul, instead of being a paid artist, became a partner with me. After a series of single concerts, all of a sudden, I was producing a concert tour all over the country, and it did very, very well.

I thoroughly enjoyed doing it, and naturally out of that, Paul said, 'This seems to be a winning combination. What else should we be doing?' We produced a couple of other shows – our own version of *The Pirates of Penzance* and *Singin' in the Rain* – that were very much vehicles for Paul to be in. Then we had the idea of producing a revival of *Grease*. Where we got that significantly right, and the opportunity that I spotted, was that nobody had ever before presented *Grease* with the movie elements in it. *Grease* was written in 1972. The movie, starring John Travolta and Olivia Newton-John, produced by Robert Stigwood, came along in 1978, and Stigwood famously got some new songs to be written for it: 'You're The One that I Want', 'Grease is the Word', 'I'm Sandra Dee' and 'Hopelessly Devoted to You'.

The rights of the movie and the stage show had never been packaged together, and I thought that if someone could present the movie, live on stage, there was a big opportunity there. Because of Paul's relationship with Robert Stigwood on *Jesus Christ Superstar* 20 years before, we all met and said, 'Why don't we produce it together?' and 13 years later *Grease* is on all over the place, and I am opening on Broadway next summer. That was the big turn: I was then a big West End producer with a big West End hit, and things rolled from there.

The first thing a producer does is to decide on the project. Then he is the man who has to get the necessary rights to present the project – that is his second job. His third job is to raise the finance to put it on and take the risk. His fourth job is to select the creative team: the director, choreographer and designer, who will create the show for him. He will also have a significant input into the casting of a show, and he will select the theatre. Once he has done those things, it is a matter of managing all those elements and relationships. Then I think his next biggest job is to sell the tickets. He is a chooser, a manager and then a salesman.

Once a show has opened he continues to manage the relationships and the artists. When you have got a hit – I have recently opened *The Sound of Music* at the London Palladium, and fortunately we have got a huge success on our hands – my job is popping into the theatre from time to time, checking that the principal artists are happy and the relationships backstage are all good. I check that everything in the show continues to be in good shape, and if I spot that something is not working quite right, I might get in touch with the director and ask him to have a look at a specific scene. I am in a lovely position with that show in that the first booking period has taken care of itself, and I have to worry about little trifles, such as when should we put our next booking period on sale? What is our next casting situation? And shall we take the show to Broadway? When it is not a success, it is much more an immediate reaction of, Gosh! We got bad reviews, we're not selling tickets, what can we do to sell tickets? Should we be continuing? What are my losses? How much more can I afford in losses before I have to close? What can I do to remedy this disaster?

A large musical costs around £4 million to put on these days. For *The Sound of Music*, Andrew Lloyd Webber and The Really Useful Theatre Company together put in £2 million and I personally, and Live Nation, together put in another £2 million. But often a producer will need to ask investors for money – I have a few regular investors. Typically they would receive 50–60 per cent of the profits on a pro-rata basis to their investment. If you haven't had a hit in a while as a producer, I guess it can be tough getting backing. Theatre investment is high risk, and there is no guarantee that you will receive any of your money back, let alone profits, so people can get wary of investing, particularly during tough financial times.

At the moment, and I use that phrase very carefully, *my* taste seems to coincide with what the public want to see. The things I have done over the past few years have been big musical tours of famous titles. I've got *Cats*, *Grease*, *Starlight Express* and *Chicago* all touring the UK at the moment. I think I have spotted that the British public very much want big Broadway and London musicals to come to their hometowns as quickly as possible, but as near to the West End and Broadway standard as possible, which is very much what I do. And in the West End I have chosen shows like *The Producers*, and a revival of *The Sound of Music*, famously cast and promoted on a TV programme. I am also not frightened, or dare I say it, too precious, about doing something that is very commercial.

I am a successful *commercial* producer, and I don't shy away from putting Ewan McGregor in *Guys and Dolls*, and at the end of his run replacing him with Patrick Swayze. That's a commercial decision, and while they may not be the most obvious choice for a musical, in terms of singing, dancing, actors, they were certainly a great commercial choice, and I *made* that work artistically sufficiently to be successful. I brought *The Producers* from Broadway with Mel Brooks, and was brave enough to put Lee Evans, who is famous as a stand-up comic, in a musical theatre lead. Casting the lead for *The Sound of Music* on a TV reality show was controversial. A lot of people said, 'How appropriate is that?' and 'How risky is that?' We have ended up with a fantastic girl, and a huge commercial success. I have made commercial decisions and judgements and been bold enough to pursue them, and at the moment, it would seem that the mass of the British public are going with what I am thinking is a good idea. There is a time when that can change, and you are no longer on the pulse of popular taste. I, unashamedly, with two kids at seven and nine years old, watch *The X Factor*. I know what *I'm a Celebrity, Get Me Out of Here!* is all about, and I promote theatrically to fit that market.

Andrew [Lloyd Webber] had wanted to do *The Sound of Music* for some time. We talked about doing it together about three years ago. We looked at doing it at the Victoria Palace at that time, but we were struggling with making the budget make sense in that sized theatre. We were talking to Scarlett Johansson about playing Maria, but we couldn't do a deal with money, timing and her movie career. Then the BBC came to us, and said they would like to follow the casting process in general, and the putting together of the musical. At that time, there were all these programmes, like *Pop Idol* and *Fame Academy* – they were the things of the moment. And in fact there was a TV programme called *Musicality* that cast the leads for *Chicago*, for one night only. And indeed, I had had a meeting about doing it with *Grease*, in the US, two or three years ago, but the copyright holders said they didn't want to do it at the time, although now they do.

Anyway, out of those lunches and those meetings with the BBC about *The Sound of Music* came the idea of casting the lead in it on television, and then out of that came the idea of doing it

X Factor-style and having the audience vote on it. Truthfully, I don't remember who was the one who said, 'Let's have the public vote!' Like most great ideas, it was really about the execution. Lots of people had thought of doing it; nobody had got it to that base and did it in that style. I think we'd all admit, the BBC, Andrew and myself, that we were all extremely shocked, albeit pleasantly, at how successful it was. There we were, middle of the summer, up against *X Factor*, on Saturday night, Andrew Lloyd Webber, Rogers and Hammerstein and *The Sound of Music*, and we were playing to six to eight million viewers.

It was a combination of things that made it work so well. Graham Norton as presenter was excellent: he loves the theatre; he has got that lovely camp, tongue-in-cheek style that fits. There is a huge affection for *The Sound of Music* in Britain, but it is almost in a 'campy' way, and Graham got that right on the button. The BBC produced it terrifically. Andrew was great on it. The whole process of judges commenting on it was intriguing, but the judges they chose were four people who really knew about the theatre, as opposed to celebrity types. I think everybody who spoke about it had integrity, and spoke intelligently, and the public responded to that. The ten contestants were all good, but different in various ways. And the prize was so significant: you can't underestimate a starring role at the London Palladium in *The Sound of Music* – an iconic role made famous by Julie Andrews. That kind of prize doesn't grow on trees. So all those things combined, plus a glimpse of, 'This is how the theatre works, and we are almost getting to see backstage process here,' all combined to create great television.

As an ex-performer it was fun for me to be on television every Saturday. It was nerve-wracking insofar as it was live: someone comes with a microphone and says, 'What do you think?' And you've got 60 seconds to hopefully be intelligent, speak with honesty, but be punchy and entertaining, and not waffle. It was not easy. There was one played joke about Siobhan [Dillon], one of the singers. We saw thousands of people, and probably, quite understandably, about five times, I said, 'My gosh! She's gorgeous.' And then, in the edit, each of those times was pushed together, as if I had said it every day. But yes, if a gorgeous lady walked in the room, I would say, 'Oh! She's extremely lovely.' I'm a red-blooded, heterosexual male who appreciates that as much as the next man; I don't think more than the next man. But it was good television. Was that part literally true? No. Was it partially true? Yes. Was it painted up more for TV purposes? Absolutely: it was entertaining.

The image that came over? Look, I go to work, and wear what I wore on television. I was trying to be as eloquent as possible, and speak intelligently and coherently. I meant everything I said. I said to the BBC, 'I will be truthful. I'm not going to *be* anything just for TV purposes.' The wrong girl might have won, and there were girls in there that would not have been very good. It protected us more and more that Andrew had a casting vote at the end of each programme other than the final one. Nevertheless, we all thought Connie was the best very early on, and the public voted for her steadfastly every week. Even when we had negative things to say about Connie, the public vote never faltered. They agreed with us, and what I thought was great about the series was that, actually the best person won. The public didn't say, 'Let's vote for the girl who has lost her dog, or her mum's ill, or whatever, we'll vote for the best.' And they saw that the judges were saying she was the best, and they felt we were right.

I watched the TV episodes, and there were a couple of times when I thought, 'What did you say that for? That was a strange thing to say.' But you are nervous, it is live, you're human, I didn't get trained to do that. And at the same time, I didn't watch it and think, 'You're coming across as someone you're not.' That is pretty much who I am, and the combination of the various personalities was good. Andrew couldn't be more different from me. Zoë [Tyler] came across as the ballsy, feisty, Birmingham singing coach. John [Barrowman] came over as the extravagant, theatrical, wonderful, handsome leading man. And if I came across as the focused, say-it-like-it-is guy, who's got two million quid in the show, that is about right.

I have spoken to Andrew about the programme, and he had his concerns when we were coming up to it, saying, 'This is not necessarily my home environment. You come from a performing background, I don't; I'm a writer and a composer.' We were all nervous, including Andrew, but then I think he was fabulous on the programme. A lot of people really saw him in a different light for the first time. He came across brilliantly and intelligently, not to mention entertainingly. And then I think he loved it. I think he would do it again without a doubt. He enjoyed it hugely, as we all did. It was nerve-wracking, extremely exciting and then the success is intoxicating.

At the time of the programme, on Monday mornings I would be spotted. That was fine, because although I had come from a theatrical, rather than a TV background, I was used to signing autographs, and what have you. But television is a different kettle of fish. You could appear on stage in front of 2,000 people for years and years, and never cover as many people as one night on the television. On the first preview night of *The Sound of Music* there were 2,000 people. All of a sudden there were 100 people round me wanting an autograph, while I was sitting in the stalls, waiting for the show to start. I was sitting there with my pad, wanting to take notes about the show and do my job, and thinking, 'Oh gosh. Yes, of course, I've got this to contend with.' But at the same time, it goes with the territory. And what is nice, and I will be quite honest, is that, as I said before, I am a commercial producer, and I view myself as a salesman, and I normally rely on artists and stars that I am employing to do interviews and promote my wares. What has changed for me is that people want to do an interview with me, because I am known off the TV, and I can promote my own wares.

As it turned out we got the best Maria, but the actor we cast as Captain von Trapp [Simon Shepherd], didn't work out. As we progressed through the rehearsal process, and got into the theatre, both we, and the actor, thought it wasn't really working. So after a fairly sensible, businesslike conversation, we mutually agreed to fix it, and find a replacement. Now we have got a great guy in Alexander Hanson. It is true that with productions that both I, and Andrew, have been involved with, an actor has been changed at the last minute, but I think that is chance. I think it has happened to others as well, but we are two of the most prolific producers over the last few years, so the odds are that it is going to happen to you more if you do more things.

I wouldn't say we are ruthless, but we are pretty focused on getting it right. It is a high-risk business, and we are both very determined to present things as best as they can be, and don't shy away from a difficult decision if it is the one to be made. I don't just wield a stick because I want to be all-powerful, it takes a lot of soul-searching to reach that decision. But if the director, the choreographer, your co-producer and your entire creative team, and indeed the actor involved, is saying, 'Its just not working, is it?' Then be brave, stand up, make a decision and move on.

As to decisions of how near to make our production to the original play, and to the movie, that is always difficult. The stage show, not seen in London for 25 years, kicked the thing off originally, and is fiercely, and correctly, protected by the writers. But then, I would argue, you have a copyright that is considerably further enhanced by a hugely successful movie. So in our production, when the children run into Maria's bedroom because they are frightened of the storm, they sing 'My Favourite Things' because it is famous from the movie. They don't sing 'Lonely Goatherd', which is what was written originally, because then the entire audience would say, 'That's the wrong song in that scene!' Actually it is not, because the script actually says, 'Let's sing a loud song to drown out the thunder.' So we cajoled, and pleaded, and persuaded the Rogers and Hammerstein Estate to let us make some changes to accommodate our audience, who would be expecting the movie on stage.

My interest in musicals came about because the first show I was ever taken to see that I really enjoyed was *Billy* with Michael Crawford at Drury Lane. I came out of that, at 13, knowing I wanted to be in the school play the next day. I like musicals and they are what interest me. Strangely enough, I have got an Olivier Award for producing a one-man straight play, *Defending the Caveman*, but that is not traditionally what I have done. I think people tend to come to me with musicals, and it is self-perpetuating. I would love to do a play, but I don't seek them out, whereas I do seek out musicals, and not necessarily revivals. *The Producers* was done on Broadway first, but here it was a new musical. And *Saturday Night Fever*, which I did, was famous as a movie, but had never been done as a stage show. It is really what has come up that I like as an idea. If Ewan McGregor, and the Donmar Theatre, and Michael Grandage want to do *Guys and Dolls*, and want to talk to me about it, fantastic.

I am pretty entrepreneurial by nature. I like the notion of how you combine various ideas, and forces, and people, in order to create something commercial and a business venture. And I like to be the person who says, 'I've got an idea, let's do something!' as opposed to waiting for the phone to ring. I think it is a reaction to having been an actor, waiting for the phone to ring for an audition. Not all theatres have a producer; subsidized theatres and repertory theatres tend to have an artistic director, rather than a producer. But at the end of the day, those are generally not-for-profit organizations, and although someone is fulfilling the producing role, it is not a producer who has got risk, so it is different.

In my own case, finding the money has been a combination of seeking from outside, and within the company, which has varied and changed as various strategies and managements have changed. I sold my original business to Clear Channel Entertainment, and the strategy was then very much, 'We want to own everything we do. We are going to self-fund everything, and we are not going to take on many investors at all.' It was pretty much, 'David, go make it happen! The money is here to back you.' A lovely situation. Then we de-merged recently, and although Live Nation is a very large *entertainment* organization, it is much smaller financially than when it was part of Clear Channel.

Now the approach, very interestingly for me, is, 'Yes, David, we will put some money in, but we also want to share the risk, and share the investment in the properties.' That's been a recent change, and you will see that reflected in the funding for *The Sound of Music*. I have produced it personally, but with my own company. So I now have an opportunity to produce with Live Nation and partner with them. So although I am chairman of the global business, I am also encouraged to produce with investors, and my own money, and the company. That is great for me, because at the end of the day most producers will admit to being gamblers, and I think you are most focused as a producer when you have got (pardon my French) your own balls on the line. It increases the sensitivity to what you are doing, and my company like that too. They think, 'If David is going into it personally, he *must* think it's a good idea. Would he be so bold if he was just using our money?' It certainly focuses one's thinking.

What's great is that I oversee an organization that has got 55 plus market places in the US, 21 theatres here – it is the biggest live entertainment theatrical business in the world. So I get to invest on both sides. *The Producers* in London came to me very much because we were the producers of it on Broadway. Similarly, I am very well positioned to take things that are successful here over to America. I have an office and contacts there; I produce there, and have venues there, which is very useful. At the moment there is a very nice trend for shows coming in *this* direction. Twenty years ago, *Les Miserables*, *Phantom*, *Miss Saigon* were going to America; all of a sudden, *Lion King*, *Chicago*, *Wicked* are coming to Britain. So being based on both sides of the Atlantic is terrific, because you can catch the traffic both ways.

I don't think it is a good idea to take being nominated as the most influential person in British theatre too seriously! I think it probably came about because of the global position. I suppose they thought I was someone producing on Broadway, running American and British theatres, and producing in London. It was great fun, and I got a lot of publicity out of it. Andrew and Cameron teased me remorselessly about it, and we had a good lunch on it. Cameron and Andrew own their businesses, and own their theatres, whereas I don't. I am a theatre producer who may own, or part-own the shows I am producing. I am chairman of a global organization, which is a public company that owns its real estate, and I oversee it and run it. I am an employee in that regard.

What I have learnt is that you are as powerful as the success you have got at the time. I think if someone opens *Mama Mia* [produced by Judy Cramer] and is rolling that out all around the world, they find themselves in a very powerful position at the time. It moves and it changes. It is really always about teamwork. It is still me going cap-in-hand to Rogers and Hammerstein asking, 'Please can I have the rights to *The Sound of Music*?' It is not me telling them I am having the rights. But I absolutely love it, and hope to continue producing theatre shows. Who knows, in the future, whether I will be chairman of a company – those things change all the time. I do know, however, that I adore the theatre; I have been in it since I was 20 years old as a singer, then actor. I am in it for the long haul. I like producing.

I like the success of it: and the success means commercially, and that people go and see it and enjoy it. *The Sound of Music* is a hit because people are enjoying the show, the reviews were sufficiently good, the TV programme was a hit, and that all escalates and provides positive cash flow, and financial success at the end. In its broadest sense, I get off on something working. A lot of people can say, 'If I do a one-man play, and four people go along and say, "This was a wonderful piece of work", and I have created a new play, and I know it was great, that is good enough for me.' That *isn't* good enough for me. That doesn't turn me on. Nobody coming, I hate. I like people going, in their droves, and all saying, 'We love it.' I am not a purely commercial animal thinking, 'I've got to make money; I've got to make money.' But I do love the fact that *The Lion King* is a massive hit in my theatre, and I don't like things not being liked, and not being a success.

So this book of yours – you said I'd get a copy? And I'd like to come to a book launch. Will you be signing it? Ooh! I'll ask for your autograph [loud laughter]. Let me know. I'll come, and embarrass you.

Production Manager

Andy Keogh

It is largely through a series of coincidences that Andy Keogh is production manager at the Abbey Theatre, Dublin. His job, put simply, is to take responsibility for the technical aspects (including budgeting and scheduling) of getting a production on stage; or, as he would be more likely to put it, to realize a designer's vision, and to make a company cohere. Andy may have got into working in the theatre by chance, but his passion and eloquence are both endearing and infectious.

The Abbey and Peacock (studio) theatres constitute the National Theatre of Ireland. Founded in 1903 by W.B. Yeats and Lady Augusta Gregory, premises were purchased on Old Abbey Street and the original theatre opened in 1904. In 1951 the buildings were damaged by fire, but were rebuilt on the same site in 1966. The theatre encourages new Irish and international playwriting and was the first ever state-subsidized theatre in the English-speaking world. It continues to receive a grant from the Arts Council of Ireland.

Selected Production Credits

La Traviata (Opera Ireland), *La Bohème* (Co-Opera), *Midden* (Rough Magic Theatre Company, Derry), *Antigone* (Storytellers Theatre Company, Dublin), *Homeland, The Bacchae of Baghdad, True West* (all Abbey Theatre, Dublin).

*　　　*　　　*

I get involved with the design ideas from the start. Here, we get a white-card model about 14 weeks before the opening night. I then talk to the set designer to try to trouble-shoot any problems there might be both technically and financially. We then get a coloured, dressed model of the set, and I am involved in costing that, sourcing all the different elements of it, and am the line manager for the stage, lighting, sound, wardrobe and stage management departments. I am involved with the whole rehearsal process, and ultimately in delivering the designs that the designers have submitted, in the way that they want them, and in a safe way, on budget and on stage for the opening night.

The key to it is to try to establish a sense of trust with the designer, and have some empathy with the design, understanding, from the designer's point of view, exactly what they are trying to achieve. Quite often designs are over-budget, so I have to try to come up with solutions to that which are acceptable to the designer. The budget is set by the director of the Abbey Theatre (who is ultimately the boss of everyone who works here), who also programmes the shows and contracts the directors. The budget depends on the duration of the show, and sometimes involves enticing international directors and designers by giving them a larger budget than other shows. There are also times when it might be important for the Abbey to make an artistic statement, for example, during the time of the Theatre Festival, or during the summer, when we have our biggest audiences.

Two of the most important things for me are: first, to try to create a positive atmosphere here, where people feel that they are listened to and are contributing, and where they all have a value; and second, to remind people that the heart of this whole building is the stage. So if it is not right there, it is not going to be right anywhere else. It can happen in some companies or theatres that other sectors seem to take on greater importance, be it administration, or the structure of the building, which might have historical significance, or whatever. But from my point of view, my aim is to imbue everybody with a sense that at the Abbey, the National Theatre of Ireland, it all happens on stage.

I have been involved here since February 2005. One of the important things that I have tried to do is to bring in people that I know from the outside world, who are very good at what they do, and try to mix those skills with the skills that were here. It is trying to constantly challenge people, and come up with something fresh. It is very easy for any organization to become quite stagnant, so I have had quite a lot of influence in getting new people to work on the shows, like stage management and crew.

The director sets the rehearsal schedule: whether it is Monday to Friday, or Monday to Saturday; what time they start and finish. But I would be involved in the production meetings. The main people involved at the weekly production meetings during the rehearsal process are the designers and the technical people: lighting, sound, wardrobe, props, the construction manager and scenic artists. At the Abbey we have our own workshops where we build and paint our own sets. So if anything changes during the rehearsal period, I need to make sure that everybody concerned is aware of it.

Another very important meeting we have here is on the first day of rehearsal. It is like a meet and greet on the first morning, with all the cast, director, designers, myself, all the technical people, but also the people from front-of-house, box office, marketing, publicity – literally everybody in the building that wants to come along. It is to give a sense that we are all involved in this one particular project, and it is important for the cast, too, to feel that there are a lot of people behind them. In the UK, there is the National, and the RSC, and several companies of that scale, with a big organization behind them, but in Ireland, there is nowhere else like the Abbey. Most smaller companies would have a read-through on the first day of rehearsal, but it wouldn't be the scale that we have it here.

The Abbey is a big fish in a small pond. It can be a source of contention, and people from the outside looking in can easily disparage it. To be honest with you, for a long time the Abbey wasn't run well, and there were articles in the newspapers about the financial difficulties, and asking where the money was going. But last year a sea change came about where two or three things happened at the same time. That cleared the table for Fiach Mac-Conghail, who is now the director, who came in last year, and is a great communicator and has great personal energy. It allowed him to start from scratch.

A lot of directors came in in the past, but they didn't have the force of events behind them to be able to effect change. Every organization needs fresh ideas, and fresh people coming in, or it will stagnate, and although theatre is one of the most 'vibrant' industries, stagnation can, and did, happen here, as easily as in a tax office. So last year was quite a big year here, and I know that from both sides of the fence. I worked freelance for quite a few years before I joined the Abbey, and the changes that I have been able to effect, not on a grand scale, but small changes along the way, have been quite positive. But any organization takes its lead from its head, and Fiach MacConghail was described in one of the papers as someone in the right place at the right time, and that is very true. Also he has no problems communicating, whether it is with one of the cleaners, or a financial controller. That sense of unification that has been created has been really positive. I think people enjoy coming in to work now – I certainly do.

I didn't really know what I wanted to do when I left school. I think that is very common in the theatre. Performers often have a strong urge to be involved in performance of some kind, but a lot of technical people *find* themselves in theatre, as opposed to having had a massive career path toward it. I did a few different jobs and didn't really like any of them, and by chance, I was taking a book back to a library, and I saw a leaflet advertising acting classes. In fact I really thought it was more of a writing course for theatre, which I was kind of interested in, just as a pastime, so I did the three-week course. I really enjoyed it, and auditioned for a performance school here in Dublin, which I went to for three years, and found myself being an actor.

I did some good work with some theatres, but it wasn't paying the bills, and I felt that if I was really going to be good at it, I would have to travel to study more. At the time, I wasn't really prepared to leave Dublin, so I found myself backstage in the Gaiety Theatre working on a pantomime. That lasted for a couple of months over Christmas, about eight years ago, and when it finished I worked on another show with that theatre. Then I got an offer to tour with Ballet Ireland, which I did, and when I came back I worked for Opera Ireland for a season in the Gaiety again. That went well, and next I worked for the company that built the set, Theatre Production Services. After that I did some freelance work at the Abbey during production weeks [the week before a performance opens, when the set goes up, lighting is rigged, stage management cues are set, scene changes are rehearsed, etc.], and I was also involved with lighting shows around the country.

I was very interested, and I picked up different things. For example, I was a flyman for the Wexford Festival Opera for a couple of months, and toured a lot with Storytellers Theatre Company. So I had quite a mix of experience, and then went into production management, where you need to know a little bit about everything. It just seemed to happen. I have never interviewed for a job that I have got in the end! By chance the Abbey were going to the Barbican in London last January with *The Plough and the Stars* [by Sean O'Casey], and an independent producer here in Dublin got my number from someone, and called to see if I was free. So I went over to the Barbican for six days before the opening night, effectively as production manager, and the managing director of the Abbey was over, and he offered me this job. It has always been chance. If I hadn't gone to return a book in a library in Dublin, I might be doing something totally different.

Now I have been here full-time for a year, and it has been good. Although in fact, as a form, I am most interested in opera. I did my first opera season at the Gaiety, when I had only been involved with theatre for about three months. We were doing *La Traviata*, which I love. I remember being in one of the scene docks [space at the side of the stage where scenery is held] during one of the shows. The set was very open; there was no masking [black cloth forming a backdrop or frame from the ceiling] or flats [screens at the side of the stage] or scenery as such. But the

Gaiety is an old theatre, with big, black brick walls, and there was a light shining on the singer, Regina Nathan, who was playing the part of Violetta. She was singing a beautiful aria, and the light shining on her was a footlight. So I couldn't see her from where I was, because I couldn't peep out, in case the audience saw me. I couldn't see her, or the audience, and there was nobody in the dock with me, or across the stage in the other dock. I was standing there, looking at this 20–foot shadow of her on the wall, created by the light, and there were 100 people in the orchestra, and 1,200 people in the auditorium, and her on stage, and I was effectively in a room with all of them, thinking to myself, 'I am getting paid to be here. And I have got the best seat in the house! Nobody else can see this.' It is a classic moment where you experience something wonderful and you wish that the people who you love were there to see it.

Another good experience has been working with a designer here, Sabine d'Argent, who is working on a show at the moment, and she designed the set for a reworking of *Antigone*, done by Storytellers Theatre Company, directed by Conall Morrison. The set was reminiscent of when you see a row of houses, and one has been demolished, and there are steel girders supporting the houses on either side. So it was almost like derelict land. We were in about four different venues, and we had these girders, again, with no masking. I think shows designed with no masking are very often more interesting than ones with masking, because a theatre space, by its nature, has an identity which you can't recreate, so if you can show that, it is absolutely fantastic. That show was a particularly fine production because Conall and Sabine are both very visual. It is not so much a concern with architecture, or structure, but the show has a *sense* of something. Conor Linehan composed the music, and he did a fantastic job with it. But there were one or two moments in that, where again, it is difficult to explain, because it is almost a musical moment rather than a dramatic one, but there was a special quality, not connected to an aural sound.

I have only worked on one show, in one venue, where I couldn't see anything technically wrong with it! I couldn't see anything that I wanted to change. It was a production of *Madam Butterfly* that I toured with, with a company called Co-Opera. They are Opera Ireland's touring company, like the world's ultimately reduced opera. It was interesting because we went to the Pharaoh Islands with that production, in 2000, and it was the first time that the Pharaoh Islands had had a dramatic opera; they had only ever had recitals before. Anyway, that particular production was in a theatre called Am Draiocht in Blanchardstown, Dublin, and it was the only production that I have ever worked on, and looked at, and thought everything was perfect. I don't think it is a matter of the budget, or the limitations of the theatre. The important thing is to have a sense of the budget at the start, and have the experience to know what will cost more than it looks like on paper, but more often, it is the tiny details of the set that are important, and also, the pressure of time.

There are so many people involved, and there is such a short time to get everything on stage. So the key is often time management during the technical week: staying in touch, and understanding what pace things are going at, and trying to pre-empt problems. Trying to trouble-shoot is a large part of what I do. So if there is something technically in a show that could potentially be quite difficult, you should try to recreate it before you get into the production week. You can never make time in the production week, only lose it, so you need to do as much as you possibly can before you get there. You also have to be able to factor in your head that, for example, you can work on something until an hour before the audience comes in, so you need to prioritize what you do. Sometimes you actually have to say, 'We can't do that before the first preview,' but then you have to be able to explain why, and be sure it is not possible.

I very seldom go to opening nights. I once went to an opening night of a play where I, and another chap, had built the set. It was in a small theatre in Dublin, and the set just had one door in it.

Everything went fine during the technical rehearsals, but on the opening night the door wouldn't open. I was stuck in the middle of the audience – there were only about 50 people there – but this actress couldn't open the door, and I was just dying in my seat! It was a long time ago, but I still don't sit in the auditorium for the opening night.

On the other hand, there are times during a show when it is fantastic. And you know yourself, whether people tell you or not, that you have contributed to it. That is a huge thing. I also really enjoy, on the opening night, that feeling that my work is done. And then in the bar, a lot of people know who I am, but a lot won't, and I enjoy that sense of anonymity as well. I take pride in my work, but it is really because of what is on stage, as opposed to anything else. And it is great for me to be able to get friends and family to see shows – and when a show goes well, it gives me pride to say, 'I was involved in that.'

Another fabulous thing I find about theatre, and especially opera, is the amount of people involved: as well as all the back-stage people and the cast, in opera you also have the chorus, the orchestra and the conductor. And it is great to see the process go from a bare stage, to the lighting rig going up, set going up, chorus coming in, repetiteur, chorus master, orchestra; it all adds up so quickly. You might have five productions of one opera, and five of another, and then it is all gone. I love the fact that it doesn't last. I think change is a good thing. The work that goes on before, and after a production to get rid of it, is never really seen by most people. But when you are there from the first day till the end, you see the entire process happening, like an arc, and then it is gone.

I love the sense, especially with a really good show, that it almost has more value by the fact that it is gone. Some things in the West End run for years. And things like Riverdance tour for years, but here in Ireland, apart from a few commercial shows that run and run, by and large shows will run for a max-imum of five weeks. It is nice to move on to new challenges, and everything is different. Generally, with every show the people involved change, and that is interesting. I am constantly meeting new people: directors, designers, lighting designers. And that is great, from a purely personal point of view; it is very difficult to feel stale.

A theatre is a totally different world. It is huge. You are talking about history, politics, philosophy, almost religion, certainly psychology, literature, art, music: you see people at their best and at their worst in theatre. People don't generally hide their emotions as much as they do outside. It is a vast world, and when you walk through the doors into it, and you realize how big it is, and how interesting and varied, that is pretty amazing. And people who don't work in the business don't really know that, but people who are inside, and have their eyes open, realize it. So it is a very valuable way to spend your time in many ways. I don't know what I will be doing in the future. Fate has looked after me so far, so I shall leave the future to it too. What I appreciate now is that sometimes, when I am working on a production that I think is a good show, I am being paid for getting a lot of pleasure.

Prop-maker and Welder

Ewan Hunter

Ewan Hunter is a multi-talented, multi-tasking Glaswegian, often maximizing his skills in improvization and spontaneity, in alternative theatre. Having trained in Environmental Art at the Glasgow School of Art, he now designs and makes puppets and props, is a steel welder and a special operations performer. Hunter has worked freelance for Scottish Opera and the National Theatre of Scotland, but most of his career has been spent with non-mainstream, small companies, in street theatre and other outdoor events, and on tour. In this regard he is different from every other interviewee.

I met Ewan after seeing The Wolves in the Walls *in Leeds, a show that was touring across the UK. Ewan plays one of the wolves (a role involving singing), but he also built the set, and made and maintains several of the props. The musical, which can be viewed on many levels, is based on a children's book. The production is extremely imaginative and well executed by the company, who are clearly very much a team. This is typical of the work in which Ewan is involved, and fits his personality: looking a little like an ex-hippy, he is someone with vision, creativity and commitment.*

Selected Production Credits

Dr Faustus (TAG at the Citizens' Theatre, Glasgow), *Shockheaded Peter* (West End, UK, European and US Tour, off Broadway, 1999–2005), *Aladdin* (Scottish Ballet, 2000), *Hikkaduwa International Parade* (Sri Lanka, 2003), *Iron* (Traverse Theatre), *Special Olympics Glasgow* (opening and closing events, Mischief La-Bas, 2005), *Der Rosenkavalier* (Scottish Opera, 2006), *The Wolves in the Walls* (UK Tour).

*   *   *

Some of the first props I made were big wobbly puppets – that is a technical term! It is a larger-than-life-sized puppet designed to have interesting movement, often used in parades. It might be a big head mounted on top of a rucksack frame, worn on someone's back, making it very tall. The reason they are called wobbly puppets is because they are not very precisely con- trolled. The big wobbly puppet heads have limited movement, a bit like the nodding of a real head. This is actually a thread that runs through a lot of the work I have done, and you can see in *The Wolves in the Walls*. For example, the wolves are not big wobbly puppets, but are nevertheless made in such a way that their movements are limited within the parameters of what something like that might actually do.

We usually made the big wobbly puppets from a frame of fibreglass rods – a kind of bendy material often used for tent poles now. It is strong, flexible and light. We would cover the rods in white tailor's, or upholsterer's wadding, to flesh the objects out, and then put muslin or calico over it. We would be given a brief, for example, to make Santa Claus, or a polar bear, and have a little team of artists, who would design it, make it and operate it. You would be the person wearing the backpack puppet because you knew how you had made it, and how heavy it was. Someone else might complain that it made them really sore to wear. Then you would put it on, and it would make you sore too, but you would keep your mouth shut!

My original interest in theatre was as a performer. But just after I left school, when I was 16, I had a fairly unpleasant expe- rience with a local dramatic company. I didn't get on with the director at all, and it made me lose some of my confidence as an actor. I had done well in art at school, and I was trying to get enough qualifications to study architecture, but then I got accepted to go to art school. I imagined everyone would be much more talented than me, so I never thought I would get in, espe- cially as I was only 17. It was in 1983, and there were grants, so you could go and enjoy yourself, and give yourself a bit of education, though not much of a training.

I came out without any specific skills, other than being able to deal with problems: for instance if there was no workshop available, or a technician who would help you out, or there were feuds between tutors or technicians. You might want to make something, and you would go to a workshop, and the technician would say, 'Oh no, I don't do that. The sculpture technician does that, but I don't like him, so if you go to him, don't expect any more help from me!' So I would decide to make the thing out of something else, and develop improvizational skills. I learnt to make things out of alternative media rather than purely sculpting out of stone.

I did a course called Environmental Art, which was a mixed media course that has since become quite prestigious, and students think of it as quite sexy. It has produced two Turner Prize winners: Douglas Gordon and Simon Starling. I came out not knowing quite what I wanted to do, but kept myself going in directions that I was genuinely interested in, and learning the skills that I needed to do that. I found myself initially working a lot in the field of outdoor events, parades and grand spectacles. At that time Glasgow was gearing up for its 1990 City of Culture events. I was peripherally involved in a big lantern parade, and that spawned many similar events because it was very successful: people liked it because it lit up the winter.

I became involved with pyrotechnics and making fire drawings, which are used by some companies in their firework displays. You make a steel drawing, or matrix out of steel rods, and put paraffin-soaked paper rope onto that, and set it on fire. I also did some big set piece finales for outdoor events: like a pyramid that caught light with shadow puppets inside. During that time I did a lot of work with Graeme Gilmour, who went on to co-design *Shockheaded Peter*. And I also did a lot of work with Julian Crouch, who co-designed and co-directed *The Wolves in the Walls*.

Graeme and I worked together for many years at Glasgow Sculpture Studios, which is an artist's resource centre that has a lovely big workshop, some studio spaces and lots of tools. It meant I had somewhere to work. By then I had stopped doing sculpture just as art, and was making things to be used in events or shows. I have always worked freelance, and in a hand-to-mouth kind of way, doing a range of jobs. Because we had a lot of space at Glasgow Sculpture Studios, we were able to make theatre sets. So people from small theatre companies, like Tag, and 784, would come to us and ask if we could make some props, and might end up asking if we could make whole sets.

These companies didn't have big budgets, so we would have to be very resourceful, and work directly with the designer to find ways of realizing their design in an affordable way. That meant that there was often quite a lot of design input from our side in order to work something out technically – like if something was made a wee bit narrower, you might get it out of a single board. We did a lot of recycling, and would make things out of driftwood, or found in skips, and use scrap metal from one job on another. Sometimes you would get a job that was a bit better funded, and would use some booty from that job – a bit of leftover steel or wood, or some fabric. If we had to buy something it would be cheap, and we might suggest alternatives to the designer. Sometimes we would do some painting too, although I am not a specialized scenic painter.

One of the most interesting, and challenging things we made was a 45–foot space rocket, which we had to design so that we could put it up overnight, and it would look like it had crashed through a railway arch in Glasgow. It was part of the Millennium celebrations. We were working with a theatre company called Mischief La-Bas (Mischief Over There), run by Ian Smith, who has been working in performance art since the 70s. The idea was that the space ship had crashed overnight, and people would wake up in the morning and see it, and it would get newspaper coverage. It was completely silly; there was no possible suggestion that anyone could believe it was true.

The railway arch belonged to a scrap merchant, so we had to negotiate with him that we could hire his archway for a night and a day. We got in at about 6.00 p.m., as soon as it got dark, and started lifting everything in with a crane. The rocket was very big, and it was in two parts. There was the arch, and a railway bridge at the top, so the bottom part of the rocket was to look like it had crashed into the ground, and there was tons of rubble around it. That part of the rocket had a door, which flipped down to form a stage, and space aliens would come out and play a tune. At the top of the railway bridge was the tail of the rocket with big tail fins and enormous booster rockets, like you get on a space shuttle.

It was all made with a steel frame, covered in plywood, and painted silver. It was designed by Graeme Gilmour, and the pair of us worked on it together to solve the technical problems. It was quite traumatic to do it all within 12 hours – to get it up before dawn. We also had to deal with lots of other people, like British Rail. They told us that the railway was potentially a military corridor in time of war, so we had to steer clear of that. Once in a blue moon you see a train going along that track, but they weren't willing to suspend that possibility, even on Hogmanay and the Millennium. Because it was a public event, we also had to involve engineers, who said things like, 'That is a 20–foot-high structure, so you will need 11 tons of ballast!' We had to use barrels of water, in case there was a 70–mile-an-hour wind, and build it so it all complied with safety regulations. There were also Mischief La-Bas dressed up as policemen: there were performances within performances, and it ran for the whole day, and it did get headlines in the local press.

Last year I did some more work for them, for the Special Olympics in Glasgow, so I still do some outdoor work, although I have also become involved with touring indoor theatre companies. In 1999 I took over from Graeme Gilmour in *Shockheaded Peter*. He wanted to do other things than international touring, and asked me to do it partly because I had a very similar background to him, and there was a lot of technical stuff to do, and a lot of maintenance on the puppets. The puppets fell apart very easily, but were also very easy to repair: rather than something like aluminium, they were made out of calico and foam rubber.

There was a bit of puppeteering to be done in the show, but I felt I was quite good with my hands, and had enough experience of theatre to know how to stand still on stage. I also had to play a banjolin, and I happened to be able to play one. It is a cross between a banjo and a mandolin. So I had the elements that meant I was able to go in and learn to do it, and get away with it, and be a reasonably pleasant person to tour with. I was with the company for 7 years, and it was an absolute treat: *Shockheaded Peter* was a brilliant show. [It won an Olivier Award for Best Entertainment.]

I first saw it because my friends were in it. At the original try-outs the show lasted about 2 hours 10 minutes, with everyone wandering about, not knowing where they were, and with all sorts of backstage panics. There was a very small audience, and the energy of the show was rather diffused. So I was watching something I thought was absolutely brilliant, but I was unsure if it was any good, or if people would like it. But eventually people came again and again, and each time they would see something a wee bit different.

In the try-out I saw, Martin Jacques [who won an Oliver Award for his performance in the show in 2002] started playing one song and singing another. It was a bit like singing 'Hark the herald angels sing' to the tune of 'Once in royal David's city'. He got to about the third chord change, and realized he was singing a different song, and just said, 'I've got to stop this!' and turned round and walked off the stage. So there was a complete hiatus, with everyone standing around not knowing what to do, and the Master of Ceremonies grabbed a skull that was used earlier in the show, and started declaiming 'Now is the winter of our discontent' from *Richard III*. He did the speech completely in character, as though it would be quite likely in the world of *Shockheaded Peter*, and that stayed in the show from then on.

Despite this, the final running time of the show was 1 hour 31 minutes, but it could vary by about 15 minutes: it all depended how long Martin would take to kill a child, or how long the audience would laugh.

Something would tend to go wrong every night, and it would just become part of the show. In my first ever performance of *Shockheaded Peter* [in 1999] I was meant to hold onto some marionettes that come dropping through some trap doors, and I dropped the whole thing, and almost decapitated Martin Jacques. That was my baptism by fire: that wasn't something we wanted to repeat again! There was a huge amount of work to be done backstage. I had built a flying system, which I then operated, so basically the set flew in and out with clouds or whatever. We just had one technical stage manager backstage, so the cast had to find a way of doing everything else. Sometimes we would repair puppets during a show. For instance, a leg might come off, or something would break, and you would think, 'I've got 59 seconds here. If the glue gun is on, I've probably got enough time to stick that back together again.'

In the spring of 2005 we did an off-Broadway run. After that an American cast came in and cloned the show, but that didn't really work out: the show had really run its course, but I went to America three times with it, and was in the last show. Touring can be quite hard. You get a kind of tour madness after a wee while. If you only have a few weeks at home between tours, you are impatient to get back on tour, and when you are on tour you can't wait to get home. Also the people you spend the most time with are your company, and they become very much like your family. You become very relaxed and casual with each other in a good way. Everybody knows how much space you all need, so you don't feel you are completely dependent on each other for entertainment.

Both in *Shockheaded Peter* and *Wolves in the Walls* the company have all been really interesting personalities as well as nice people. In some companies there is a sense of the turns [actors] and techies [technical staff] and they don't have anything to do with each other. There is none of that here. There are times when people want to go and do stuff on their own, but there is a very healthy company atmosphere. Everyone has had experience of practical theatre, rather than coming in as a diva. We all maintain the puppets now. It creates a good spirit if everyone is responsible for what they are using, and everyone involved has input at all levels.

I built the set. It is made of a steel frame covered in printed cotton canvas. [There are the walls of a room, and doors, and also freestanding walls that are moved around by the performers.] The design on the canvas was on a disk and sent away to be printed. It goes with the design of the book illustrations by Dave McKean: Julian Crouch [designer] wanted to keep that feel, so the design is a mix of collaged scanned images and photographs. A scenic painter might have done it, but this has a lovely consistent quality and transparency that would be hard to achieve.

I also made the shadow puppets. We had a two-week development time, when the designer, the director, the composer and I all experimented with things. Neil Gaiman, the author of the book, was also there for some of the time. I spent most of the time making things, many of which were never actually used in the show. We started with the book, and Julian Crouch made a storyboard of all the main action that needed to happen, and then we would decide where to use puppets, or projection, or whatever.

Julian also made some wolves' heads, and in the process of playing about, I remembered that at art school I had used some jodhpurs and stuffed the thighs, and made some satyr-like costumes for a fashion show. The puppeteers in this show are called the hypotheticals, because we are agents of Lucy's imagination, and we are also there to operate the show, moving things around and making things happen. Julian's idea was that we should look a bit wolf-like as well as holding wolf puppets, so you couldn't make a distinction between where the puppet started and where the person ended. I brought in an old jersey, some old jodhpurs, some pillows, and dressed up as a wolf with big thighs. We were unsure how to make the wolf puppet, and Julian drew a prototype of a solid head and flexible body to be made out of wire and hessian. So then I thought maybe we could stick one arm into the body of the wolf, like a huge glove puppet, with our hand in the head. It meant we could wrap the body around us and it all seemed to work.

A lot of us made the wolves. It was a really nice process, because so many of us were involved, in the same room, making the show, whether it was the content of the scenes, or making puppets, or details of the set. It was a holistic process, which is really why you see me on the stage: it is not because I am desperate to be an actor, but it makes sense as part of creating the show. I don't really see any difference between what I have to do backstage and on stage. In this show I am doing as much backstage as on it, and have done as much in preparation, to make the whole show work, before coming anywhere near the stage. It is a bit like being a weatherman on TV, which is just a posting by the Met Office to do the weather at the end of the news.

I enjoy the variety, and the fact that I am always in control of where I want to take my work. There are always different decisions to be made about what jobs to do. Will I do this job where I might make a bit of money, or will I do this job that I will enjoy the most? My work can vary from finding myself on the stage, to doing a really satisfying day's work cutting bits of steel and welding them together in order to make a frame for a set. Sometimes it is really nice if a designer has given you a lovely drawing, and all the sizes are right, and everything works, and every morning you know exactly what you have got to do. That can be really restful. In other situations, you might have a thumbnail sketch, and the designer doesn't know quite how the show will work out, so you are realizing something from a tiny kernel of an idea, and it becomes very creative, but also very technically demanding. That is also nice because it is appreciated by the designer, and they wouldn't come to you if they didn't feel you could do it.

The work I have done for Scottish Opera has been mainly trouble-shooting. For example, they re-mounted [in 2006] an absolutely beautiful production of *Der Rosenkavalier*, directed and designed by David McVicar [originally in 1999]. In the second act a big golden curtain comes down, and at the time of the first production they didn't have the resources to build a carved curtain, and just had a fabric one. But when they re-created the production they decided to have something more like an Austrian eighteenth-century theatrical curtain would have been, and they called me in to build a framework for it to be mounted on. I worked with the scenic artist who would be carving and painting it. The set had been built, but there weren't any drawings, and it was all in bits, so I had to work out how big the frame had to be. The whole set was on a rake, and the set was like a semi-circular cone, and nothing was straight at the bottom, and there was a false perspective at the top, and I had to take all of that into account. I also had to build about 80 metres of catwalk along the back, suspended from the existing metal set, so that the stage-hands had access. It was difficult but really satisfying.

One of the reasons why I like working in the theatre is that you are always working as a team. There is always a bigger picture, compared to being a fine artist, where you are expected to work on your own, and come up with your own ideas, and provide all your own fuel for inspiration. I find it much more satisfying and productive to be working with a large team of talented people. You are constantly learning and sharing your skills. I think that is fantastically rewarding, and the reason why I keep on choosing to do things like *The Wolves in the Walls*. I hope I continue to be involved in productions from the very initial idea of the thing. I would like to be as involved with theatrical invention as much as possible in a collaborative way. Whether that involves being a permanent member of a theatre company, or continues to be working freelance, I don't really know.

I am finding myself making more and more puppets. I don't consider myself to be a puppeteer, but I am interested in the use of inanimate objects and apparatus in theatre. I work long hours when I am in the workshop and have a deadline, and I don't make a fortune. Sometimes you get several jobs that pay well, and other times you do a job because it is a project that you want to see realized. I wouldn't really have it any other way. So far I haven't been seduced into putting up trade exhibitions. The people I work with in Glasgow, in particular, are very special. Over time you carve your life and environment out of people you like to work with.

I am glad that I am still making a living out of what I was trained to do. I feel there is still a very strong thread of what I learnt at art school, and what that gave me in terms of the principles by which I work, and what I plan to get out of my work. I am still quite pragmatic: if I can't afford to do a job, I won't do it; or if someone is taking the piss and offering you so little that you are taken for a ride. That doesn't happen to me very much because I am asked to do things by people I respect and like, which maybe is a measure of success. I chose to go to art school because it was what I wanted to do, not what I thought I ought to do, and I feel I am certainly still surviving, and getting plenty of succour, out of what I do.

When *The Wolves in the Wall* finishes its tour I am going to Sri Lanka. Some of the time I shall be doing a residency, doing a bit of personal development as an artist or practitioner. I have been there before, when I was working with Neil Butler, a producer of outdoor events and parades, who runs a company called UZ Events in Glasgow. He has been going to Sri Lanka for many years, and started involving himself with the community. In the wake of the Tsunami he went to see what he could do. As well as people being drowned, there were people who were homeless, and people whose boats had been smashed so they didn't have a livelihood. He helped set up a temporary boatyard, and got hundreds of boats back into the water.

Now he is hoping to make the building that was used as a boatyard into a creative centre, as a resource for visiting artists who can seek funding to try to build up an artistic exchange. So I am going in that capacity, and also I am going to attend a puppet festival in Ambalangoda, a mask and puppet centre. It is a small town where the biggest concentration of mask-makers traditionally live. So I will be working with some Sri Lankan puppeteers, and we will try to get a wee show together. You can't really anticipate what will happen until you get there. I find the best way to learn from people is to work with them. When I was in Sri Lanka before, I worked with an artist there who I brought back to Glasgow, and we did a big outdoor event in a beautiful park in Falkirk. It involved a lot of roaming companies who work in transient theatre – not so much street theatre, but people who work with non-captive audiences.

The events that I tend to do involve making something and then throwing it away, or setting it on fire, or it breaks as part of the performance. I find that fascinating. I also find the idea of engagement with a captive audience interesting, and I enjoy watching companies who know they are not going to get them all the time. They might get everyone who passes for around ten minutes, but those people will enjoy those minutes before they wander off. Other people will arrive halfway through a show, but might still become engaged in a wee bit of it. Some companies have gone from doing theatre-specific stuff to site-specific artworks, and have failed miserably because they have not understood the conditions. You can't expect too much from your audience, so you have to be fairly spectacular and impressive if something is transient. I haven't got the ego to be a visual artist who sells their work and needs everybody to like it. I have been very lucky in the work I have done, and it is very important to enjoy the job you do.

Stage Manager

Trish Montemuro

Stage management is one of the most fascinating jobs, since with it comes the privilege of seeing a play develop from initial read-through to final performance, but it is also a difficult job. Director Sir Peter Hall said, 'Ideal stage managers not only need to be calm and meticulous professionals who know their craft, but masochists who feel pride in rising above impossible odds.' Stage managers are responsible for everything that happens on stage: they look after a production artistically and technically during all performances, and they are also responsible for the scheduling and smooth running of rehearsals. They normally oversee the work of a deputy (DSM) and at least one assistant (ASM).

A natural progression for a stage manager would be to become production manager or company manager. Some, however, such as Trish Montemuro, who works at the Royal National Theatre in London, prefer the 'hands on' part of their job. She, perhaps more than most stage managers, gets very involved with rehearsals, and forms close bonds with writers, directors and actors. I met Trish in her small, shared office, down a long corridor of red-painted doors (each floor of the rabbit-warren backstage is colour-coded) at the National Theatre. To get there, we walked through the Green Room canteen, where our progress was slowed by various actors rising and hugging Trish, exchanging bits of news. She is clearly exemplary at her job, yet for someone whose work depends on efficiency and precise communication, Trish has a slightly scatty air about her. But she was very generous with her time with me, and was eager to help with the book and make this interview good. Nor did she disappoint: her effusive nature, and her deep interest in modern playwriting, as well as acting, are very evident, and she tells wonderful stories of her experiences.

Selected Production Credits

A Midsummer Night's Dream (1982), *The Mysteries*, *Arcadia*, *Dealer's Choice*, *The David Hare Trilogy*, *Skylight*, *The Invention of Love*, *Hamlet* (2000), *The Trackers of Oxyrthyncus*, *The History Boys* (all at the National Theatre).

*   *   *

I joined the National Theatre in 1982, when Peter Hall was artistic director, so I've worked with all four artistic directors to date. I started at the NT as an assistant stage manager and my first production was *The Beggar's Opera*. It was directed by Richard Eyre for the Cottesloe Theatre. Paul Jones played Macheath. My enduring memory of my first day was walking into the rehearsal room and hearing Paul Jones – the lead singer of Manfred Mann, of 'Pretty Flamingo' fame – singing the opening, and I thought, 'No one will believe this!' Eventually I worked as a deputy stage manager, and in 1986 I was promoted to stage manager. I took over from Diana Boddington [1921–2002], who was Laurence Olivier's stage manager. She was an institution, nearly a legend, very funny and a terrifying example to follow. This was her office and the walls were covered with pictures of the royal family. She was also a devout catholic who went to mass every morning and swore like a trooper.

I took over Diana's team and the NT's production of *King Lear*, with Anthony Hopkins, directed by David Hare. Tony Hopkins is a more instinctive than intellectual actor: he has incredible power and presence on stage. He hadn't done theatre for quite a while – at that time he was mainly doing films in Hollywood. I think he found it quite a challenge to suddenly be performing every evening, and rehearsing *Antony and Cleopatra* with Peter Hall in the daytime.

At the National there are six stage management teams, each with a stage manager, a deputy and two assistant stage managers.

The teams work on different productions, in all three theatres, often performing one play while rehearsing another. Because the plays are in repertory, one doesn't have to work every night. This is one of the advantages of working in this kind of theatre. Our hours are based on a 44–hour week, although this is an average, and each week varies. Often, especially when we are putting a play on the stage, and while on tour, the hours can be considerably longer. In the West End, you would have eight shows a week plus frequent rehearsals of the understudies and new cast members. There is not nearly the variety. Here, you get to work with the best writers, directors, designers and actors, and do plays that the commercial theatre might not be able to afford to do, so for a stage manager, the National Theatre is probably the best job you could hope for. I still count myself amazingly lucky, and still get a buzz from it even after 23 years.

My team and I have worked on new plays with nearly every playwright in the English language in the last 20 years, including: David Mamet, David Edgar, David Storey, Tom Stoppard, Alan Bennett, Peter Gill, Stephen Poliakoff, David Hare, Tony Harrison, Charlotte Jones, Nick Dear, Robert Lepage and Patrick Marber. All this has made for a very exciting time. My very first experience of a 'new writer' was Tony Harrison, on *The Mysteries* in 1985. I thought, 'So this is a writer!' and instinctively produced a small table in the rehearsal room that could be solely for his use. He often reminds me about that. I think that writers who spend any time in rehearsals like to have their own bit of space.

The next project we worked on was *The Trackers of Oxyrthyncus*. This was based on fragments of a lost satyr play by Sophocles, which was discovered in Egypt by two British archaeologists in 1904. It was a parable about the god Apollo. He had a satyr flayed alive because he had learned to play the lyre better than the god. This instrument was reserved for the more educated and grander members of society. Tony took the theme of high and low art, and wrote the play around it. Before coming to the Olivier theatre, the play was first performed in Delphi, in Greece. I performed more the role of a hands-on producer there. There was just one performance in a week-long international festival, and we had the honour of closing in the festival. This lost Sophoclean play was being performed for his own countrymen: it was a very special experience for everyone involved. The play was later performed in the Oliver Theatre and it was a big success. In so many ways my career has been punctuated by very interesting and widely diverging experiences like this.

I would say that with Tony Harrison, I had more of a collaborative role. Normally, a stage manager does what the name implies, and manages the stage. You work closely with the director, and are responsible for putting together the technical requirements for a play. You have to know what is in the director's mind or at least be able to make a pretty good guess. I go to pre-production meetings, so I know in advance what the set is going to be like. My team and I then mark up a rehearsal room to represent the scale of the set on stage. Sometimes there is not enough room in the rehearsal room for the set so we use a card model to show the actors exactly how the set will work. As parts of the set, costume or props get made, the directors and actors can see how things are progressing because our workshops are located on site. Items of scenery sometimes get constructed off site, but they inevitably get worked on here during the final stages. This way the people in the workshops can try things out and make adjustments where necessary, and most importantly, be involved in the project with the acting company and directors. We have notoriously short technical time on stage before a first performance, so this kind of involvement is hugely advantageous.

Another large part of my job is to communicate with those outside the rehearsal room about everything that might affect them. Watching rehearsals, we are able to pinpoint all the technical aspects, such as when a dresser might be needed for actors' quick changes, as well as various props, wigs, sound and lighting, and we will relay this information to the appropriate departments. With my team I gradually chart all this information for staff who won't join the production until we hit the stage. Generally the deputy stage manager is in rehearsal all the time, and runs the show in the evening. The assistants are in and out of the rehearsal room, getting props, or stand-in props for rehearsals, organizing wardrobe-fitting calls and setting up the scenes as they are rehearsed. The stage manager troubleshoots by keeping an eye on all aspects, and trying to divert any problems before they arise.

I also look after the acting company, and schedule each day's rehearsal calls, arranging the rehearsal day around wardrobe fittings, wig calls, singing, dancing, voice and dialect coaching, etc. Another complication at the National is that often actors are cross-cast with other plays in the rep, so they have matinees, word rehearsals, and breaks to be taken into account. Once the play gets into the theatre, a few days before our first performance, the DSM sits in a room at the back of the stalls. I would normally be based in what is known as the 'prompt corner', which is in the wings at the side of the stage. But I move around wherever necessary for the smooth running and safety of company and crew.

The job of a stage manager is exciting because we get to see the whole process. I personally, like to involve myself in all areas of the production. Also, my job doesn't stop with the first night. I am there to ensure that the production stays technically as it was set during the previews and on the press night. Performances inevitably develop and become richer, but occasionally an actor might get quieter, or something might get forgotten, and I am able to comment. I enjoy being a part of this process, and feel that in so doing have participated in the event of that particular performance.

Peter Gill [director and writer] once paid me a huge compliment in saying that I was able to picture the vision of the director, knowing where a production is headed. Whether that is true or not, it has been something to aim for. I think it is essential to try and do this. Technical and artistic aims usually overlap: observation is very important and gives me much satisfaction. Once a production is up and running the director usually stays in touch, and is there to ring if any difficulties develop either technically or artistically.

Directors can make a big difference to my work. They all have different styles and work in many different ways. Lyndsay Anderson was a director I had enormous respect for. He always asked one's opinion about things. I also enjoyed working with Richard Eyre, although stage managers must often accept with good grace when their ideas get taken over. Directors often do this. For example, when Richard Eyre was the artistic director, running the building as well as rehearsing, I suggested to him that the actors' contracts would allow him to work for five hours without a full lunch break, and that he might consider this type of schedule. It would allow him to spend the mornings for meetings, and the enormous workload of an artistic director, and still allow for a generous rehearsal time. He took this suggestion on as 'his' way of working. It became a joke between us, because Richard always took full credit (even publicly) for this idea. Subsequently, other directors followed suit. This is what you often find as a stage manager: you have to be a generous facilitator.

Years ago I would never have imagined I would be a stage manager at the National Theatre. I emigrated to England from Canada nearly 30 years ago. No one in my family was involved in the theatre, apart from my grandmother, who was an actress before she was married and moved, with my grandfather, to a tiny town in the prairies where they raised a large family. There is a framed photograph of her, an Edwardian lady on a billposter for a play called *The Kerry Gow* in 1904. As a child I can remember her giving elocution lessons in the dining room of her home. She had a very loud voice, always wore elaborate hats, and sang in the church choir. But most of my family are doctors, and I was never taken to the theatre as a child. I seem to remember taking ballet lessons for a while. There is a photo somewhere of me posing in costume as a bunny rabbit.

I went to university and did a humanities degree, and by accident really, I started working in the equivalents of fringe theatres in Ottawa. I used to read the plays, try and work out what they would need, and collect the props in my flat. Through this I met a couple of people who had worked in London, and I decided to come to the UK, initially for six months. I applied for a place on the technical course at RADA, and was amazed I even got an interview. I thoroughly enjoyed my time at drama school. We learnt about all aspects of technical theatre from set building to sound and lighting. We looked at different architectural styles and historical accuracy with regards to props, costumes and scenery.

It is no longer essential to have an equity card, and some assistant stage managers have no formal training – they might get taken on by a theatre after a work placement. Very fortunately, when I left RADA, I got work very soon at various fringe theatres and in the West End. One of my early jobs was as a stage electrician on *My Fair Lady* at the Aldwych theatre, and in fringe as resident stage manager at the Tricycle Theatre. After this apprenticeship I went for an interview at the National, and I got a job as an ASM.

From then on, work has never stopped being exciting. My job has enabled me to work with directors and writers who are fantastic. My team and I have always preferred to do new plays. It is fascinating because the first time a play is ever performed starts from a blank page. The writer is always in attendance in rehearsals and the play usually develops in rehearsal as well. For example, we did the world premier of David Mamet's *Glengarry Glen Ross*. That was really thrilling, because at that time we didn't have the luxury we do today of the script on line. I would sit down with the writer and take the rewrites. David would count the beats to the line, and if you listen to the rhythm of his words, you can hear that. Every little 'Um' and 'Ah' is a beat.

Doing that kind of work was exciting. I would often come in on a Sunday before the first rehearsal with Tony Harrison, and he would work on an Olivetti typewriter with golf balls for English and Greek letters. We would literally cut and paste the rewrites into a script and then photocopy it, and it would be the rehearsal script. Gradually over the years everyone's life has been made easier with computers and emails. Now an author has everything on a memory stick. Apart, that is, from Alan Bennett, who still uses a manual typewriter.

When we rehearsed *The History Boys* by Alan Bennett it was a very happy time. We had a group of young actors playing the boys, and there was a lot of catching up to do with regards to World War One poetry, numerous literary references and knowledge of history. Alan was there almost every day. I think writers like rehearsals because it gets them out of the house. Writing is such a solitary existence. Alan was a totally unassuming person, and so warm and funny. All the boys loved him and would crowd around him whenever he arrived.

But each rehearsal period is different. Tom Stoppard would always ask for a table in the corner, where he would sit and listen. He is extremely clever, but totally and genuinely accessible. I'm sure he is aware that he might be thought of as frightening, so he is never lofty. On the other hand, Harold Pinter was very scary. We did a production of *The Trojan War Will Not Take Place*, a French play by Giraudoux, which Harold directed, with Brewster Mason, Annette Crosbie and Martin Jarvis. For fun, the actors called Harold 'Sir' behind his back. Anyway, he smoked these little cigar-like things, and he didn't like any build-up of cigarettes in his ashtray. So at every break one of the stage management team would empty the ashtray into a metal bin, which we kept handy. One day at lunchtime I looked at the ashtray and said to the team, 'Oh! Who cleaned this ashtray? Sir would *not* be pleased!' And they were all looking at me and laughing, and Harold was watching in the doorway. But he laughed too.

I worked a lot with Peter Gill, and in some ways I learnt more from him than many directors. He is very unique. Peter doesn't always appear to be working on the text in rehearsal. It is not really improvization; it is more the ambience in the room. By talking in a group about something, which is seemingly unrelated, you can tap something in the play, which you couldn't otherwise. So you learn that what the director is looking for is not always obvious.

They are all different. I remember when I first worked with Patrick Marber on his new play *Dealer's Choice*, which won him a couple of Best New Play awards. He was directing it as well. Sometimes that works very well, but often writers are not the best directors of their own work. In rehearsals early on, if he didn't like the way an actor did a move or said a line, instead of waiting, and suggesting another approach, he would sigh, lean over and say to me in a not-so-quiet tone, 'Do you really think he's going to do it like that?' In the end, though, the actors adored him.

It is the actors who have to make the play live for the audience, and if you like actors, you can learn so much from them. They, on the whole, are very brave individuals. They put a lot on the line, especially in new plays, where the actors have no prior frame of reference. For example, I worked with Maggie Smith in a new Poliakoff play, *Coming in to Land*, directed by Peter Hall in 1987. She didn't like being at the National very much and she didn't really like the Lyttelton Theatre either. But she had a wonderful sense of humour which made working with her a treat. In rehearsal, she was like a sponge – she just soaked things up, and created a very rich tapestry. It was almost invisible; she wouldn't try things different ways, but in talking about a role, she would somehow assimilate it and just do it. She was quite amazing, and completely mesmerizing to watch.

Another fascinating actor was Paul Schofield, with whom I did *A Midsummer Night's Dream* in 1982, very early on in my career. He was from another generation of verse speaking, often doing long speeches in one breath. Like the one which starts: 'There is a place where the wild thyme grows . . . ' Words would just flow, and make absolute sense. Susan Fleetwood as Titania was wonderful as well. I was young, and had never seen anything like that before.

I learnt a lot from watching Michael Bryant on the numerous times we worked together. I remember soon after he received the CBE, I was standing with him when the curtain was about to go up after the interval. The audience was very close, just the other side of a masking flat. We heard two elderly gentlemen discussing the programme biographies. One said, 'I see here that Michael Bryant has won the Best Supporting Actor award.' The other said, 'Oh really? And he's also a CBE.' The first responded, 'Do they give CBEs to supporting actors?' His Gloucester in the David Hare/Tony Hopkins *Lear* was outstanding. The blind scene was the very best I've ever seen.

Michael hated doing any exercises like improvization, or 'trust' games, and method acting was anathema to him. When he was playing Badger in *Wind in the Willows*, the movement director brought in a videotape about badgers' behaviour, and suggested he watch it. The next day Michael turned up for rehearsal and said, 'You know, I have discovered one very important thing about badgers: they are very much like Michael Bryant!' He was a very private actor in terms of the emotional or intellectual side of things. He just was what he was. He is known to have a place, a position, on the Olivier stage, where he would always find himself. It was the best place on the stage. He worked on a role in his own private way, but he somehow just 'magicked' a performance up with very little apparent effort. He was just brilliant, and he had enormous confidence.

Working with John Wood, on the other hand, was a very different experience, because he is unlike any actor I have ever seen: he is so intellectual and intense. He is a bag of nerves, and yet every moment is completely precise. He is wonderful to watch, trying new things all the time. Of course he was 'high maintenance', in the sense that he really required you to be there for him. The rewards were rich though. Eve Best was also very intense, and needed a lot of encouragement, but her performance in *Mourning becomes Electra* was like an explosion. It was acting at its best. Other actors might be very quiet and composed and still wonderful. Helen Mirren is one of those. She is quite analytical about her role and very focused. Helen plays things very close to her chest, in that she doesn't keep trying out things in a flamboyant way. The questions she might ask would be more intellectual than emotional. I think she finds her way into a part in that way.

I have done several plays with Judi Dench. She sometimes finds it difficult to learn lines, and she finds that frustrating. Once she has learnt her lines, though, she will usually sit in a corner of the rehearsal room and do the crossword. There is a real little community of actors round the building who do *The Times* crossword. First I did *Antony and Cleopatra* with Judi, and then I did another 'dead playwright one' – *The Seagull* by Chekhov. It was directed by John Caird in the Olivier. Rehearsals for this play were extremely relaxed, and we'd rehearse a bit, then stop for a theatrical anecdote or two, then rehearse, then play lotto like they do in the play, and segue into another rehearsal and so on. Work got done, but I remember one day, Judi, ever mindful of learning the text, announced, 'These rehearsals have been so enjoyable, like a long tea break, but I think now, with two weeks to go, we had better get down to rehearsing the play!'

All went well until the press night, when I had to stop the performance. A huge piece of scenery on a computerized flying system got stuck half-way in, and I had to walk on stage and make an announcement to the audience, although did manage to get it going after a few minutes and carried on. This is the worst-case scenario for a stage manager. It is fine if that sort of thing happens at a preview or even a normal performance, but not a press night.

When we opened *The History Boys* we had a fire backstage on the press night! Since the debacle of *The Seagull*, I am usually now acutely nervous, privately, of course. It wouldn't do to let anyone backstage know. We normally have a little rehearsal, and then do our first night good-luck cards. I have taken to staying close to the theatre. I usually have a sandwich in my office, which I did that day. Then I heard something over the sound system that was like water, and went to the stage, and one of my team was coming off saying, 'There is a waterfall on the stage!' I went on, and it was like a monsoon pouring down all the lighting slots on one side of the proscenium. One of the lighting racks had caught fire, and the sprinkler system was activated, and we couldn't get it turned off, because at first we didn't know where the fire was.

In retrospect it was quite funny. It was about 6.15 in the evening, and we were going up at 7.00. We went on stage, raised all the alarms, and contacted the creative team, including importantly, the lighting designer Mark [Henderson]. I put out a call on the tannoy saying, 'If anyone has any spare time, come to the Lyttelton with towels!' Eventually we got the water mopped up, but it had been pouring down for 20 minutes. All of the downstage area was soaked, and half the carpet and seats in that area. We had to turn the lights off, and work with little torches, while the fire brigade and everyone checked all the circuits to see if we could turn them on again safely. People from wigs were running about with towels, and it was really quite an amazing event. People from all over the building came down and found little lights to work with.

Nick [Hytner, director] and Mark talked about what to do, and decided to go if we could. So everyone front of house was given a drink, and we aimed to start at 8.00 p.m. Mark Henderson is an incredibly un-precious type of lighting designer, and he was quite calm about his design being potentially ruined until we knew which circuits were involved. So we all worked like mad, and at about 7.45 we switched the lights on, not knowing what would be short-circuited, and what would stay on. A lot of the lights never did work, so they were re-lighting as they went along. I watched from the wings, willing lights not to blow, or for anything else to go wrong. But we got through it, and although it was a nightmare for us, often audiences seem to enjoy it if things go wrong.

All the company were terrific. Rarely have I known actors to be really grumpy. I think almost all actors, writers and directors are, to an extent, self-obsessed, but in a way they have to be. Some actors are semi-neurotic, and more frightened than others. What they have to do requires tremendous courage, and so if some of them are frightened, it is understandable. You have to adapt to different people's foibles, and the way they work, and what their fears are. But I feel really happy to have had the career I have had in this theatre; it couldn't have been better.

Presently I am rehearsing *The Life of Galileo* by Brecht, in a new version translated by David Hare, directed by Howard Davies. Simon Russell Beale is Galileo. I stage-managed Howard's very first play for the National, *Cat on a Hot Tin Roof* by Tennessee Williams in 1989. Eric Porter was Big Daddy, Lindsay Duncan was Maggie, and Ian Charleson was Brick. Sometimes I just feel, 'How could I have been so lucky?' Simon and I did Hamlet together a few years ago, and toured the production in Europe and America. His performance was wonderful and I never tired of watching it. In rehearsals, now as then, he brings a richness to the character and many, many layers. It is lovely to watch it emerge.

To sum up, as a stage manager, you are backstage, and not in the limelight, like other people in the theatre, but I wouldn't want to be. I love the fact that there is so much to see from the vantage point of backstage. On the first night of *The Trojan War Will Not Take Place* [1983], Harold Pinter gave us a little book he wrote, called *Mac*. In it he writes about his time as an actor in the early 50s, travelling around Ireland, playing in church halls. Pinter describes watching a matinee performance of *King Lear* from the wings one rainy Saturday afternoon. They are in a one-horse village, but Mac gives a thrilling, electric performance. Coming off stage, the actor asks Pinter, 'What did I do different?

Did you notice?' Pinter writes that the actor never did it again, not quite like that. But who saw it?

In a way, for me, that says everything about my career in the theatre. It is always a moment. You might see Simon Russell Beale play Hamlet on a particular night, when everything works perfectly, and the question is, who saw it? It is not like a movie, which thousands of people see. An audience that sees a limited run of a great play with a wonderful cast is very lucky. But the joy of working in a theatre is being in that special place at a specific time and being able to see something unique.

Voice / Speech / Dialect Coach

Deborah Hecht

The voice is our most powerful communicator, and it is language and words that drive theatre. Voice coaches help to develop the voice's potential dynamism, clarity and flexibility. They teach breath control, resonance, pitch, how to project and sustain the voice. If they are dialect coaches too, they might teach, for example, Irish, Texan or French accents. Speech coaches also make the language of the classics accessible to modern actors and audiences, freeing the voice so that it can inhabit the language. They help actors extend their expressive range and bring words to life.

In England and America few theatres have a voice coach on their permanent staff: the Royal Shakespeare Company is unusual in having several, and in giving coaching to the whole company. More often someone is brought in to work on a production with particular actors. This is the way Deborah Hecht works. She has coached actors in numerous Broadway and off-Broadway plays, as well as regional productions in the US. Hecht has also worked for the RSC and the National Theatre in England, and for film. She teaches at NYU's Graduate Acting Program, is approachable and sensitive, working in a field where teaching and technique are mixed with tact and timing.

Selected Production Credits

Angels in America, The King and I, Titanic, The Crucible, Long Day's Journey Into Night, The Color Purple, Festen, The Wedding Singer, Tarzan (all on Broadway).

*   *   *

Like many in the theater, I started out as an actor. I was living in San Francisco at the time, and took a summer program at the

American Conservatory Theater. While I was there my speech teacher was a woman named Edith Skinner, and she had a protégé called Tim Monich, who is now a voice coach for films, but who was teaching at Juilliard at the time. When I finished my course in San Francisco I came to New York for a year, and Tim was teaching a private class, and fortunately I took that class. The following summer I went back to San Francisco and was offered the opportunity to take another class with Edith, and this time it was training teachers of speech.

At the end of that summer I started looking for a job in the theater, and wanted to be either in San Francisco or New York. Circle in the Square [theatre and school on Broadway] was looking for a speech teacher, and I guess Edith recommended me, and I literally got hired after a 20–minute telephone conversation. So I started out with a trial by fire. It was a really lucky break for me, because it tapped into things that I happened to be good at. I was good at languages and linguistic things; and I grew up in a large family that was very musical. I played piano and drums, so I was lucky in that I had both rhythm and melody training as part of my preparation. I also grew up without a television, which I think is significant, because I grew up listening to things – to dialects and recordings. So that is how it started. I didn't have any more formal training than that.

While I was first teaching in New York I continued studying with Tim Monich, and I also eventually went back to school and got my MSA in acting. It is definitely helpful to study as an actor, because you get training in voice and speech and acting and movement, and if you decide not to act, you can focus on one of the other areas, as I did. And I believe training as an actor is a very good background for vocal specialization. My next job was teaching at the Yale School of Drama. While I was there I was called upon to do more coaching of dialects, in particular in their professional repertory shows. So I begun to beg, borrow and steal whatever materials I could get my hands on in terms of books and recordings, and I learnt by doing. At that time the field was smaller, and there weren't as many voice and speech coaches as there are now – it has really grown over the last 20 years. Tim thinks that was partly because of Meryl Streep's success in *Sophie's Choice* [1982] doing a Polish accent. I also think that since the world has grown smaller there is more call for accuracy in dialects.

In America theaters do not generally have a resident voice coach unless the theater is connected to a training program. Usually we are brought in show by show. I work freelance on Broadway, off-Broadway and sometimes in film. There are more female voice and speech teachers than men, and I don't know exactly why. My fear is that it fits into the traditional belief that women tend to be better verbally, and men are better at math, although I don't think that is necessarily true. When people find out what I do, they often ask what accents I can do, and want me to do one, or they ask me to guess where they are from, which I am OK at, but I am not one of the people who is great at it. I am not aware of my own speech most of the time, but when speech and voice coaches talk to each other, our speech seems to perfect itself on the instant!

It is usually the director who requests a coach. As a voice and diction coach, you are occasionally called in to work on the show as a whole, as I did years ago in a production at the Lincoln Center of *Abe Lincoln in Illinois*. That was an unusual situation where I went in three times a week and would warm up the company vocally. That theater is pretty vast, but vocal warm ups are more common in England than in America. With a dialect, it would be obvious from the start that a coach will be needed. However, with voice coaching you are usually called in a week or two into rehearsal, to work with one or two particular actors, when it has been discovered that someone needs some help. Then you tend to work individually with that actor doing exercises. It is very different building a voice over a two- or three-year training program and trying to build a voice in three weeks.

I try to be selective about what exercises will work best with an actor to try to get them where they need to be. Does it have to do with building resonance or strength? Or is it the extremes of a role, which might involve yelling, screaming or crying? Another problem is diction, which is often a big part of being understood and heard in the theater. That can be improved by doing full-body physical exercises, perhaps involving yoga positions, which force the body to open up and develop resonance. We do exercises that may involve singing, and for diction there are a lot of patter exercises that one can use to help articulation, and build strength and flexibility in a particular area. We also work with the ear and the physical structure of the mouth to adjust vowel sounds, or inflection, or whatever it needs to be.

You often schedule the work with the stage manager, frequently working in a less than helpful space. If we are lucky we get to work with the actor in the rehearsal hall. If we are very lucky, we get to work in the theater space itself, which I just did with a production of *Festen* [by Thomas Vinterberg]. But sometimes we just work in a small room, and then you observe the actor in the rehearsal hall, and see what is working and what needs to be adjusted. I might work from points on the floor, or in the room, creating greater and greater distance that they have to project their voice to. In the theater the voice needs to get past the overhang above the orchestra to the back wall. With speech coaching, it depends on the nature of the play and the size of the theater, and whether or not the actor has had previous training. I have also been called in to work with actors because they can be heard, but they cannot be understood. With younger actors in particular, there is a tendency for speech to sit back, sort of 'horizontally' in the mouth. Sometimes they are not as muscular with their lips, or the tip of their tongue, so they cannot find the necessary 'bite' or the expressive musicality within the language.

In my work a good ear is essential, but so is a good eye, as one has to notice what the whole body is doing and how that is reflected more microcosmically through the mouth; also one must notice what is happening with the facial muscles for both speech and dialect. With the voice, it is more about the body: where it is open and free; where it is holding or tight; where the sound is resonating, or *not* resonating; and what the correlation is between physical movement and the sound which results from that movement.

I have also worked with singers on musicals. It is the musical director who usually works with the singers to open their voices, but I enjoy working on the parts where they are not singing. I grew up with a lot of singing training myself, so it has been easy for me to work with the musical director, and I like doing that. I can also make use of what they are doing, because singing is a direct help to the voice, and I can work with diction to place a note or open up a sound. Occasionally, I have worked on the actual singing per se, but it is quite compartmentalized here in terms of who does what, and so I try not to tread on anyone's toes. I might make suggestions to the musical director, as opposed to the singer. Knowing what to say when, and who to say it to, is very important.

I usually leave the actors alone the first day or two that they go into technical rehearsals, because the move into the theater causes so many other things that they have to deal with. But if it is a difficult transition as regards voice, I will try to get some time with the actors individually or collectively to do some work in the space. Then I will stay until the final dress rehearsal, and go in at least once a week during the previews. After opening, occasionally, I will come in and check on the show and make sure everything is up to par.

I have probably worked most as a dialect coach. Then I work with the phonetic alphabet, and if an actor is familiar with this, it becomes a very easy shorthand. You look at sound shifts, vocal placement shifts, rhythm shifts and find all sorts of ways of making it happen. Whatever you do with your voice affects your whole body, so often with a dialect, altering the way one stands, moves and uses the voice are important in addition to shifts in sounds. We have tapes, and sometimes I recommend videos, so you can listen and also watch. Sometimes it is useful to watch with the audio turned down so they can observe the person's face.

I write up sheets of all the different sound categories both for the dialect itself and for the specific play. For example, between British and American, we say 'pass' and 'ask' [with a short 'a' as in 'apple'] that needs to shift to the [longer] 'ah' sound, so I list all the words in the play that make that change. Sometimes if it is a big cast it is helpful to get some of the work out to actors before formal rehearsals even begin. With regard to classical plays, our attunement to regional accents is less about class and more about the specific region, than it is in Britain. There is a desire to make the world of the play somewhat uniform, so unless a character is specified as being from a particular region, everyone would aim for a more integrated sound, which to me means consonants are specific and strong, and vowels are closed, opened, rounded, as needed. This will lift the images from the text and also make clearer and stronger the emotional action being conveyed through those particularly chosen words.

I don't have a preference between voice, speech and dialect coaching – I enjoy it all. It is rare that you do a significant body of work in each area on one play, but sometimes you get to do more than you signed up for. For example, I am working on the musical *Tarzan* right now on Broadway, and I am doing dialect work and some voice work with the main actor [Josh Strickland], who is a novice to the theatre. But it also enabled me to do some singing vocal work with the lead young woman singer [Jenn Gambetese] with the music director in the singing rehearsals. That was an unexpected bonus and a lot of fun, and we got this young singer to do some things with her voice that I don't think she had done in the past. It opened her up, and I think gave her a more mature and more interesting sound.

One of the productions I enjoyed working on most was *Long Day's Journey Into Night* [by Eugene O'Neill] with Vanessa

Redgrave, even though it was a bit nerve-wracking to start with. I love working with Vanessa. I had previously been attached to a production of *Antony and Cleopatra* with Vanessa, so I knew how she worked – that she is idiosyncratic in how she develops a role – and it is wonderful when it comes together. I am not timid with actors, and I don't think actors need to be coddled. I think sometimes in America we tend to be overly careful of actors. Actors want you to be truthful with them. But I think the part of Mary Tyrone in *Long Day's Journey Into Night* was a very challenging role for Vanessa – as an English person coming here, speaking American, but with some Irish influence in the background.

I was not sure at the start whether she could sustain an American accent, but she managed it. We would slide around and find her American accent, and then it would fall away when they were off book [not using scripts to read any more, having learnt their lines] and on their feet, and then it would come back. Then it would fall away again with the transition into the theater, and then come back. It fell away a little, too, with the first audience, and came back. But she knew when, for example, it would slip into just Irish, and then she really got it. She let the Irish come in just in one particular scene when she was reminiscing about a nun that she had loved.

Vanessa is a very strong-willed person. She came to the rehearsal wanting to do an Irish accent throughout. I knew that if I said no it was not a good idea, and she would hang on to it, and not give it up. So I just agreed with her, and then surreptitiously started moving her in another direction. I partly used my own mother as an example, because my mother had gone to similar schools, and came from a similar background to the character in the play. So I was able to use the sacred heart nuns from Chicago as an example. It was a matter of trying to steer Vanessa away from what she initially wanted to do towards a direction that we felt she needed to go. In fact she was wonderful.

That production was a very interesting, potent piece of work that really spoke to me. Vanessa had very particular ideas that really served the role. She ended up playing it essentially as a morphine addict, in the sense that a child, coming home, would-n't know what it was going to find. I felt that for the first time I understood about the effects of an addiction on the destruction of a family. Philip Seymour Hoffman was also in that production, but I think I just literally gave him one note [advise an actor ver-bally how to improve]. It was a word that would have been pro-nounced differently from how we pronounce it today, and he took the note and used it, so it was great.

The whole Redgrave family is wonderful to work with. I worked with Vanessa's daughter, Natasha Richardson on *A Streetcar Named Desire* and with her sister, Lynn, on *The Constant Wife*. They work so hard and are just the most open group of people; they are really fun to work with. Another play that had a wonderful cast was *The Glass Menagerie* on Broadway in 1994, which I did a little bit of voice work on, mainly with Calista Flockhart. She actually started her career in theater, and I had worked with her before. *The Glass Menagerie* also had Julie Harris in it, who was one of the people who, when I was a child, made me want to be an actor. Just being in the same theater with her was a real treat, and she is a lovely, gracious person. The son was played by Zelijko Ivanek, who I think is one of the really wonderful, and somewhat underrated American actors – he is not a household name, but he is a great actor, and he played the lead in that.

Most actors who get voice coaching like the attention, appre-ciate the help, and just want to do their best. It is a rare exception where someone would not want to do some work. They are the ones who are facing the public, while we can safely hide out. They are the troops in the trenches. You have to be careful how, and when, you give the note, and you have to be sensitive to the actor. If it is a novice, or more nervous actor, you don't want to bombard them with a lot of notes that are going to make them insecure. So you have to find a way to introduce a positive, and then say 'and also this'. Most of the greater actors, people like James Earl Jones, are incredibly open and grateful to get notes.

Another interesting project was *The King and I*, because it dealt with a language which is less familiar to the public. There was one person in the cast who was Thai, and knew the language, and we had tapes to listen to, and by the end it was quite good and accurate. But the producers came to the first run-through and said the dialect would never work because the Thai language is very soft, and they tend not to finish the ends of words, and they don't have plurals. We were using a lot of the reality of the Thai dialect, but it was simply not going to work in the theater. So the finished product had a much more generic sound, and it was not a Thai accent. It made no difference because it was a really good production, but it was a good lesson in life truth versus theatrical verisimilitude.

A production that was also challenging to work on was Tony Kushner's play *Homebody/Kabul* [2001, directed by Declan Donnelan], because it involved British dialects, Farsi and Dari accents and languages. We were working with two languages and three dialects, and the Afghan was not at all familiar to me. We brought in an older gentleman as consultant, and he was incredibly helpful, and we would talk and I would record him, and he was there when we were working with some of the actors. I learnt something about what felt to me like the dead centre of Indo-European languages. You could see in those Afghan languages, in their structure, and even in some of the words, the origins of European languages. Tony Kushner was not around all that much during rehearsals, but I had worked with him before on *Angels in America*, when it was done on Broadway [1993], and he is very, very intelligent. He knows what he wants and is very specific, but also very generous and open. If there are questions, he is easy to talk to and ask.

Writers like him can be a help, but directors can also make a huge difference to my work. When a director understands the place and the importance of voice and speech work it is much easier. Sometimes there are directors, and some of them will freely admit it, who know what they want, but don't always realize how much work goes into it. And this has a lot to do, frankly, with casting. One is always better off if one casts a trained actor, as opposed to someone who may be charming, and look the part, and be a perfectly lovely person and a very hard worker. But without the training it is harder for the actor, and for the support staff, which I am part of. There are directors who are well aware of that, and directors who are simply more accessible than others.

Jack O'Brien is a great director, who did *The Full Monty* on Broadway, and runs the Old Globe in San Diego. He came through the repertory training system and really understands the whole, and so is great to work with. You can have a very specific conversation with him about voice, or speech, or dialect, and he will understand exactly what you are talking about. Another director who I adore is Richard Eyre. I am about to work with him on *Mary Poppins* here. I have worked with him before, and he really understands the entire process and is wonderful to work with. It is definitely a help when the director is involved with everyone and you have access to him.

You do have to be judicious: the director has a bigger job than I do, and far more things to worry about, so as a coach, you cannot be running to the director all the time with this or that problem. You have to try and work it out for yourself, and check in with the director and the stage manager. A good stage manager is very helpful because they are your liaison with the director, and will also be running the show once it has opened. So a good stage manager is also very important.

I prefer working in theater to film because it is a different social construct and I also like being in a theater. Film is more technical, and actually I have less experience in it. I like the rehearsal period in theater, whereas in film you usually have to work much faster. When I worked with Uma Thurman on *The Producers* I was able to do some work ahead of time. That was a good experience and Uma is actually very, very funny. I think she is even funnier than she realizes – I mean she has a real comic gift. But even on that, I had to make notes on every shot, and tell the script supervisor which were the best takes for the dialect. Interestingly, often everything works together. The shot that the director likes best for acting is also the shot that is best for dialect.

I have always wanted to work in the theater since I was a child. At the time I thought that meant I wanted to be an actor, because you are drawn to what you see, and what I have realized is that really I want to work in the theater in another way. Someday, I don't know if it will happen, I would like to make use of this voice and speech work that I do, and add to what I do already in working with children in regular schools, not theater schools. I am also interested in the possibility of working with incarcerated young people. Another thing I am interested in is working vocally with women politicians, because I think that in some cases their voices hamper their career. Many of them are incredibly intelligent, and I think the world would be a better place if some of them had a better voice.

But I love what I do. It has to do with the human voice speaking to other human beings, and I think it is a really important part of theater. I don't know what it is like in other countries, but here the arts are in some ways less valued than they once were. I think they are incredibly important and it is a worthwhile field to go into. I was lucky enough to work on the play *Festen*, which was not as well received here as in England. People seem to think of it here as a little domestic play, whereas I see it as a piece about tyranny that speaks to us in America right now. It says something important, and I think that is the biggest pay-off for me. Other things are fun, but when you work on a play which really has something potent to say, you feel that your work is more than just entertainment: you realize the importance of the theater.

Wig and Make-up Co-ordinator

Claudia Stolze

Claudia Stolze has had a fascinating career path, and now runs a department responsible for all wigs (head and body), make-up and prosthetics seen on stage at the Royal Opera House, Covent Garden. This includes transforming European looks into Japanese Kabuki-style, with black hair and white faces for Madama Butterfly, *creating strategically placed wigs for nude Rhinemaidens in* Das Rhinegold, *making a prosthetic nose for Placido Domingo in* Cyrano de Bergerac, *and changing Wayne Sleep and Anthony Dowell into comic ugly sisters for the ballet* Cinderella.

The Royal Opera House is the third theatre on the Covent Garden site. It opened in 1732 as a playhouse, and the first serious musical works heard were the operas of Handel, who gave regular seasons there between 1735 and 1759. The building went through various incarnations, including being used as a Mecca Dance Hall during the Second World War. The Royal Opera House as it is today opened in 1999, and is now both beautiful and functional, and is home to two of the most renowned companies in the world: the Royal Opera and the Royal Ballet.

Claudia Stolze works from an airy, tidy office. On the shelves is a library of reference books on artists, opera and make-up, as well as rows of plastic boxes bearing labels such as 'MAC sheer coverage'. She has a big glass window that allows her to view her large team of workers, beavering away in an adjoining room. Claudia is passionate about her work, but she has a sense of humour too, and chuckles intersperse her words, which are spoken with a very slight German accent. She is petite and pretty with tied-back hair and very subtle make-up. But I couldn't help being transfixed by her top eyelashes, which although extremely natural looking, seemed just a little too fabulous to be real.

Selected Production Credits

Othello (Royal Shakespeare Company, 1999), *Afternoon of a Faun*, *My Brother, My Sisters*, *Gloria* (all Royal Ballet revivals), *Rigoletto* (2001), *Wozzek* (2002), *Madama Butterfly* (2003), *Orlando* (2003), *Sweeney Todd* (2003), *Cyrano de Bergerac* (2006) (all Royal Opera House).

*   *   *

My work here is always different. For example, on a production we did here of *Das Rhinegold* in 2004, the Rhinemaidens wore 30–inch-long blue wigs. They did not have any clothes, but they had little blue 'merkins' – pubic wigs. You don't often get to do merkins! The designer went to great lengths to explain his thought processes to the singers, and that it really made sense, so they said it was fine. The maidens are supposed to be children of innocence, and as soon as someone appears they put clothes on to protect their modesty. There is a long tradition of them seeming to be nude. It was an intelligent concept, and if people understand that, then they are usually ready to go along with it. We took precautions to make sure the singers were covered until they went on stage, and the pubic wigs were made on a kind of thong or see-through G-string, so they were kind of wearing something. Their whole bodies were made-up with pearly white make-up too.

We do face and body make-up, wigs and prosthetics. There are 22 people under contract in this department, and up to 15 extra freelancers depending on what shows we are doing. We do new productions and revivals of both opera and ballet, and cover the Linbury Studio theatre as well. We also do photo shoots for posters, and BBC recordings, where they go in closer with a camera, and make-up may need to be slightly altered. It is the biggest wig and make-up department in this country. I have worked here since May 2000, and what I do has changed slightly over the years. As we expanded, to help run the department, I was given two team leaders, one for the ballet and one for the opera, who each supervise their own teams, and a workroom co-ordinator. I am able to do much more fundraising now, with the development department, and more promotional work to raise the profile of the wig and make-up department in the Royal Opera House, and as a profession in itself.

I am present at the initial design meetings, which on a big show might be a year in advance of opening. For example, something like *Faust* has 150 wigs in it, and it has a lot of quick changes involving a lot of staff. If there is a show with only a few people on stage, we might know what is required about three months in advance. I do the first costing on the basis of the talks I have with the designer. This is then looked at by the people who decide about the money, who might get back to me and say, 'We have to cut down the budget. You will need a second meeting with the designer to see what he or she is willing to sacrifice.' Then I will suggest ways in which we might be able to save money, and come up with several costings until we have juggled all the needs for the show.

For some designers it is extremely important that the wigs are prominent and costly; for others the set is what matters most. Some designers have extremely clear ideas, and are very know-ledgeable about what can be done with what material. In those cases, we just follow their brief. If they also have an idea of how much things cost, then we have a really easy life. But there are many designers who develop as they go along, and want our input and suggestions. If a designer gives us drawings of hair and make-up from the front, side and back, it is wonderful, because it makes our life extremely easy.

For example, Tanya McCallin is a fantastic designer, who is a great researcher, and she has a very fine eye for combining period with modern. Although she may want something to look stylized or period, she will also want it to look absolutely con-vincingly natural. She always brings us big folders of back-ground information. We will discuss in detail the skin tones that she wants to achieve, and she is one of many who take our work very seriously. On the other hand it is also very exciting to work something out with a designer who has less formulated ideas. We have a really fast turnover, so we have to be really on the ball to be so flexible. We have curtain up on a different show every week: it is such a big repertoire house. Even with revivals of older shows, if the principals change, you sometimes have to redesign a hairstyle for the person who is coming.

Most of the wigs are made from real hair because it is recyclable and also it looks much more convincing. Nowadays, unless it is meant to look artificial, the tendency is towards natural looks. So you want to have believable fronts, which look as if the hair has grown out of the person's head, rather than something slapped on. The hair is all European hair unless it is for an Asian production like *Butterfly*. European hair is very expensive, but it is the only thing which looks right on European people.

The cost depends on the colour and the hair length. If someone wants a light-blond 30–inch wig, which is the longest you can get in European hair, you need 14–16 ounces of hair, which costs [Claudia quickly checks a chart on the wall above her desk] £66.50 per ounce, so just the hair would cost £800–£1,000. Long hair is very rare, and if it is blond it has gone through a lot of processing: the hair merchants put a lot of work into it to make it blond without disintegrating.

All the complicated wigs are made here by our staff. The more normal wigs are sent out to be made, with knotting instructions, so that the fall of the hair looks natural, and the makers know which colour goes where. A wig is hardly ever just one colour, and we have very clear diagrams and instructions, like '2–3 hairs per knot'. We have big storage rooms in the basement where we have over 20,000 wigs in store. If they are well made and well looked after they can last up to 50 years. There are wigs that are older than me! But once a show is completely scrapped from the repertoire we recycle the hair.

Another thing we do here is prosthetics. For example, in *The Ring Cycle*, Albrecht had a diseased arm, which throughout the cycle became increasingly diseased so he ended up with a glove-like prosthetics arm where it looked like the skin had all come off and all the muscles were exposed, which was quite gruesome. In *Rhinegold* the props department made exposed brains, but we had to put them on the singers' heads and put blood round them and incorporate them into the face. That sort of work is more like film work, which I have done, but I don't like all the waiting time involved with films, and being completely uprooted from home. From that point of view being resident in a theatre is very nice.

I also made the prosthetic nose for Placido Domingo in *Cyrano de Bergerac*. The show opened in New York, and he had a false nose there, but they have different materials, and I asked if he would be happy if I could make my own nose because I was used to a different material. He said that was fine, so we took a face cast, which I still have here on my shelf. It is a plaster cast of half of his face, which is all that I had time to do in the 20 minutes he could give me. First I gave him a bald cap to protect his hair, and then I used alginate, which is the same stuff dentists use when you have a cast of your teeth. I poured it over his face, making sure that the nostrils were clear. If you make a full cast, you put straws up the nostrils. Then I put plaster bandages over to make a casing, because it is flexible.

Next I modelled a variety of nose shapes in clay on top of the cast, to see what would look best, and made a positive and negative cast into which I poured some foam, which, when set, is a bit like a very, very fine bath sponge. It is glued onto the face with prosthetics glue and blended with make-up. We looked at the different shapes, and decided on one that we were all happy with, and which didn't affect the resonance of his voice. Some people don't like anything alien on their faces when they are singing, and others don't mind. Some people actually stick things behind their ears to make them stick out so they can catch the sound better – singers are very sensitive.

You must never impede their singing, hearing or vision. So when we did prosthetics for Wotan's gouged-out eye in *The Ring Cycle* it was actually done over gauze, and he was able to see through it although it looked very gory. With dancers, too, it is vital that they see properly and have spatial awareness at all times, even if they are wearing a mask. If they jump in the wrong direction it might trigger a whole lot of injuries and accidents. How many tasks someone can do while singing or dancing can also vary. For example, one person might be able to loosen their hair and some can't. We can facilitate something by saying 'This is the easiest way to do it.' The designer says, 'This is why I need it to *look* like that.' The director says, 'This is why I need it to *happen* like that.' And the performer says, 'This is why I can't do it!' But we usually find a way that makes everybody happy.

I need to have technical, organizational and people skills. We are usually the last people, together with wardrobe, to see the artist onto stage. We do the last tweaking of their curls, give them a pat on the shoulder, and say, 'Right; fine; off you go, you look great.' They need that reassurance that they look just right for the part. They don't necessarily have to look beautiful, and they know that. Wardrobe makes sure that everything is fastened properly, and we make sure that no make-up is smudged and everything is glued down well.

We are quite crucial for their looks, and in providing a reassuring voice before they go on stage. We do not aggravate them, but actually calm them down and support them. They need to be able to trust us. So we have to be very calm and sure in ourselves, and be quite psychologically insightful not to take things personally if someone is nervous. Some artists get giggly, some people become very serious, some don't want to be talked to. There are various ways in which people deal with the stress of going on stage and presenting their art to 2,000 people, which is no mean feat – and in this house perfection is expected.

From a make-up point of view, not only is the theatre big, but there is also the orchestra pit between stage and audience, so everything has to be slightly more enhanced. You wouldn't want to wear what you wear for a performance out on the street. Some things might look wrong from close up, but they work from a distance, although over the last 20 years make-up has become much less crude. We constantly check our work, going into the auditorium and seeing it under the lights. The lights might wash everything out, or enhance everything. White light tends to bleach everything so you don't see contours, and red light too, makes everything look very soft. If there is yellow light, the person will never look healthy, so we need to work very closely with the lighting designers.

Everything is prepared up here, because colour rendering has to be done in daylight, and then the application is done in make-up rooms and in the dressing rooms. We are sponsored by MAC and use a lot of their products, but for specialist things we go to theatrical suppliers. We also use different suppliers when we need effects, like blood. We have a variety of stage blood colours and thicknesses and tastes – some taste of mint, some like strawberry! Sometimes we use weird things like yoghurt. We are going to do the world premiere of *Bird of Night*, which takes place on a Caribbean island in the 1950s. There are two narrators who have to look slightly strange, as though they had been made-up with mud. But as they are singers, we cannot use anything powdery that floats and might go into their airways. So we need to concoct something that will break and flake as though it was dried earth, but doesn't powder, so we are experimenting at the moment with a mixture of yoghurt and clay.

But even with normal stage make-up, we make up almost all the principals, except for a diminishing few who like to do their own. They know nowadays that there are very well-trained people to look after them. In the past people did more of their own make-up, and in the ballet still, it is part of their tradition to get into character by putting on make-up. Many of the dancers are trained to do make-up, and are used to doing it, but we come in when it is specialized, like skulls, or aging, or warts, and we also do their body make-up if they can't reach. They don't mind that at all. If they had hang ups about their bodies I think I would hang myself! They really don't mind. Of course you don't touch their private parts – it is like with a doctor. You don't get shy in front of a doctor, because they are used to it, and we are used to body make-up, and they are used to having it done. We have seen many bodies, warts and all!

We also put most of the wigs on for the singers and dancers, although the chorus and resident people do themselves unless it is something very specialized. Often we show them and teach them. So there is a lot to do. Opera houses usually need a much bigger wig and make-up department than straight theatre. I used to work at the Bavarian State Opera in Germany, and their department was as big as this, and I think the Hamburg State Opera is probably this size too. Straight plays usually have smaller casts, and in this country it is normal that actors make themselves up. I used to work at the RSC, and except for specialized make-up, the actors did it themselves, as they do at the National Theatre.

I was in an amateur dramatic group at school – we did Shakespeare in German. I was Hermia at one point, but I did all the make-up for them. When I left school we carried on the group, doing mainly modern writing. Then I started studying languages, but realized that I was not an academic, so I gave that up after two years, and decided to become a wig and make-up artist. I did an apprenticeship as a hairdresser, which was obligatory in Germany, and then I did two years in the theatre as an apprentice: I learnt on the job rather than at drama school, which I think is much better. In England I would advise anyone interested in hair and make-up to do the City and Guilds in hairdressing. Then you can do a course at the London College of Fashion, which is more to do with design, but that is what is available. There are also some private colleges – some good, some a waste of money.

My first proper job was at the Opera House in Bonn, still the capital of Germany. Then I came to England, without a job. I applied to Covent Garden, but the boss then didn't want to know me: he wasn't having me, for whatever reason. So I worked in a restaurant in the National Gallery. Then after three months of being in England, I met someone from Madame Tussauds, and they happened to have a job open, and I got it. I worked there for two years as a wig-maker and colourist. I inserted the hair, coloured the heads, inserted the eyes and made wigs. Among others, I worked on waxworks of Nelson Mandela, Tina Turner and Harold Wilson, and it was very interesting. I learnt a hell of a lot about colouring. It is such fine, intricate work there, and I got my bearings with colour, and saw what it does under light, which was invaluable for me.

But I missed the opera world. It was all very quiet there. Everyone was very busy and the models wouldn't talk to you! It was a weird place: we had cupboards with hands, cupboards with eyes, cupboards with arms, with legs – and we had a whole cupboard full of heads. It was quite alien! After that I worked freelance as a wig-maker, and as a freelancer at English National Opera, and then I went back to Germany for family reasons. I ended up in Munich for five years, first at the Bavarian State Opera, and then I was deputy head of department at the equivalent of the ENO in Munich. Then I became homesick for England and came back here. I did a few films and some television work, and then I toured with the Pet Shop Boys, which was completely new to me. I did the wigs for them on the British tour. A separate lady did their make-up. It was great fun: a completely different world, and they were really sweet – two men who were really nice. To be on tour with a pop group was exciting and extraordinary!

After that I was offered a job at the RSC, which I took on for half a year, and then I toured with them to Plymouth. I really enjoyed my time with them, and I was involved in some very good shows, with some very good actors: It was around 1999 and they were doing *Othello*, *Volpone*, *Timon of Athens* and *Anthony and Cleopatra*. While I was there I saw an ad in the newspaper for the job here as head of department, but I thought, 'They'll never take me. *Royal* Opera, and I am German; I don't think so!' But the girls in the department said, 'No. Try for it.' And I replied, 'Do you really think I should? They wouldn't take a foreigner.' But they insisted, saying, 'You never know.' So I thought I might as well try, and I sent my CV. They rang me a few days later asking if I would like to go for an interview.

I was interviewed, and I got the 'yes' the very same day, which bowled me over. I was in a restaurant celebrating my farewell from the RSC, because the season was ending. I got a phone call on my mobile. It was from Personnel saying, 'Miss Stolze, we have deliberated very briefly, and we would like to offer you the job. Would you like to take it?' I said 'Yes!' and put the phone down and ordered a bottle of champagne. I shall never forget that moment. And I had somebody to celebrate it with. I really didn't think I would get it. I thought there must be so many other wonderful people applying for this job and I was really chuffed to get it.

Then I realized that I had really taken on a lot. It is a hard job to get your head round, to keep up the quality, to keep everybody in the department happy. It is constant give and take, negotiation and organization. What keeps me going is being able to listen to and see those wonderful performers every day. I love classical music and we are immersed in it. Also, I can really get a kick out of something looking just right: when we followed a designer's brief and managed to get it to look exactly like he wanted it to.

I get a kick out of beautiful hair. I am very strange: a weird one! I like working with hair, making it flow, and making a wig look like it is real hair. People come to me and say, 'I thought she was blond and short-haired, but now she is dark and long-haired.' When I tell them it is a wig, and they haven't realized, I get extremely proud. Or if we just manage to create something which is in itself a thing of beauty: I get a kick out of that big time. Something stylized like the otherworldliness of the Queen of the

Night in *The Magic Flute*, which was the fantasy creation of John McFarlane, whose designs were absolutely beautiful. Also the new opera *The Tempest* which is designed by Moritz Junge is really funky and cutting edge in its design. Everything had to be very fresh and new, with luminescent colours, and I really enjoyed working on that.

One of the operas I am most proud to have worked on was *Madam Butterfly* [2003]. That is partly because I am so interested in the whole Japanese Geisha culture. I find it absolutely fascinating, and Agostina Cavalca's costume designs really captured that look: the white make-up and the artifice of that world. I think we achieved exactly what the designer wanted in a medium that I absolutely love. I really thrived on it, and I was very proud of my department – their talent and passion.

I also enjoy the challenge of a period piece where you try to be as true to that period as you possibly can, and have to do a lot of research on how hairstyles were achieved. For instance in Rococo times they used a lot of hairpieces, and hair was greased down with beef fat. We wouldn't do that, but we would try to emulate it. Another challenge is to make a long-haired person look like a boy. We have got Mozart's *La Finta Giardiniera* in the repertoire now, in a modern-dress production. Sophie Koch is a very beautiful, feminine woman, with very long hair, and she is meant to look like a boy. We had to make a very short wig for her, and to make that wig look like real hair on a woman who has got very long hair is difficult. We pin-curl or wrap the hair to make it as close to their head as possible, so it doesn't create any bulk. Then we put a stocking top, or net over it, depending how see-through the wig is going to be, and then the wig over that. That is something I really enjoy doing: making a beautiful feminine woman into a gamine boy.

I never get bored. Some people come here from working on a West End musical, doing the same thing every single day – it would drive me nuts! Although those cast and crew become like families because they work together so intensely. But I like constant change. I do the odd show still to keep my hand in, and I have got a few singers who I always look after when they come, and it is an honour for me. I immensely enjoyed doing Placido Domingo for *Cyrano de Bergerac*. He is the most professional and charming person to work with. It used to take about an hour for the whole look: to put on his nose and wig and do his make-up. Then I would follow him wherever he went, and saw him onto the stage. Whenever he came off I was there to see that the hair was still right, the nose wasn't coming off and to repair the make-up. He is one of my big time favourites. Whenever he comes here, I am there for him.

Ballet dancers have different needs. For instance they need their wigs and headdresses really fixed. If it doesn't hurt, it is not fixed well! They really need to know it is on, so they can completely forget about it. If they concentrate on anything other than their dancing it can be very dangerous. If something starts to wobble, it might put them off kilter. Dancer's make-up is generally more traditional, stylized and artificial. It also needs to be better powdered, because they sweat more, and they tend to be made up much earlier. They will make up, and then have class because they want to be warm before they go on stage. So we tend to look after them before they warm up, and then they just come for a quick touch up. Because the dancers are a resident company they tend to like to work with the same people. They get used to a certain person looking after them. I have never been quite as present with them as I would have liked; my role has been more organizational.

Scheduling the work is a big task in itself, as you have to take into account which singer or dancer gets on best with which make-up artist. I would never deliberately put people together who don't get on. Whereas I used to run the department and do the shows, I delegate more now. I also do lots of in-house teaching, which I enjoy immensely. My long-term aim is to put in place an apprenticeship for our profession, which is something close to my heart. I have found that students do not leave colleges job-ready. We don't need designers, but people who can transform design into reality. They don't have the skills and dexterity. What makes you good is not only talent and a good eye, but experience, repetition and a knowledge of materials and colours, and how to use them.

At present we can't take on students, and we don't have the space at the moment to take on work experience people, who usually just come for a week, which is just a waste. I am writing a handbook for wig and make-up artists, and then I am going to write a curriculum, which will hopefully involve the colleges and a two-year stint here, as well as a two-year City and Guild hair apprenticeship. It would be a long learning period, but it would mean that the people who did it would be dedicated, and you need to be dedicated to be good. I want people in this department who have a passion for it, and really love what they are doing. We get a new pool of knowledge as new people enter the department. Some of the old skills must be upheld, but they must be mingled with the new. It is an interesting profession that is constantly developing, and it is an integral part of the theatre. Take away wigs and make-up and people just look ordinary. Or take away costume, or light – no magic. If you take away any part of the production process it all collapses. They are there to make the whole illusion work.

When people know what I do they are usually intrigued, but it sounds more glamorous than it is. At the end of the day it is hard work. My staff are very tired at the end of the day. Very often we have 13–hour days and six-day weeks. Sometimes we even have seven-day weeks. Only after 12 days are we obliged to give a day off. We do rehearsals in the morning, and then maintenance, and then the show. It is a hard job, with odd hours, so we tend to have friends within the theatre business, and one's private life can suffer a bit. Sometimes I sit on a bus and look at peoples' heads and think, 'That is an interesting double crown.' Or, 'If we made a beard that colour, nobody would believe it was real!' I keep looking at people and they must think, 'What is she staring at me for?' They wouldn't guess what my job is, especially as I don't really wear that much make-up myself; mind you I have got eyelashes on today.

But although our job is hard, we are blessed. I wouldn't want to work anywhere else. It is wonderful to make people up, and listen to beautiful music, and be creative in an environment like this. Everything at the Royal Opera House is of such a high standard. But I like to keep the mystery a little bit as well. As much as people would like to know exactly how things work backstage, I wouldn't like them to know how a quick change is managed. A really difficult opera was *Sophie's Choice* [2002]. There were quick changes for dress and wig that were 30–seconds long! We had to find ways to make that happen, and I am not going to tell you how. You need to make people wonder, 'How on earth did that happen?' And you mustn't tell them! Not every detail, just a little glimpse. I like people to think 'Oh, how fantastic!' That is the mystery of theatre, which I feel should always remain. You need to suspend disbelief. You need to do magic on stage; otherwise it is not theatre.

Index